A Guide to Haunted West Virigina

A Guide To Haunted
West Virginia

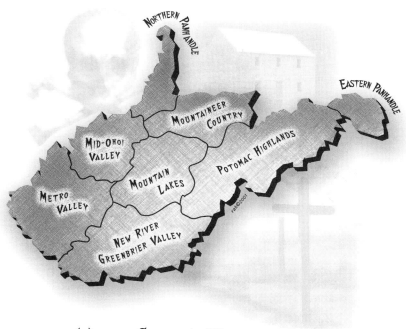

NORTHERN PANHANDLE

EASTERN PANHANDLE

MOUNTAINEER COUNTRY

MID-OHIO VALLEY

POTOMAC HIGHLANDS

MOUNTAIN LAKES

METRO VALLEY

NEW RIVER GREENBRIER VALLEY

rs4©2001

BY WALTER GAVENDA AND
MIKE SHOEMAKER

© 2001

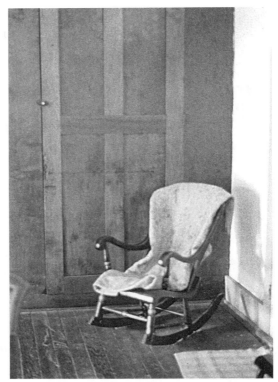

A heart-shaped pool of water appeared underneath this chair in the Prickett's homestead.

Published by Peter's Creek Publishing
A Division of Gauley Mount Press, Glen Ferris, WV.
Layout by RK Graphics, Reston, VA.
http://www.rkgraphics.com
http://www.hauntedwestvirginia.com

ISBN 0-9628218-8-8
Library of Congress No. 2001129166
Printed in the United States of America

TABLE OF CONTENTS

LIST OF PHOTOGRAPHS

Chapter Four ~ Mountain Lakes

Chapter Five ~ New River/Greenbrier Valley

Chapter Six ~ Northern Panhandle

Chapter Seven ~ Mid-Ohio Valley

Chapter Eight ~ Metro Valley

Index

INTRODUCTION

IN MEMORY OF
ZONA HEASTER
SHUE
GREENBRIER GHOST
1876 — 1897

A GUIDE TO HAUNTED WEST VIRGINIA

INTRODUCTION

It was a rainy Sunday afternoon in late October. We were cautiously creeping our way down Route 10 going to Sarah Ann looking for the grave of Devil Anse Hatfield, which, according to our research, was haunted. We had few stories for this part of the state, and since the Hatfield Cemetery was clearly marked on our map, we felt that the site should be fairly easy to find.

The river on one side and steep cliff on the other left little room to maneuver. Occasional coal trucks would loom up out of the driving rain like the phantoms that we sought, engulf us in coal-dust-laden spray, and then slog on. It was as though we were being swallowed up by time, then spit back out into reality, over and over again.

Through the mountains, down by the narrow river gorges and past guard rails, bent by collisions that had happened in the distant past. The rain howled, and the soggy autumn leaves swirled by like demented bats. Through Oceana (hey, the familiar glow of the golden arches of a McDonalds) then on to Logan and finally, Sarah Ann.

We pulled off the road next to the Hatfield Cemetery sign. Mike looked at me and said, "Look, it's pretty bad out there. You don't have to come if you don't want to."

I pried my white-knuckled fingers away from the steering wheel. The rain pounded on the car with a machine gun-like rhythm and showed no signs of letting up. Normally I like poking around cemeteries. You have to if you are a ghost hunter. But in my mind I was still fighting Route 10, the sludgy road spray and the coal trucks. So, for the first and only time on our quest, I decided I would stay in the car.

I watched Mike trudge up the hill, trying to keep his camera dry. He was wearing my Washington Redskins hat to keep the rain off his glasses. As I fiddled with the car radio in a fruitless search for a football game, my mind went back to the day I ran into Dave Phillips, our publisher.

We were both having a quiet lunch and began to talk. I told him of my plans to write a book about haunted Western New York, which is where I was born. Dave looked me in the eye and said, "How about a book about ghosts in West Virginia?"

I thought about it a moment. True, I had never been farther into West Virginia than Harpers Ferry and Shepherdstown, and my knowledge of West Virginia could comfortably fit in a gnat's eyeball. But I'd taken the ghost tour in Harpers Ferry so I was that much ahead. I was an experienced writer and researcher, well educated in ghostly lore. Driving around West Virginia might be fun. "Sure," I said, "How hard could it be?"

I would quickly find out.

First, I discovered just how big West Virginia is. Then, since I was starting from scratch, hours of library work lay ahead of me before I could set one foot into West Virginia. Early on I knew I needed help, so I called on Mike, who was not only an expert editor and researcher but learned in ghostly matters and a compiler of guidebooks to the Appalachian Trail. We decided to make the book a guidebook and Dave readily agreed. Thus began the odyssey that would take us over 7,000 miles of West Virginia roads and through hundreds of books, magazines, newspapers and interviews and eventually to Sarah Ann in the pounding autumn rain. We slipped and skidded our way on to Welsh, Princeton and finally back to Beckley. We got our pictures and the book continued forward.

Why We Wrote This Book

This question goes beyond the simple fact that a publisher asked us to write a book about ghosts, a subject in which we were both knowledgeable and interested. Every culture has its stories and legends that are as real to the people of that culture as the land on which they live. Yet most historians tend to ignore this part of cultural history and dismiss it out of hand as mere superstition and unworthy of their lofty consideration. If ghosts or the supernatural are mentioned at all, it is in a disparaging or demeaning way.

Folklorists, on the other hand, collect ghost stories but are generally interested in them only as stories and delight in pointing out that the crossroads spook story they collected has its roots in ancient Egypt. Many folklorists don't recognize the truth behind some of these tales and tend to treat them as bucolic tales of fiction. Thus the story is taken out of context, and the real significance to the people is blurred sometimes beyond recognition.

The U. S. Park Service, in particular, seems to go out of its way to discourage interest in supernatural occurrences on its sites. We found this to be particularly true at Harpers Ferry. One historic reenactor at another site told us that the Park Service "Didn't want to attract the wrong sort of people to the sites." The fact that the "wrong sort of people" pay taxes to support park activities doesn't seem to carry much weight.

We are also not seeking to prove the reality of ghosts. But we are not trying to explain them away or debunk them, either. We strongly feel that if people believe that a ghost haunts a crossroads or hollow, whether one actually does or not, then that alleged haunting is as real to the inhabitants of the area as the last local election, a Civil War battle, or a conflict happening on the other side of the world.

Since ghosts are rejected by most proper historians and relegated to primitive fiction by folklorists, we decided to create our own discipline, which we call "parahistory." Parahistory is the study of paranormal events (events not in the range of normal experience or scientifically explainable phenomena, in other words ghosts) in a particular area and their relation to the other historical events in the area. Parahistory is hidden history; hidden not by the people who believe it but by historians who dismiss it and folklorists who reduce it to quaintness.

These stories, myths and legends are important to a people and their culture. They represent the very heart and soul of a people, and when the stories and tales die out, something inside the culture dies with them. The historic preservation movement is becoming very popular nowadays and is an important force in preserving the history and heritage of our country. *A Guide to Haunted West Virginia* is an attempt at parahistorical preservation, to save these scattered bits and pieces of the past and preserve something important in the local culture.

We strive to make our work more than just the retelling of old tales. Where appropriate, we provide historical detail that puts the stories into context. For example, it does little good to tell the stories about the spooks that haunt Droop Mountain if you don't explain a little bit about the battle. Further, by giving directions to these sites, we allow our readers to become active participants, if they wish, by actually going to see where these things took place. Thus the parahistory of West Virginia is being preserved.

How We Wrote This Book

Any good fisherman will tell you that, to be successful, you have to drop your baited hook where the fish are. Otherwise, all you have to show for your efforts is a pile of waterlogged worms. Thus the first thing we had to do for our guidebook was to find where the ghosts were. When you're fishing in strange waters, a good guide will help you find the fish. Guides to ghosts also exist in the form of folklorists, local historians, magazine writers and newspaper reporters, who collect and publish tales of hauntings. We had to consult these people in order to know where to drop our bait, so the first six months of our effort was spent in various libraries, seeking out the stories. And we hit the motherload. We found so many stories that we had to set up criteria to choose those we would consider for our book.

First, we had to be able to find the location of the story on our maps. Many of the stories had indefinite locations or none at all, so they were ruled out right away. Further, the names for some of the locations of some of the older stories are no longer used today. A ghost at an unspecified location is not what you want to put in a guidebook. So if we couldn't find it on a map, it didn't get in.

Second, assuming we had a good idea of location, the site had to be accessible to the public. This ruled out tales of haunts in the middle of the wilderness or so far in the backcountry that they could be reached only with great difficulty. We didn't wish to put our readers in any sort of danger. (We also didn't want to put ourselves in the way of trouble. We may be intrepid ghost hunters, but we're not fools.)

These two criteria ruled out lots of stories. But as we analyzed the remainder, we realized we would have to weed out more. So we didn't include personal apparitions because they generally were of limited duration and usually significant only to the people who witnessed the haunting. So if your Great Uncle Zeb appeared at the foot of your bed one night to tell you that his last will was under a loose brick in the fireplace, we didn't include it because it would have very little meaning to anyone else. We also tended to shy away from ghosts haunting private residences because we were sure that most homeowners would not want hoards of spook hunters banging at the front door at all hours or wandering through the flowerbeds.

While this eliminated many stories for consideration, we were still left with a ton of tales from all over West Virginia. The only way we could start further elimination was to get out in the field and see for ourselves. So we said, if we could find the haunt, it was in, if we couldn't, on to the next place. As it turned out, for every haunt location we found there were three that we couldn't find.

We divided the state into areas and surveyed them one by one. Sometimes we had to visit a particular area twice. It became a great game with us. Finding an obscure location was a triumph while not finding a place that should be easy to locate was a defeat. But serendipity guided our hunt, because even when we couldn't find a particular haunt, local people would give us leads on new and often more interesting stories than the originals. Thus not only did we preserve parahistory; we added some new chapters as well.

Before we go on, we must make it clear that we do *not vouch* for the authenticity of any ghost we write about. If we conducted a complete parapsychological examination of each site we visited, we would finish our research sometime during the autumn of 2020. We also did not set out to debunk any ghost tales, although in the course of our fieldwork, we ended up doing just that.

We can say, in all truthfulness, that we have been in or as near as you could get, to every place we've written about, and if you follow our directions, you should be able to find each place. This assumes, or course, that there haven't been any radical changes in the landscape. We aren't responsible for floods or landslides or strip mining or building fires that occurred after we visited a site. We further take no responsibility for accident or injury suffered by anyone following our directions.

We did two years of long weekends' worth of field investigations. We traveled thousands of miles and in the process saw more of West Virginia than many people who were born there. As you read the book, we think you'll find that we violated every one of our selection criteria at least once. In some instances, stories such as the Zona Shue case were historically important and to exclude them would be inexcusable. Other stories were just so interesting that we felt you would enjoy them, whether you could actually visit the spot or not.

What Are Ghosts?

This question has puzzled mankind ever since we achieved self-awareness. Do we go on after death, and more importantly, can we come back? And if we do come back, can we communicate with the living?

Our ancestors seem to have had a profound belief in ghosts. Ghostly tales were told in ancient days. The Romans, in particular, had a fascination with ghosts, and the belief that the souls of the dead prowled the world of the living continued throughout the Middle Ages.

Then came the rise of science and technology, and belief in ghosts was shunted off as primitive superstition at best, and fraud and stupidity at worst. Men of science and reason laughed at the idea of ghosts and consigned them to the backwaters and odd corners of our culture. If ghosts were spoken of at all, it was generally in a humorous vein.

Then the bloom began to fade from the rose of science, and serious consideration of the supernatural became more common. Ghosts became quite popular. In some circles it was considered chic to have a spook skulking about your house. Soon books and television specials on ghosts and hauntings were sprouting like toadstools in the September mists.

But all this doesn't answer the original question: just what are ghosts? Our trusty Webster's Dictionary defines a ghost as "A disembodied soul, the soul of a deceased person conceived either as the denizen of an unseen world, or appearing to the living in bodily likeness hence, specter or spook." This is really an old-fashioned definition that describes literary ghosts, spooks that appear in stories or in movies. Real ghosts, and we believe that there are real ghosts, usually don't act like that at all.

We think that there's a lot more to hauntings than a dead person returning from beyond the grave, although we wouldn't rule this out as a possible explanation for a few of the haunts that we've looked at. To us, ghosts are sensory phenomena that have been witnessed by credible individuals but have no readily apparent or believable rational explanation. These phenomena probably involve natural processes that aren't readily understood or may have supernatural causes. So, are ghosts tormented souls that reach across vast barriers of time and space to send a message to the living? We reply with a resounding maybe—and maybe not.

Let's take a closer look at our definition. "Sensory phenomena" is just our shorthand way of saying, things that you see, hear, smell, feel or sense. As far as ghosts are concerned, these range from strange lights, disembodied footsteps, crashing noises, voices, being touched by invisible hands, smelling things that are not there, finding cold spots in places that should be warm, seeing apparitions to a whole host of other strange things.

The second part of our definition deals with the credibility of witnesses. Credible witnesses aren't prone to hallucinations, playing hoaxes or practical jokes, or wouldn't benefit commercially from faking a haunting. Would people fake a haunting to have a laugh, become the center of attention or to make money? You betcha! History is full of such incidents.

So how do you judge credibility? Most hauntings usually follow a pattern. If a story deviates from the pattern it may have been added to, spiced up a little to make it better, or completely made up. Both of us have read enough haunting reports to judge the credibility of a story. You get a feel for the tale, and if something about it doesn't seem quite right, then it's probably a phony. With all of our experience and expertise, could a knowledgeable hoaxer fool us? You betcha!

Finally, the event must be inexplicable. Theories without proof don't offer an explanation. We're positive that some of the hauntings in our book could be explained by natural causes, if they were strictly and carefully investigated. For example, the settling of houses, underground water, wind in the chimney—all could cause some of the sounds we report as part of hauntings. When pipes expand and contract, they sometimes sound like ghostly footsteps in the hall. But expanding pipes generally don't trod down the hall, throw open the bedroom door, pull off your covers and leave you shivering in the dark. The proof must be readily demonstrable, and with ghosts, that isn't easy. "Probable," "possible," "maybe," and "could be" just won't cut it. So if you can't really explain a haunting, then it's inexplicable and grist for our mill.

Types of Ghosts

There are three basic types of ghosts; ghosts that haunt people, called poltergeists, ghosts that haunt places and ghosts that haunt objects or things. Poltergeists (a German word meaning noisy ghost) attach themselves to a single individual and follow that person wherever he or she goes. The victims are usually children in their early teens, although this isn't always the case. Poltergeists do nasty things to their victims and surround them with inexplicable events. Loud noises and crashes occur, and objects float across the room as if moved by invisible hands. Uglier poltergeists have caused fires to break out spontaneously, showers of stones inside rooms and walls that weep blood.

Sometimes poltergeists physically attack their victims, slapping them, biting them, pulling their hair or even levitating them. Despite all of the destruction, poltergeists are very seldom seen. Fortunately, these infestations usually last a few weeks or months, rarely more than a year. Then they vanish as mysteriously as they appear. The spook in our Wizard Clip story was probably a poltergeist.

The vast majority of spooks in our book are ghosts that haunt places. The places that they haunt can be as small as a single room in a house or as broad as a stretch of highway or a mountain. A few, such as the Mothman, seem to haunt a whole section of the state and the neighboring states as well.

Ghosts that haunt places manifest themselves in a wide variety of ways, but they are more often heard than seen. The noises they make range from bumps, bangs, moans, and mysterious voices to, in one instance, a whole troop of cavalry horses moving across an old battlefield.

Then there are the full-blown apparitions. Some ghosts look just like real people, until they suddenly vanish or walk through a wall. Some are translucent or transparent. Some lack various body parts, most particularly their heads. Some apparitions follow mindless patterns, over and over again. Others often acknowledge witnesses and, in rare instances, attempt to communicate intelligently.

Sometimes ghosts that haunt places act a lot like poltergeists. They slam doors, fool with the lights, make loud noises and move the furniture around. But there is a pronounced difference between the two. Ghosts that haunt places never leave the places they haunt.

Poltergeists always stay with their victims. No matter where the victim goes the poltergeist follows.

It's true that certain individuals seem to set off or attract ghosts that haunt places. But a true poltergeist is only set off by one individual: its victim. So while certain people seem to wake up sleeping spirits, active ghosts don't need any psychic prodding to perform. Anyone can set them off—even you.

Ghosts that haunt things act much the same as ghosts that haunt places. Ghosts can haunt pictures, items of furniture, cars, and even airplanes. These ghosts are bound to objects, and if you move the object, you move the ghost.

Why Do Ghosts Haunt?

Once you weed out the obvious hoaxes, expanding pipes, bats in the attic and hallucinations, you are left with an indigestible wad of impossible events. So why are there ghosts and why do they haunt? Why are some places haunted, and others not? What is the mechanism that sets off a haunting?

The classic spiritualist answer is that ghosts are souls caught between universes, who don't realize that they're dead or that are so attached to people and places on earth that they are reluctant to leave. And while some haunts seem to fit this explanation, others do not.

Some scientists and investigators feel that certain places store emotions like psychic storage batteries that some people can unwittingly trigger. This explanation might account for the sightings of John Brown's ghost or for the activity at Droop Mountain. But it does not explain why the Droop Mountain battlefield is veritably crawling with spooks while the Point Pleasant Battlefield, which was as bloody as any battle in the Civil War, has no ghosts that we know about. No spectral Shawnee attack the Virginia Militia or skulk around the park at night even though Point Pleasant is an area where lots of weird stuff happens.

Perhaps ghosts are the result of some perfectly natural cause that we have yet to discover. The realm of quantum physics contains many strange things that we don't understand. Perhaps some future Einstein will make a discovery that will explain it all.

Now if you really want to let your imagination run wild, try this on for size. Perhaps time doesn't move in a straight line, but curves back on itself. That might cause the boundaries of the time continuum to become thin. If the boundary becomes thin enough, maybe ghosts are bits and pieces of the past, or future, that make it into our universe. Or perhaps there's a parallel universe that exists next to ours and occasionally, they cross paths. Or maybe we produce the ghosts ourselves, from somewhere inside us. There has been research that demonstrates that this is more than just speculation. And maybe none of these answers are right, or maybe all of them are.

Ghost Lights

Reports of ghost lights associated with hauntings are quite common in West Virginia, so common, in fact, that we decided to include a special section in the introduction just to deal with them. Ghost lights are not unique to West Virginia but are seen all over the world. They've been widely studied by serious scientists who have arrived at several conclusions as to what these mysterious lights really are. Various explanations depend upon where and when the lights are seen.

Explanations for ghost lights fall into two basic categories. The first, and by far the most common, is that these ghostly lights are mirages caused by automobile light reflections; distant lighthouses; or lights from trains, planes, towns, searchlights or any other artificial source. Of course the fact that some of these lights have been seen long before there were any planes, automobiles or other artificial light sources doesn't seem to daunt proponents of this theory. And in all fairness, we will readily admit that some ghost lights are misidentified artificial light sources.

The second explanation is that ghost lights are one or more natural phenomena. Let's take a quick look at some of the more common theories:

• Will-o-the-wisps and foxfire: Will-o-the-wisps or jack-o-lanterns are caused when methane gas from rotting vegetation is ignited in the air over swamps, marshes, bogs and other stagnant water. This so-called swamp gas was a favored explanation for UFO sightings in the mid-1960s. Foxfire is also the product of rot and decay. Logs and stumps sometimes begin to glow because of a luminescent fungus. Foxfire therefore is really a sort of fire in slow motion.

• St. Elmo's Fire: Most commonly seen by sailors at sea and in the air, this is an electrical discharge from pointed objects such as ship masts, radio antennae on planes and sometimes even people. It is usually sighted during thunderstorms when there is a lot of static electricity in the air. It generally doesn't harm people, and the literature is full of reports of St. Elmo's fire clinging to hair, beards and fingers of individuals. (St. Elmo is the patron saint of sailors who believed they were under his protection when St. Elmo's fire was visible.)

• Ball Lightning: A relatively rare type of lightning may be formed when electrical forces, usually in thunderstorms, create a glowing ball of plasma in the air. It can take on many shapes, forms and colors and can even appear in a closed room. Witnesses report that sometimes the ball lightning seems to act almost intelligently, going down hallways and climbing stairways. But when these plasma balls explode, they can cause lots of damage, and some witnesses say they leave behind a sulfurous stench (a possible explanation for the Keyser Devil).

• Andes Lights: In the Chilean Andes, thunderstorms are a rare phenomenon. There are, however, luminous charges of electricity that shoot from the mountain peaks to the clouds. These discharges are silent, but they sometimes can be seen from 300 miles away. The Andes isn't the only place where these phenomena occur. In the September 1919 issue of *Scientific Monthly,* Dr. Guy Hinsdale reported that in western Virginia—where there are numerous parallel ridges separated by deep, narrow valleys—silent bursts of electricity occasionally discharge from the peaks into the air. There is no explanation for the cause of these electrical discharges.

As we roamed the highways and byways of West Virginia, we would occasionally hear reports of fireballs going from mountain to mountain or into the air off of mountaintops. And southeastern West Virginia is no different from western Virginia, so maybe the wild part of wild and wonderful West Virginia is a bit wilder than the West Virginia Department of Tourism sloganeers imagined.

• Piezo-electrical phenomena: Here's where we get a bit technical, so read closely. If you take granite rock, with its high quartz content, and put it under intense pressure in a laboratory you can produce an electrical charge, usually when it is crushed from the strain. This charge is called piezo-electricity. Many ghost lights appear along earthquake faults, where granite rock is under pressure deep underground. There is another phenomenon known as earthquake lights that occur just before or just after earthquakes. These are probably piezo-electrical discharges.

Many ghost lights appear on mountain ridges, near or on top of earthquake faults or along railroad tracks, particularly those that run near or at earthquake fault lines. There's one class of ghosts that appear as balls of light around railroad tracks. We call them railroad ghosts. The common explanations of these hauntings usually center around a railroad employee who was decapitated on the job. The specter walks up and down the line with a lantern, looking for his or her lost head. (Just why a ghost without a head, thus without eyes, needs a lantern to see is never really clear in these tales. But then no one would notice a ghost wondering around in total darkness, and ghosts like to be noticed.)

The late Bob Jones, the founder of a paranormal research organization called Vestigia, conducted a complete investigation of just such a haunt along an abandoned railroad in New Jersey. By mounting an instrument package on a small rail car and sending it into the ghost light, Jones was able to determine that there was an electrical charge where the light was shining. Jones wasn't sure what caused the charge, but interestingly enough, the rail bed was made of pieces of granite. (See the chapter on the Fairmont Ghost and the Screaming Jenny section in the Harpers Ferry chapter for examples of just this kind of ghost.)

Then there's always the possibility that ghost lights really are ghosts. Floating balls of light are common in areas said to be haunted and have even been captured on film or videotape. Are these ghosts really little understood electrical phenomena, or do the misunderstood electrical phenomena provide spirits with the energy they need to cross over from their dimension into ours? Just thoughts to ponder as you're sitting on the road near Walnut Bottom, waiting to spot the Cole Mountain Lights.

Grateful Thanks

We would like to take this opportunity to thank all the librarians, motel workers, gas station attendants, store clerks, park rangers and personnel and those who work for local historical societies and museums. Without their help, this book could never have been finished. They were a tremendous help to us and more than generous with their time. Most of all we would like to thank the wonderful people of West Virginia, who took pity on two obvious flatlanders and went out of their way to assist us no matter how crazy some of them undoubtedly thought we were. Their kindness, politeness, their obvious pride in their heritage, and love for their mountains was a welcome change from the cynical urban environment we are used to. We hope we've repaid you by writing this book the best way we know how. And we hope you enjoy reading it as much as we enjoyed writing it.

EASTERN PANHANDLE

MORGAN

BERKELEY

81

JEFFERSON

340

rak©2001

CHAPTER ONE

JEFFERSON COUNTY

Harpers Ferry Haunts

Harpers Ferry National Historical Park has the scariest ghosts in West Virginia. The mere mention of them terrifies the park rangers, sending them into quivering fits of denial. The Park Service, you see, wants to teach you about the history of The Hole, as Harpers Ferry was first called; about how Peter Stephens, a squatter on Lord Fairfax's land, established a ferry across the rivers here; about George Washington's choosing of the site for a national armory; about the growth of a vibrant manufacturing town; and about John Brown's attempt to spark a slave revolt with his raid on the Federal armory. This is serious history, you understand, and there's just no room for ghosts in the rangers' earnest lectures.

But ghosts do stalk Harpers Ferry. Not only ghosts from John Brown's raid but spooks from other parts of Harpers Ferry's colorful and violent history. The Harpers Ferry Ghost Tour was one of the first in the nation. Park Service denials aside, the dead still walk, some of them seen by National Park Service employees. Here are a few of them.

John Brown's Ghost

John Brown was a fanatic abolitionist who decided to seize the Federal Armory at Harpers Ferry to arm and set off a slave rebellion throughout the South. A veteran of the wars in bleeding Kansas, Brown convinced elements of the abolitionist movement to give him assistance. In between fund-raising jaunts, he scouted Harpers Ferry as the most likely spot to begin his great crusade. He rented the Kennedy farm in Maryland to serve as base and jumping-off point for his invasion of the Old Dominion. Here he gathered arms and ammunition as well as men. When he felt the Maryland authorities were getting suspicious, he launched his attack on Sunday, October 16, 1859.

In the dark of the night, Brown's men seized the arsenal as well as several luckless townsfolk. The hostages included Colonel Lewis W. Washington, the great grandnephew of George Washington. The local slaves did not rise to Brown's banner, and he soon found himself trapped in the fire engine house, surrounded by a thoroughly aroused mob of locals that peppered the building with steady musketry.

The engine house, where John Brown and his black dog are seen.

The Federal government sent Colonel Robert E. Lee and Lieutenant James E. B. Stuart along with a company of U.S. Marines to take back the arsenal and rescue the hostages. Brown refused to surrender, and after a three-minute fire-fight he was captured and the hostages were freed. Brown was confined to the Charles Town Jail, tried and convicted and sentenced to be hanged. On December 2, 1859 he was executed, striking the spark that set off the explosion that tore the Union apart. If witnesses are to be believed, psychic echoes of that explosion reverberate today around Harpers Ferry, where John Brown's ghost still walks.

Today, virtually everyone who visits Harpers Ferry comes because of John Brown, but it's safe to say that no one ever expects to meet the fiery abolitionist. Yet a number of tourists believe they *have* met him. They describe an elderly, bearded man in antique dress who wanders the streets of the restored historic section. Since he looks like Brown, everyone thinks he is a Park Service reenactor, so they ask him to pose with them for a photo. He kindly obliges, and the tourists depart satisfied. But when they develop their film they realize that he is missing from the picture, a blank space occupying the place where he stood.

Other tourists tell a somewhat different story. They've seen a man who looks like Brown, accompanied by a black dog, strolling down High Street along the storefronts. When the two reach the fire engine house, also known as John Brown's Fort, they vanish into the closed door.

These stories raise several perplexing questions. Brown was hanged in Charles Town and, not surprisingly, he haunts that town as well (see John Brown Marches On). He also haunts the Kennedy Farm in nearby Maryland, which served as his headquarters for the raid. Can the ghost of one man haunt three places at the same time? And while Brown's ghost has every reason to return to the fire engine house where he was besieged, why should he haunt a scaled-down replica that doesn't even stand in the original location? Are wandering spirits so undiscerning? Maybe people's cameras malfunction and that's why he doesn't appear in the picture. Maybe. Perhaps people are simply overcome by the spirit of the place and see what they wanted to see. Perhaps. And if that's all there is, we might not bother to report this.

However, several strange events connected with Brown's raid give it supernatural overtones. For example, take one of Brown's men, Aaron D. Stevens. Stevens was a desperate character who advocated killing the hostages they had taken and burning the town. Strangely enough, he was severely wounded when the enraged townspeople disregarded a flag of truce he carried. He was captured and taken to Fouke's Hotel, where an angry crowd gathered around him. One man put his gun to Stevens's head and said he was going to kill him. In his memoir, *The Strange Story of Harpers Ferry*, Joseph Barry reported that Stevens "fixed his terrible eyes on the would-be murderer and by the sheer force of the mysterious influence they possessed, he compelled the man to lower the weapon...To this day the magnetized man avers that he cannot account for the irresistible fascination that bound him as with a spell." It seems that Stevens, was a practitioner of Spiritualism, as were several other raiders, and he met his fate on the gallows on March 16, 1860.

Does Dangerfield Newby haunt Harpers Ferry, loyal to Brown even in death? Given the gruesome circumstances of his death, we would not be surprised. Newby was a tall, strong mulatto about 30 years old. His white father had freed him, but he burned with the desire to free his wife and seven children, still slaves in Warrenton, Virginia.

On the morning of October 17, the Charles Town militia arrived by rail and boated to the Maryland shore. From there they drove the raiders off the B&O Railroad Bridge. At the same time, a mob of armed citizens from Charles Town came down Shenandoah Street and took positions alongside armed townspeople in houses near the armory, cutting Brown off from escape into the Virginia mountains. About 11 a.m., someone from an upper floor of a house shot Newby through the neck with a six-inch spike, killing him instantly as he stood near the armory gate. The spike was probably fired from a musket. He was the first of the raiders to be killed, doubly ironic, for the raiders' first victim had also been a free Black, Heywood Shepherd.

Newby's body lay where it fell for more than 24 hours. The citizens of Harpers Ferry left it, and the local hogs almost devoured it. That evening, after Brown's capture, some local heroes decided that Newby wasn't dead enough. One fellow shot him again, and another kicked him in the face. Perhaps because Newby's body was too far from the source of their whiskey, the mutilators dragged it over to Hog Alley, a short, narrow passage between High Street and Potomac Street. Today his ghost—dressed in baggy pants and a slouch hat and with a gaping hole in his neck—wanders Hog Alley.

John Brown's Prophecy of Doom

Perhaps the most uncanny aspect of the raid was Brown's statement that Harpers Ferry would be destroyed in the near future. Immediately after Brown's capture, Governor Henry A. Wise of Virginia interviewed him for more than two hours in his jail cell in Charles Town. According to witnesses, this is when Brown made his dark prediction.

Others point to a note Brown slipped to one of his guards on the day he was hanged. It said, in part, "I John Brown am now quite certain that the crimes of the guilty will never be purged away but with blood!"

You might argue that this was just righteous fist shaking or that Brown had a clear view that the raid would ultimately touch off the Civil War. For whatever reason, John Brown's prophecy was right, and throughout the war the people of Harpers Ferry dwelt upon Brown's bloody prediction as they watched their once prosperous town disintegrate.

Even the fulfillment of this vision was filled with weird coincidences. First among them is the dual role played by Major Hector Tyndale. The Major accompanied and protected Brown's wife as she traveled from Philadelphia to Charles Town to retrieve her husband's body and arranged for the transportation of the body to North Elba, New York, for burial. A little more than two years later, in February 1862, Tyndale supervised the burning of a substantial portion of Harpers Ferry, as a reprisal directed at the numerous Confederate saboteurs and spies in the city. Later that year, the town was further devastated when it was besieged and captured by Stonewall Jackson's troops during the Antietam campaign.

It was The Great Flood of 1870, however, that sealed its fate as a thriving town. The raging waters completely wiped away the many industrial works on Virginius Island in the Shenandoah River.

There were two spooky incidents concerning the great flood. On the evening of the flood, a Professor Kidd was lecturing the local teachers' association in the schoolhouse on Shenandoah Street. As he discussed the poor construction of schoolhouses in general, he stated that the very building they occupied was the worst planned he had ever seen. As Joseph Barry writes, "he expressed a wish that some convulsion of the elements would take place for the special purpose of destroying this house, so that another might be erected on a better plan." Although no one at the lecture suspected that a flood was coming, within hours the professor's wish was fulfilled, for the schoolhouse was demolished.

The other event concerns a death premonition or perhaps a bit of fun that turned into a macabre joke. Mrs. Overton was a widow who lived in a house on Overton's Island, adjacent to Virginius Island. On the Sunday preceding the flood, she was in an unusually excited state while attending a church class. She made a point of shaking everyone's hand and bidding them farewell, saying that she probably would never see any of them again this side of the grave! And she was right, for the muddy waters of the Shenandoah swallowed her up and swept her away.

Camp Hill's Phantom Fife and Drums

At this point you may think that Harpers Ferry is a place of high strangeness, but few *bona fide* ghosts. Have no fear. Better still, have a little fear, for witnesses have seen and heard numerous ghosts in the historic district.

One of the oldest and strongest hauntings concerns Camp Hill. This ridge between Harpers Ferry and Bolivar got its name from the encampment there during the Undeclared Naval War Against France. What has a naval war, and an undeclared one at that, have to do with Harpers Ferry?

The revolutionary government in France had been attacking American commerce at sea since 1793. President John Adams authorized American naval vessels to defend themselves against French attacks. American ships won several battles. So while the two nations were never officially at war, a naval guerrilla war proceeded apace.

It appeared that the conflict might become a full-scale war, so in 1799 a military force commanded by General Charles C. Pinckney was stationed on the ridge to protect the armory. As it turned out, the only battle these men fought was against disease—always the biggest killer of the armies of that time—and the western slope of the ridge became the final resting place for many of them. Far from home and in forgotten graves no longer marked, it's no wonder their spirits wander. And as ghosts often do, it seems they reenact the familiar

Sidewalk at Camp Hill - actual location of the camp.

routines of their last days, drilling to the piping of the fifes and the beating of the drums. As Joseph Barry, our oldest source, records, townspeople on still nights often heard "the weird notes of their fifes and the clatter of their drums...." Even in modern times, people have heard this phantom fife and drum corps parade down the street from Camp Hill. But no one has ever reported seeing them.

Because of this spooky marching and drilling, many fine houses in the vicinity of Camp Hill became vacant and remained that way for many years. In some of the houses, doors opened and slammed in the night by themselves as people heard the sound of footsteps. There's even a story that a sword fight between two ghosts drove one family from their home. The houses might have remained unoccupied indefinitely, but new people moved in who had not heard the tales, didn't believe in the haunts, or weren't bothered by them.

In 1867, the New England Freewill Baptist missionaries bought Camp Hill and established Storer College on the site. Founded for the education of the newly freed slaves, but open to all students, the college operated successfully until 1955, when West Virginia integrated its schools and colleges. The campus was later acquired by the Park Service, which now uses part of it as a training facility.

Today the stately college buildings stand amid tall trees on the verdant hill. Generally deserted and quiet, they offer an opportunity to commune with the past in more ways than one. The ghosts are seldom heard in recent years. We're not surprised in a noisy tourist town. But if you walk the lane along the ridge and sit quietly on a bench there, you might yet hear the lilt of the fifes and the rhythm of the drums, the last remaining sounds of a forgotten war that never was.

Harper House

The Park Service may be squeamish about ghosts because two of the houses it manages are haunted. The first is Harpers Ferry's oldest standing structure, and the last home of the town's founder, Robert Harper. Born in Oxford, England, about 1703, Harper came to Philadelphia at the age of 20 and worked as an architect and millwright. Engaged by the Quakers to build a meetinghouse on the Opequon River, he fell in love with the scenery of The Hole and bought the squatter's rights and ferry service from Peter Stephens in 1747. The next year he purchased the land from Lord Fairfax. After losing a house on Shenandoah Street to a flood, Harper built the present stone house on the hill overlooking High Street. Because of the delays caused by the American Revolution, construction took six years, from 1775 to 1781. Harper died in 1782. But something in the house lingers on and there's some confusion as to who or what it is. One of Harper's friends, named Hamilton, supposedly died in the house in an accidental fall, so the neighbors all believed that Hamilton haunted the house. Another story says that Harper's wife, Rachel, fell from a ladder and died. Rachel supposedly took with her the secret of where the Harpers' fortune in gold was buried. Many tourists claim to have seen her specter—a woman dressed in 18th-century style—gazing down on the Harper house garden from the uppermost window. The ghostly guardian of a treasure—the only example we've found so far in West Virginia—or a clumsy man who took a header? Maybe neither or maybe both.

Does Rachel Harper's ghost guard a treasure at the Harper House?

The Wager House

The Park Service's other "problematic" building is known as the Wager house. It stands next to the Harper house, on property that the childless Harpers gave to their niece Sarah Wager. From her, the property passed to her son and then to three grandchildren, one of whom built the Wager house. The owner went bankrupt, however, causing the house to be sold at auction to Dr. Nicholas Marmion. The house remained in the Marmion family until the Park Service acquired it.

The Park Service first used Wager House as a guesthouse for visiting officials and researchers. Those people who thought they were due for a pleasant stay in a period house were in for a big surprise. We have a mass of reports from various guests describing several different ghosts. Unfortunately, none of these ghosts has been identified, and the causes for their haunting the house remain unknown.

Our first source is a researcher named Marguerite Thayer. One evening she saw a handsome man in a brocade vest standing at the top of the servants' stairway. He gave her a "dark and menacing look." Terrified, she turned to flee the room. Just as she opened the door to escape, she felt a hand push her from behind. Looking back, she saw that the room was empty. On another occasion, she saw the phantom of a woman on the stairway, in a long gray-hooded dress in the 18th-century style.

Dave Williams, a Park Service employee from Denver, also saw both of these ghosts. He was staying in the Wager house while working on a park development plan. One night he stepped into the hall and saw the woman in the gray-hooded dress. This time the phantom was holding the hand of a young girl, about eight years old. They stood there a moment, then vanished before his eyes. Subsequently, he also saw the man in the brocade vest at the top of the servants' stairway. The man also wore a top hat and carried a walking stick. The man gave him "an evil look," the same as he gave Marguerite Thayer, before vanishing.

In the early 1970s, researcher Horace Fuller was relaxing on a couch in the living room when an eerie feeling overcame him. Sitting up, he saw a 19th-century laborer cross the room, with what looked like the body of dead man slung over his shoulder. Horace sprang from the couch and followed them out into the large hallway where the ghost and his grisly burden both disappeared.

Today the house serves as the park library. This naturally gives far less opportunity for the ghosts to be seen, since no one is there much of the time. The Park Service has effectively buried the ghosts in books.

The Ghost of Father Costello

The ghost at St. Peters Roman Catholic Church, at the top of the famous stone stairway, is a comforting one in contrast to the rest of Harpers Ferry's haunts. Built in 1833, on the site of a mission established in 1792, St. Peters was the only church in Harpers Ferry to escape destruction during the Civil War. It was, however, renovated and enlarged in 1889. With its impressive neo-Gothic architecture and Tiffany stained-glass windows, it is considered by many to be the most beautiful building in town.

St. Peters survived the Civil War due to the courage of its priest, Father Costello. He alone of Harpers Ferry's ministers remained in his church throughout the war, personally defending the property by courageous appeals to morality, from the threatened

St. Peter's Roman Catholic Church, where the dying Yankee soldier whispers.

depredations of both sides. Appropriately, some say that every now and then, a strange glow seen in the threshold of the entrance is the spirit of Father Costello still looking after his beloved church.

Another story about the glowing threshold attributes it to an incident from the Civil War, when the Union Army used the church for a hospital. A wounded Catholic soldier lay in the yard outside the church, waiting to be treated because his wounds seemed less severe than those of others. While he waited for treatment his wound continued to bleed. When his turn finally came, he breathed his last

The walkway where Father Costello's ghost walks.

as they carried him into the church. They say if you see the threshold glowing, listen closely and you'll hear his dying whisper, "Thank God, I'm saved."

Visitors to Jefferson Rock have also seen Father Costello. While passing the church about six o'clock in the evening, people tell of seeing an old priest in black robes and a black friar's hat making his way from the rectory to the church. They stop to speak to him, but he ignores them, and then much to their amazement he disappears through the sidewall of the church at the place where a door existed before the renovation. These stories apparently date from a time when the road was at the same level as the church. The level of the road was raised, creating a very narrow walkway between the road's retaining wall and the church wall. If this ghost still walks, he must slip down the slim passage beside the road, or else tourists would see little more than his head rising above the new road level. Or if the ghost has adapted to the new conditions, he must fly or leap across the space between the road and the church wall. Unfortunately, we have no recent reports of this ghost's exact movements to gain entry to the old church.

Screaming Jenny

Perhaps the most horrifying Harpers Ferry ghost story is the sad tale of Screaming Jenny. Soon after the railroad came to town in 1833, a destitute woman named Jenny took up residence in one of the armory's abandoned storage sheds, beside the tracks near today's train station. While trying to stay warm one cold winter night, Jenny got too close to her fire. Her sackcloth dress caught fire and blazed up

Screaming Jenny appears coming down the tracks at Harpers Ferry.

in an instant. Hysterical with terror, Jenny ran out of her shack and down the tracks screaming for help. The wind fanned the flames, turning her into a veritable human fireball, but her agony ended quickly as the night train struck her. To this day, engineers sometimes tell of seeing and hearing a screaming fireball racing down the tracks toward them. Some even say they hear and feel the thud of the train striking a body, although no body is ever found.

A variation on the Jenny story claims that she's a colonial housewife who got too near the fireplace and caught fire and that the screaming fireball is seen running along the top of Maryland Heights, the cliffs across the Potomac River. But there's another story that may account for that fireball. Since the Civil War, weird lights seen on the heights are thought to be the ghosts of the 100-day men, short-term volunteers from Ohio who helped defend Harpers Ferry early in the war. Though gallant and brave enough, these men lacked experience in military matters, to say the least. Lacking suitable dry ground to build a campfire, one rainy night they used some live cannon shells to construct a hearth. The fire was lit, and a terrific explosion killed many of them. Their ghosts now light the heights, a constant reminder of their foolishness.

How to Get There: The park visitor center lies on US-340, west of the Shenandoah River crossing. A free shuttle bus runs on a continu-

ous schedule between the visitor center and the park's main historical section.

John Brown Marches On

> *"John Brown's body lies a-moldering in the grave,*
> *But his soul goes marching on."*

John Brown has certainly lived up to the Civil War song, *John Brown's Body*, for his soul still marches on the Kennedy Farm in Maryland, in Harpers Ferry, and in *two* places in Charles Town. It's as if John Brown is re-enacting every stage of his raid, trial, and execution.

So we went off in pursuit of John Brown's ghost. We rolled into Charles Town on what turned out to be the hottest day of the year. We started our search by visiting the Jefferson County Museum, which was well worth the trip. We took a tour of the Courthouse where Brown was tried. Our guide, Nan Furioso, proved to be an invaluable source not only about Brown, but about Charles Town as well.

Charles Town Courthouse.

On October 26, 1859, just ten days after his raid on Harpers Ferry, John Brown went on trial in Charles Town for treason, murder, and inciting a slave revolt. During his capture, Brown was battered with the hilt of a sword. His injuries were slight, but to inflame public feeling in the North, he pretended to be an invalid. He forced his jailers to carry him on a cot every morning from the jail to the courthouse, and then reclined on the cot during his trial.

The jail was located on the southwest corner of George and Washington streets, on a diagonal from the courthouse. A post office replaced the jail in 1919. The courthouse still stands on the northeast corner, although it has been expanded and renovated over the years.

According to Nan Furioso, Brown's little drama spawned an interesting tale. Whenever Charles Town is blanketed in snow, the diagonal from the jail site to the courthouse melts rapidly, before any adjoining roads or sidewalks. No one can account for this strange phenomenon, for there are no heating pipes or other natural causes to explain it. Some people say John Brown's ghost treading back and forth from the jail to the courthouse causes the melted path. Now that's marching!

On October 31, Brown was condemned to be hanged. His appeal failed, and on December 2, 1859, he was taken out of jail and, riding on his coffin, hauled in a wagon to the gallows. You can see the wagon in the Jefferson County Historical Museum.

The execution procession traveled to the empty field of a nearby farm where a scaffold had been constructed. Colonel John T. Gibson of the 55th Regiment of Virginia Militia commanded about 800 troops who enforced martial law at the hanging. Even though the worried authorities excluded the general public from the vicinity, many watched from the nearby house of the site's landowner, Rebecca Hunter. Her house still stands at 534 South Samuel Street.

Because Brown saw himself as a martyr serving God's purpose, witnesses claim he exhibited "impressive serenity" during his last days. He declined what he called the "hypocritical prayers" of local ministers at his "public murder." On the scaffold, he displayed a stern dignity. His last words were, "Be quick!"

But the hangman wasn't. Brown took a very long time to die. Some 35 minutes passed before his pulse ceased. Even then, the soldiers who attended to his body were not convinced he was dead. His piercing blue eyes still seemed alive, so the soldiers poured hot wax on them! But this did little good, and witnesses said that Brown's eyes continued to "glow."

It is a curious fact that this haunter of so many places was interested in Spiritualism, the religion based on séances with the spirits of the dead. Even while in jail, Brown read a Spiritualist newspaper, which could almost make you think that he planned his own haunting!

As you might expect, Brown has not left the place of his death. Some say he haunts the red brick Victorian house that stands almost on top of the hanging site. Colonel Gibson built this house in 1892 as a kind of perpetual celebration of Brown's death. A fanatic in the Southern cause, Gibson served with distinction in the Confederate army and was presented a Southern Cross of Honor by the United Daughters of the Confederacy. But he never really accepted the Confederate defeat. For a time, after building the house, Gibson produced picture postcards with the hanging site marked by a cross. From these postcards we know that the site was probably in the yard on the left side of the house as you face it, a few feet to the left of the old "well."

In a sense, Gibson was dancing on Brown's grave, and he seems to have known that he might provoke some retaliation from beyond the grave. To protect himself, he introduced every paragraph of the deed to the property with the Lord's Prayer. Despite this precaution some say the ever-combative Brown struck back. Nan Furioso told us that if you go to the house at sunset, you might see Brown's death agony. As the shadows deepen, look to the third-story window on the right. There Brown's ghost appears with his head tilted to the side in the act of strangulation.

But there are other unearthly presences in this house besides John Brown. We learned of its other ghosts from the present owner, the congenial Gene Perkins. A devoted historical architect in his spare time, Mr. Perkins bought the dilapidated house in 1987 and set about restoring it. During a bout of flu that autumn, his five-year-old son Philip saw a male ghost in the upstairs Grape Room. After that, he refused to sleep upstairs. Well maybe poor Philip was having a hallucination brought on by fever. Not so. While no one else in the family has seen it, the ghost is often heard walking up and down the upstairs hall, proof that the sighting was not the one-time effect of the sickness. Other than being male, this ghost has no characteristics to distinguish it as Brown, and so sounds much more authentic to us than the spook at the window. Mr. Perkins feels that the ghost is probably some casualty from the Civil War or a member of Gibson's family (perhaps Gibson himself).

Other phenomena plague the house, too. Occasionally items are oddly "misplaced" and then suddenly found again in places previously checked. Then there are the doors that like to unlock themselves. This is not some prankster's trick, either, for the locks are all skeleton locks, and Mr. Perkins keeps the ring of keys with him.

Mr. Perkins has never seen any apparition, nor heard one, except once in the autumn of 1997. In a strange repetition of the circumstances a decade before, a ghostly presence made itself known as Mr. Perkins's son Philip lay ill on the first-floor couch. While in the kitchen, Mr. Perkins heard a female voice call "Philip!" He thought his wife had returned home from an errand and went out into the hall to see her, but no one was there. He then went to the pantry and again heard the voice distinctly call out "Philip" three more times. No one knows who this solicitous spirit is.

Perhaps the oldest ghostly tradition of the house tells of mysterious flickering lights seen in what was the servants' quarters upstairs. (As it is the only room in the house without a fireplace, it was probably the servants' room.) These sightings began in Gibson's own time. The lights always appeared on winter nights after the Gibson family had left on their annual trip to warmer southern climes. These lights continue to appear, for an elderly neighbor of Mr. Perkins, Rosie Keyser, has seen them in recent winters when the house was unoccupied.

No one knows what these lights represent, but one remarkable suggestion links them with the man who assassinated Lincoln, John Wilkes Booth. Booth reportedly attended Brown's hanging dressed in the borrowed uniform of the Richmond Grays. Further, Booth and Gibson were close acquaintances. Gibson gave him Brown's personal Bible and Brown's copy of the Chatham Constitution, which Gibson had confiscated when Brown was executed. Booth also gave dramatic readings during his time in Charles Town, and Gibson hired Booth briefly to oversee his theater and coach some performers in Shakespeare. Obviously, the two men were quite friendly.

Some believe Booth escaped the manhunt after the assassination and lived secretly for some years under Gibson's protection, perhaps in this bedroom over the kitchen. Whole books have been written to argue that Booth lived long after his supposed death in Garrett's barn on April 26, 1865, but we have not heard of this angle before. Mr. Perkins told us that some Booth family representatives visited him a few years back to look into the matter, and they told him that animal bones were found in the grave where John Wilkes was supposed to have been buried.

Perhaps the most wonderfully mysterious aspects of the Gibson House are some details of its construction. First, the house has no foundation. Instead it was built using an old French bricklaying technique that allows the house to safely expand and contract, as if "breathing," depending on the season. Second, the "well" in the yard is actually an "escape" exit, connected to the house by a now mostly filled-in secret passage. Finally the house has a literal connection with Charles Town's biggest "secret": a vast cavern that lies below most of the city. The main entrance to this cavern descends from the back of the Old Opera House, on the northwest corner of George and Liberty streets. At one time, the cavern—with its large subterranean pond, beach, and paddleboats—was a popular attraction. It was closed, at least officially, after some children drowned there. Perhaps not, for Colonel Gibson's house originally had a double outhouse, one side of which actually concealed an entrance to the cavern. What purpose this may have served, we shall probably never know.

How to Get There: The courthouse stands on the northeast corner of Washington and George streets (US-340 and Route 9). To reach the Gibson house from the courthouse, go one block east on Washington Street and turn right on Samuel Street. The Gibson house is on the left at 515 South Samuel Street.

The Haunted Inns of Charles Town

Where do you go in Charles Town when you want to get a good meal in pleasant surroundings? You could try the Charles Washington Inn, set in an old house, nicely furnished with plenty of room for a large group. Or you could go downtown and try the Iron Rail Inn, a large brick building not too far from the courthouse. There's a nice restaurant upstairs and a fun pub downstairs. But if you go to either place, you might get a surprise with your shrimp cocktail, for both places are said to be haunted by very active spirits.

The Charles Washington Inn was named after the founder of Charles Town, who also happened to be George Washington's youngest brother. As far as we know, neither George nor his brother haunt the inn. The resident spook is a feisty 13-year-old named Miss Emily. Feisty? Yes, and we can personally attest to her feistiness.

Strange things happen at the Charles Washington Inn. The lights go off and on of their own volition. Doors slam by themselves and locked doors are often found wide open. The owners had to stop putting bud vases on the dining room tables because when their employees arrived to start work in the mornings, the vases were turned over. The perplexed owners called in a psychic who claimed that the ghost was that of a young girl named Emily. Miss Emily died in the Pink Room, which is now an upstairs dining room. This may have happened when the house was used as a hospital.

There have been reports that Miss Emily responds to the mention of her name by dimming the lights in the downstairs dining room. There allegedly is a window upstairs that can't be cleaned because a child's handprint is always found on it. Finally, one waitress, who no longer works there, reported that she was literally thrown out of an upstairs closet by some unknown force.

Walt had his own personal experience with Miss Emily and her jokes. The first time we visited the inn was a boiling day in August. We had been trooping around Charles Town and, hearing that the inn was haunted, decided to have a late lunch there. As we ate, we talked with our waitress and asked her about the stories that we'd heard. She was very forthcoming and confirmed many of the tales. She also mentioned that Miss Emily had been fooling around in the kitchen that afternoon. Then she asked if we wanted to look around. Of course we did.

When we got upstairs to the Pink Room, the center of the hauntings, Walt decided to have a little fun. (It helps to have a sense of humor when you're a spook hunter.) "Miss Emily," he said, "I know you're here and I've seen your kind before. There's nothing that you can do to me that will scare me because I've seen it all."

Nothing happened. So we chuckled and went downstairs. Before we left Walt decided to use the men's room. As he stood before the urinal, a heavy thump sounded on the wall, just over his head. "Miss Emily," he said, "it's not polite to do such a thing when a gentleman is engaged in so delicate an operation. You shouldn't be in here."

He hurriedly washed his hands and looked out into the hall. No one was there. The only people anywhere were Mike and the waitress, and they were both near the front door, far from the bathroom.

"Did you hear a bang on the wall just now?" Mike shook his head no, and the waitress looked at him with a knowing smile.

As Walt later stated, "Somewhere, deep in a hidden recess in my mind, I could sense a 13-year-old girl who was giggling." As we've said before, when you look for the supernatural, sometimes you find it looking back at you. And we may have a picture to prove it!

We took pictures of the Charles Washington Inn in the spring, after our encounter with Miss Emily. Look at the upstairs window to the left of the door. You'll see what could be a person, standing, looking out the window...the window of the Pink Room...Miss Emily's alleged headquarters.

Charles Washington Inn - Miss Emily in upper left hand window?

An odd reflection on the windowpane? Perhaps. A real person? We didn't see anyone looking out the window when we took the picture. The inn was closed and no one was around, no one alive, that is.

Nothing like this happened to us when we went to the Iron Rail Inn. According to the owner, the haunts there would give Miss Emily a run for her money, because unlike Miss Emily, you can actually see them, although in the case of Charlie Skinner you can't see all of him.

Charlie Skinner owned the building where the Iron Rail is now situated. Charlie, who was described as a little weird and a bit of a recluse, haunts the pub downstairs where he used to live. He usually is seen by the cigarette machine near the door to the men's room. Sometimes only half of Charlie appears, usually surrounded with a green glow.

One lady customer saw Charlie's lower half walk through the wall in the room behind the bar. As seems to be usual in these sorts of cases, there used to be a door where the ghost went through the wall. The bartender confessed that when he's in the pub alone he feels like he's being watched. One time a disgruntled former employee broke into the pub and set fire to it. But the fire put itself out. People who work at the Iron Rail say that it was just old Charlie looking out after his old home.

The second ghost in the inn haunts the dining room. Sometimes diners see a lady clad in a 1950-style formal gown. She always sits at the table nearest the front dining room window. No one seems to know who she is or why she's there.

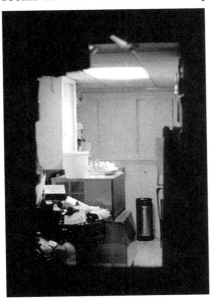

Iron Rail kitchen, where the lower half of a man was seen walking through the wall.

Finally, there's a red translucent cloud that appeared to a man working at a computer in the office upstairs. The man simply looked at the cloud and it vanished. Witnesses reported that the upstairs hall was ice cold although it was a hot summer's day. Again another glitch on the ethereal highway to other dimensions?

So go have a nice lunch or dinner at these fine establishments. (The Charles Washington Inn is closed on Sundays, so you might want to call ahead.) But you never know if or when the ghostly inhabitants will pop up and surprise you, so treat them with respect, particularly if you have to use the facilities.

How to Get There: *From the junction of US-340 and Route 9, in the center of town, go one block north on Route 9 and turn left on West Liberty Street. The Charles Washington Inn stands at 10 West Liberty Street, between Charles and Lawrence. The Iron Rail Inn stands in the same block as the courthouse, on the northwest corner of Washington Street (US-340) and Samuel Street.*

The Truth About Wizard Clip

The sleepy little town of Middleway hardly seems like a place where a vast supernatural upheaval has occurred. But over 200 years ago, one did, and you can see some of its effects even today. As you drive down the street, notice the little wizard's caps on the street signs. There also was a Wizard Clip Inn, but when we looked for it, it had gone out of business. When we investigated the remarkable events that allegedly occurred in this town, we found additional material that makes it even stranger than the traditional tale told in most books. Here then, is our version of the story of Wizard Clip.

The traditional version of the story goes like this. One night in 1794, a mysterious stranger sought lodging at the home of Adam Livingston, a prosperous farmer of Smithfield (now Middleway) who kindly obliged him. In a few days the stranger fell deathly ill and asked Adam to find a Catholic priest to administer the last rites. As a pious Lutheran in those non-ecumenical times, Adam refused and remained unmoved by the man's pleas. The stranger soon died. On the night of his death, Adam hired Jacob Foster to sit up with the corpse (a custom of the time). As darkness fell the two men tried to light candles, but the candles kept flickering out, though the air was perfectly still. Other candles were brought in, but they too wouldn't light. Unnerved by this, Foster fled the house.

After the stranger's burial, poltergeist phenomena began to plague the Livingston family. Dimitri Augustine Gallitzin (1770-1840), a Russian prince who emigrated to America and became a Roman Catholic priest, described some of the phenomena in an 1820 letter: "...stones were seen moving across the room held by invisible hands, fire bursted [sic] repeatedly out of their beds at broad daylight, strange and frightful apparitions and strange noises terrified them very often at night." In addition to the noises and the fires, dishes flew off the shelves and broke, the barn burned, and cattle mysteriously died.

But the thing that scared the Livingston family the most was the audible clipping of a pair of shears. The invisible shears left half-moon shaped cuts in clothes, sheets, boots, and other objects. And the phantom clipster did not confine its activities to inanimate objects. On one occasion the shears beheaded Adam's chickens and turkeys, and on another they destroyed a favorite flock of ducks.

In an 1839 letter to Mrs. Catherine C. Doll, Father Gallitzin tells of an old Presbyterian lady who lived in Martinsburg who went to Livingston's house "to satisfy her curiosity." Before she entered, "she took her new black silk cap off her head, wrapped it up in her silk handkerchief, and put it in her pocket, to save it from being *clipped*. After a while, she stepped out again, to go home, and having drawn the handkerchief out of her pocket and opened it, she found her cap cut up into narrow ribbons." These events became so well known in the area that the name Wizard Clip was soon commonly substituted for Smithfield.

This narrative, told and retold in collections of ghost stories, has a solid historical basis. John Adam Liebenstein, later anglicized to Livingston, was born in Lancaster County, Pennsylvania, on February 16, 1739. He inherited his father's land in Virginia, totaling 350 acres in Smithfield, and moved to the property with his wife and family about 1772. He was indeed attacked by the poltergeist. However, the mysterious stranger and Jacob Foster are probably apocryphal details that first appeared in *Hardesty's History of Jefferson County* in 1883. What really happened was much more extraordinary and complicated than the traditional story.

According to the account of a neighbor, Mrs. Richard McSherry, the poltergeist actually appeared sometime before 1790. She said, "They were alarmed by strange noises in the house, like horses galloping around." Then their barn burned, the livestock died and the rest of the happenings contained in the traditional tale occurred.

The poltergeist pestered the Livingstons despite Adam's many attempts to send it away. He read in his Bible that ministers could cast out evil spirits, so Adam sought help from the Rev. Christian Streit, the Lutheran pastor of Winchester from 1785 to 1812. Streit told him such powers existed only in early apostolic times and that modern pastors had no such power.

Next Adam tried the local Episcopal minister, the Rev. Alexander Balmain. A prominent citizen, Balmain tutored in the Lee family, served in the Revolutionary army, and married one of James Madison's relatives. But the poltergeist was no respecter of important connections. When Balmain tried to exorcise it, the ghost abused him and carried off his prayer book, which was later found in a bedpan.

According to Fr. Gallitzin's letter to Mrs. Doll, a Methodist preacher and some members of his congregation tried their hand and were "driven away by a shower of stones thrown among them by invisible hands." In addition, Father Thomas Mulledy, later president of Holy Cross College, tells of three men from Winchester who came to end the haunting but were quickly frightened away when a stone flew from the fireplace and whirled about the floor for 15 minutes!

By this time Adam had nearly concluded that all ministers were humbugs because they didn't have the power described in the Bible. Then a prophetic dream gave him encouragement. He dreamed that he was struggling to climb a high mountain. Upon reaching the top, he saw a beautiful church and a man dressed in robes, and he heard a voice say, "This is the man who can relieve you." He made inquiries and, as a devout Lutheran, must have been disconcerted to learn that the only clergy who wore the robes he described were Roman Catholic priests.

There was no Catholic Church in the area at that time, but Mrs. McSherry told him that a traveling priest would say Mass in Shepherdstown the next Sunday. Adam went to the Mass and to his surprise recognized the priest, Father Dennis Cahill, as the man in his dream. Father Cahill, who ran a mission in Hagerstown, Maryland, laughed at first and said that Adam's neighbors were probably playing tricks on him. Eventually Richard McSherry and others convinced Father Cahill to go to Adam's house. On this first visit he sprinkled holy water in each room of the house and said some prayers. This temporarily halted the haunting. Soon the noise and destruction returned, however, and Father Cahill had to consider an exorcism.

The Catholic Church is reluctant to conduct the rite of exorcism; so before authorizing its use, it investigates the situation to verify that exorcism is warranted. So in the autumn of 1797 the church sent Father Gallitzin to investigate, and he spent three months doing so. Ordained only two years before, he was probably chosen because he was fluent in German (the Livingstons' daily language), well educated, and of noble birth.

Father Gallitzin's investigation convinced him that the haunting was real and he decided to undertake an exorcism. According to his friend, the Rev. James Bradley, as quoted in Sarah Brownson's *Life of Demetrius Augustine Gallitzin*, when he started the exorcism "the rattling and rumbling as of innumerable wagons" filled the house and "worked so upon his nerves that he could not...read the exorcism." Knowing he was outclassed, he then sent for Father Cahill.

When Father Cahill arrived he had everyone in the house kneel. Then he "commanded the evil spirits to leave the house without doing any injury to anyone there." The spirit put up a "stubborn resistance," but eventually obeyed. Father Cahill concluded the exorcism by celebrating Mass. This put an end to the haunting.

Afterward, Cahill occasionally visited the Livingstons and in time received them into the Catholic Church. He left for Ireland about 1806 and died there in 1816.

These early sources give no reason for Adam's ghostly persecution, but a possible cause came to light shortly after the Civil War. John Gilmary Shea was writing a history of the Catholic Church in America, and he got some details of the story, which were handed down to Mrs. Mary Ann Taylor by her parents, who had lived in the neighborhood at the time of the haunting. Mrs. Taylor said that during the exorcism "the spirit confessed to have murdered his predecessor [i.e., the previous landowner], and that the spirit could not find rest until he had made restitution and had given to the murdered man a Christian burial. The spirit also made known the spot where the body lay. Witnessed by a great number of residents and strangers, it was disinterred. The property was restored to the rightful owner and the spirit was at rest."

The Stranger's Grave.

This testimony is supported by the fact that Livingston eventually donated 34 acres, subsequently called the Priest Field, to the Catholic Church. While gratitude may have played a part, the spirit's demand for the restoration of property to its rightful owner would explain why this particular parcel was donated. That parcel of land had originally been surveyed for Andrew Hamton in 1735. In 1760, however, Edward Thomas obtained the parcel in a grant from Lord Fairfax. He subsequently sold it to Christian Fox, who in turn sold it to Adam's father. What became of Hamton and why he didn't obtain a patent on the land is a mystery. If Hamton was the murdered man and had no heirs, then only giving the land to the church would fulfill the condition of the exorcism. This was common practice in those days.

Adam did not deed the land to the church until February 21, 1802. Adam's wife, Mary Ann, had written a letter published in the *Potomak Guardian* on September 12, 1798. She bitterly opposed donating the land to the church, denounced "priest craft," and claimed that the exorcism had not entirely eradicated the haunt. Thus the restoration of the land was necessary to completely finish the exorcism.

Mrs. Taylor's testimony also offers an explanation as to who lies in the so-called Stranger's Grave, located in the Priest Field. Since the stranger is probably an apocryphal addition to the Wizard Clip story, the grave's most likely occupant is the murdered man.

The successful exorcism of the spook did not mean an end to the strangeness for the Livingstons. Afterward, the Livingston family often saw a brilliant light and heard a voice that instructed them in the Catholic religion. At times, the voice sang beautifully in Latin and English. On one occasion, a ghostly arm appeared and taught them to make the sign of the Cross. The voice also frequently awakened them at night and told them to pray for sinners, sometimes leading them in saying the Rosary.

In the midst of these visions, another kind of "stranger," allegedly an angel, appeared on the scene and instructed the Livingston family for three days. Accounts of the visit come from Father Mulledy, Mrs. McSherry, and Mrs. Helen Nicholson Scharmann (McSherry's granddaughter).

One day the family was startled by the sudden appearance of a beggar at their door. He was poorly dressed and barefoot, though the day was cold. They took him in and gave him clothes and shoes, which he said "were not needed where he came from" because "there is neither heat nor cold in my country." When they asked where he came from, he answered, "from my Father" and said he had come to teach them "the way to my Father." You might think that this episode was a clever hoax by a beggar who knew the local story. But when the man left, the family reportedly saw him disappear before their eyes as he passed through the gate.

Visitations by the light and the voice continued for many years. No one knows when they ended or if they ended. In March 1809, Adam sold the rest of his property and moved to Bedford County, Pennsylvania, to be near some of his children. There, Father Gallitzin often held Mass in Adam's home, until Adam died in the spring of 1820.

Livingston's house in Middleway was in ruins by the Civil War and is gone today. Stories about the place probably scared potential buyers. The Civil War artist James Earl Taylor (the son of Mary Ann Taylor), writing about the legend, observed "that the people of Smithfield are so superstitious that many of them will not pass the right of the field."

The Priest Field was first used as a Catholic cemetery, apparently located on the northeast side of the field. Taylor speaks of "another burial place," probably the murdered man's grave that was separate in the woods. For some 50 years, a rude stone marked this grave. Today a wooden cross marks it.

Descendants of one of the original trustees eventually disputed ownership of the Priest Field, but in 1922 the court ruled that the church's deed from Livingston was valid. Bishop Dennis J. O'Connell of the Diocese of Richmond gave thanks for this decision by celebrating three Masses on the site on All Soul's Day (November 2), 1922. A small chapel was built there in 1923, and Masses were held every year on All Soul's Day. In the 1960s the Masses were moved to another location due to the small size and disrepair of the chapel.

It seemed as if the site would never fulfill the prediction that the voice made to Livingston: that the Priest Field would become "a great place of prayer and fasting and praise." But on May 30, 1978, the Diocese of Wheeling established the Priest Field Pastoral Center to provide believers a quiet place for prayer and contemplation.

Although many aspects of the Wizard Clip story—the stranger, the dream, and the voice—may be apocryphal elaborations, the main points of the haunting, the exorcism, and the deeding of the property are all well documented. Few hauntings leave behind tangible traces, but there is no doubt that the legacy of the Wizard Clip poltergeist is the Priest Field Pastoral Center.

How to Get There: *Go west from Charles Town on Route 51. The Pastoral Center stands on the left side of the road just before the* *road crosses Opequon Creek. To the right of the parking lot, a memorial sculpture of Livingston stands beside the entrance to a path leading into the woods. Take this path; go right at the fork, and cross a dry creek. About a quarter-mile from the beginning of the path, a large wooden cross supposedly marks the grave of "the stranger," or rather, the unknown murdered man.*

BERKELEY COUNTY

Haunted Hedgesville

Hedgesville is a small town located on Route 9 between Martinsburg and Berkeley Springs. It's a quiet, peaceful country town that's slowly turning into a suburb. But just drive a few miles down Route 901 to a small hamlet called Spring Mills some foggy October night and you may discover something quite frightening.

Route 901 is a typical West Virginia country road that meanders through relatively flat (by West Virginia standards) countryside dotted with small farms and houses. In places, bedrock shoulders its way up through the surface, giving some of the pastures a hard scrabble look. The area is starting to fill up with townhouse developments and new single family homes, but in the fog and during the night, this road can still be a lonely place.

Several years ago, during one late October evening, a man and his wife were driving down Route 901 from Maryland towards Hedgesville. The autumn mist formed patches of fog that forced the driver to slow down. He was used to the ways of the hills and fog was not unusual at this time of year.

He came to another patch of fog on the curve by the Spring Mills plantation house. As he slowed the car down, it became so cold inside that he had to turn on the heat. The swirling fog began to take on a greenish glow. Then the headlights went out and the car engine quit.

Suddenly a short, bearded man with long amber hair, dressed in a Confederate uniform with a sword at his side, stumbled out of the fog. The man was clutching his back with both hands as though he was wounded. Much to the amazement of the driver and his wife, the soldier seemed to notice them. He hit the hood of the car with a thump. They could see that his hands were covered with blood. He looked at them as if pleading for help, then slid to the ground, leaving bloody handprints on the hood of the car.

The driver leaped out of the car to help the stricken man. When he reached out to touch him, the soldier disappeared and the bloody handprints on the hood of the car vanished. The car engine restarted itself, the headlights came back on, and the fog vanished—just like the soldier. The petrified couple raced on to Hedgesville, vowing never again to take Route 901 at night. According to Susan Crites, the noted West Virginia folklorist and ghost hunter, several other people have met the wounded Rebel soldier at the same place under similar conditions and have had the same thing happen to them.

So just who is this wounded soldier? No one seems to know. The Civil War was fought all over this area. We know that Spring Mills was used as a headquarters by both sides. *The Civil War Day by Day Almanac* indicates that there were skirmishes in Hedgesville on July 18, 1863 and, perhaps more significantly, October 15, 1863. But since this area was the scene of many raids,

Spring Mills Plantation on Route 901, where the Spring Mill phantom soldier appears.

bushwhackings, ambushes and murders, these dates may not relate at all to the haunting.

Just up the road from Spring Mills is the Falling Waters Cemetery. The graveyard is located next to a Presbyterian Church that was founded in 1745, and some of the tombstones carry dates that go back before the American Revolution. Falling Waters Cemetery contains one major oddity. In most cemeteries you will find tombstones located at the head of the casket, thus they are called headstones. The grave markers in Falling Waters seem to be placed at the foot of the casket and thus are footstones rather than headstones.

Whether this unusual arrangement was dictated by topography or some other factor was not readily apparent.

Further, we found at least one Civil War veteran buried in the graveyard. He is John Scott Harlan, who served in Company C of the First Virginia Cavalry. Harlan was born on March 5, 1841 and died on October 12, 1902. The ghost usually appears right around this date. Does this mean that John Harlan's ghost haunts Route 901 on foggy October nights? Probably not, but the coincidence is rather interesting.

Spring Mills may be one of those places that attract strange, unworldly things. For example, some people say that if you stand near Spring Mills at dusk, you can hear horses clatter over a wooden bridge that no longer exists.

This apparition must be truly startling to those who encounter it. But what a shock it must have been to a dying Rebel soldier, desperately seeking help, whose last conscious vision was the hood of a Buick, protruding from an unearthly green fog. The thoughtful among you might raise this question. Does he haunt our world or do we haunt his?

How to Get There: *From Route 9 in Hedgesville, turn onto Route 901. After about 2.5 miles, the road crosses Harlan Run. The old Spring Mills Plantation stands on the left by the creek.*

MORGAN COUNTY

Berkeley Springs' Haunted Castle

West Virginia is the last place you'd go to find a castle, particularly one with a ghost. But if you go to the historic town of Berkeley Springs, you'll find one nestled against the side of a mountain, just outside of town. The castle is a half-size replica of Berkeley Castle in Bath, England, the original home of Virginia's third colonial governor, William Berkeley. It is the only example of an English-Norman style castle in the United States and was built in 1885 by Colonel Samuel Taylor Suit to impress a 17-year-old girl named Rosa Pelham.

Side view of Berkeley Castle in Berkeley Springs.

Suit, a 46-year-old, wealthy businessman who fought for the South in the Civil War under Robert E. Lee, was the Minister to England under the administrations of Grant and Hayes, both former Yankee generals. Suit became smitten with Rosa Pelham, the daughter of Congressman Charles Pelham. After an ardent pursuit, Rosa agreed to marry him if he would build her a castle. So Suit began the construction of the castle, and the two were wed. They had three children, a daughter who died of typhoid fever in her teen years and two sons who survived into adulthood.

The castle's construction cost a considerable fortune in the 1880s—about $100,000. The walls are three feet thick and the entry hall is 17 feet high. Unfortunately Colonel Suit died before his project could be completed. His will stipulated that Rosa would not inherit his fortune if she didn't finish the castle. Rosa finished the job, and then took 30 years to finish off Suit's fortune.

Rosa entertained on a lavish scale. Sometimes she would rent railroad passenger cars to bring her guests into town. Rosa's friends came from Washington and New York, and she put them up in a local hotel where they sometimes spent a week or two. Parties lasted from sunset to sunrise, and an orchestra was often imported for dancing.

When Rosa reached her mid-50s, the fortune was gone and the music stopped. She had to take out a mortgage on the castle, but then lost it when she could not make the payments, even though she owed only $4,000. Rosa moved to the country, where she tried to make ends meet by raising chickens and selling jellies and preserves. One of her sons, who moved out west, took his mother with him. Rosa never remarried—although she may have lived to be 90.

Despite, or maybe because of all the parties and gaiety, ugly rumors began to spread about Rosa. It seems that Colonel Suit died just after changing his will in which he left everything to Rosa, except for $1,000 for each of his sons. Some said Rosa poisoned the Colonel to get his money, but this was never proven.

The Colonel wasn't the only man who died in Berkeley Castle under suspicious circumstances. One of Rosa's lovers died when he "accidentally" fell on the tip of Rosa's parasol as the two struggled on the grand staircase. A second lover "accidentally" fell to his death from the roof. Like any good castle, the edge of the roof is surrounded by battlements, so "accidentally" slipping off this roof is considerably more difficult than it would be from an ordinary house.

The castle fell into disrepair until it was purchased in 1954 by Walter Bird, a direct descendent of James I of England and James IV of Scotland. Mr. Bird restored the place, but since the original furniture had long since been sold, he filled it with antiques. These include a canopied bed that once belonged to Revolutionary War General Horatio Gates, the victor at the Battle of Saratoga, and a sofa that is reputed to be over 1,000 years old.

Like any good English castle, Berkeley has its share of otherworldly residents. The haunting seems to be quite typical being heard more than seen. Sometimes there are loud crashes upstairs, but when the staff goes up to investigate, nothing is disturbed. And what haunted castle would be complete without the sounds of footsteps when people aren't there. And sometimes the furniture is moved around, but not by human hands. And then there's the sound of the laughter of children that floats out of the downstairs dining room on the odd occasion, but only when the room is empty and there are no children visiting the castle.

Perhaps the most haunted room in the castle is Colonel Suit's second floor combination office and drawing room. Tour guides feel uncomfortable there. In 1993 people working in the room saw a quill pen rise up seemingly of its own volition and twirl round and round. They fled in terror. When the staff was kind enough to let us look around the room and take some pictures, the lights seemed to dim a little. Old wiring or somebody saying "Hi"? It's interesting to note that the husband and wife desk, which occupies a prominent place in the room, was one of the few pieces of furniture actually owned by the Suits that is still in the building.

Being a town landmark and open to the public, the castle hosts many weddings. Strangely enough, it seems subject to mysterious power failures during the ceremonies, but never during the receptions. A comment on the holy state of matrimony from beyond the grave or just that old wiring again? Or maybe the spooks like to have a little fun at parties.

No one knows just who or what walks the castle halls at Berkeley Springs. Sam or Rosa are good candidates. Or maybe it's the teenage daughter, trying to make up for being struck down in the prime of youth. Then there are those two lovers who died mysterious deaths. Or maybe it doesn't have anything to do with the Suits at all. Maybe old Horatio Gates is prowling around, wondering just what his bed is doing in an English castle in West Virginia.

How to Get There: *The Berkeley Castle stands on Route 9, a short distance west of the junction with US-522.*

POTOMAC HIGHLANDS

MINERAL   HAMPSHIRE

340

GRANT

TUCKER

HARDY

rak©2001

RANDOLPH

33

PENDLETON

250

POCAHONTAS

CHAPTER TWO

HAMPSHIRE COUNTY

The Laughing Boys of the Cacapon River

If you drive a little way over the West Virginia line down Route 50 in the direction of Romney, you come to the hamlet of Capon Bridge. The Capon Bridge spans the beautiful and scenic Cacapon River, which meanders through Hampshire and Morgan Counties until it joins the Potomac at Great Cacapon, near Berkeley Springs. Cacapon State Park is noted for fishing, hiking and white water rafting and even has an 18-hole golf course. The Capon Bridge is farther up river.

We saw the river at its best. As it flowed by in the sparkling autumn sun, it didn't seem that a peaceful place like this would be the haunt of restless spirits. But in the world of the supernatural, appearances can be deceiving. If you don't think so, consider this story.

Shortly before the start of World War II, a boy and his dad were camped along the banks of the Cacapon near Capon Bridge. They'd had a successful day of fishing and were just nodding off to sleep when they heard something hit their boat with a loud thump. They quickly ran to the boat, moored by the bank, but found nothing wrong. Puzzled, but not particularly disturbed, they tried to get back to sleep. About 10 minutes later, they heard another loud thump, and their boat suddenly shot into the middle of the river.

Shocked and surprised, the boy and his dad swam after the boat, caught it, and pulled themselves in. As they rested from their unexpected swim, they noticed laughing boys riding in old-fashioned wooden washtubs surrounded them. As the children frolicked and laughed all around them, something hit their rowboat with such force that it was knocked four or five feet shoreward. They noticed that the rowboat was hitting one of the wooden tubs. The father got up and tried to push the tub away with an oar, but it wouldn't budge. All the time the boys around them laughed and shouted.

When the father finally stood up to move the tub, he noticed a boy floating face down in the water. As he lifted the lifeless body into the boat, the laughter around him ceased, and the other children disappeared. The father and son strained to get the boat ashore, but when they landed they looked back and the body was gone. Neither of them had seen it disappear.

This all might be dismissed as a campfire ghost tale or a caprice of the imagination. But noted West Virginia author Susan Crites, who collected this tale, says she has seen the boat and the two gouge marks made by the collision with the tub. And if that isn't enough, she says she has seen three other boats whose owners claim they had collisions with floating washtubs. All three boats have two deep gouges on the same side of the boat. The gouges are exactly the same size, color and shape. Are the stories a hoax perpetrated by local fishermen perhaps to protect a favorite fishing spot or just for the sheer fun of fooling the credulous?

Perhaps. But consider this final, chilling bit of information. Ms. Crites reports that an 1892 edition of the *Martinsburg Daily Gazette* contains the story of an 11-year-old boy who was lost during a "Boys Washtub Race" at a church picnic on the Cacapon. The body was never recovered.

And now it seems that somewhere in infinity, the ill-fated race continues. Somewhere beyond, a long dead, long forgotten little boy reaches across the decades to try and find some peace. Perhaps it is true that the dead never forget.

How to Get There: *Go down Route 50 to Capon Bridge. On the side of the Cacapon nearest Virginia, there's an area that looks like it might have been a park or a picnic area. There are several places on either side of the bridge where you can pull over. We didn't notice any boat rental places in case you really wanted to go looking, but a quick call to Cacapon State Park could tell you where you could rent or launch a boat.*

MINERAL COUNTY

The Old Stone House at Keyser

During the Civil War, Keyser, West Virginia, then called New Creek, occupied a strategic position astride the Baltimore and Ohio Railroad. In order to protect this vital lifeline, Union forces built Fort Fuller, which is located at the site of the Administration Building of present-day Potomac State College. Keyser served as a base for several Union forays into West Virginia, including General Averell's great raid on Salem, Virginia in 1863. (For more on this event, see The Ghosts of Droop Mountain.)

On August 4, 1864, Confederate troops under Generals John McCausland and Bradley T. Johnson attacked Fort Fuller but were repulsed. On November 28, 1864, the Confederates came back with vengeance in mind. Cavalry wearing Union Army overcoats, under the command of General Thomas Rosser, captured Fort Fuller along with considerable supplies and 400 prisoners. A confused sentry let them in thinking that they were a returning Union patrol. Rosser's men destroyed the railroad bridge and then pulled out. With such a history there are bound to be a few ghosts skulking around Keyser. And the Old Stone House is where some of them may have lingered.

The Old Stone House at Keyser, viewed from the street.

The Old Stone House, built by Edward McCarty in 1815, is the oldest house in town. It was appropriated by the Union forces to serve as a prison and hospital. Other sources say that the Confederates also used the Old Stone House as a hospital. In Keyser, as in the rest of West Virginia, the Civil War was truly less than civil, splitting families and communities, and giving rise to atrocities that today would be considered war crimes. It was just such an atrocity that gave rise to this tale of a rather unique haunting.

There are two versions of the haunting of the Old Stone House, one Rebel and one Yankee, but we shall report them both.

According to the Rebel version, the Old Stone House was being used as a prison for captured Confederate soldiers. The conditions were harsh, and food was poor in quantity as well as quality. Knowing this, the brother of a slain Union soldier decided to use them to exact revenge for his loss. He came to the Stone House with a basket full of small loaves of bread, in the bottom of which he hid a pistol. The prison guards didn't detect the weapon, so he went in and passed out the loaves of bread to the hungry prisoners. While his victims were eating, he pulled out the pistol and killed seven prisoners. Just as the last shot was fired, the roof over the southern corner of the cell blew off. It was as though nature itself was outraged at the perfidious act done in the guise of charity. After the war, none of the subsequent owners could keep a roof on that part of the house. Finally, a descendant of one of the murdered prisoners purchased the house, and he had no more trouble with the roof.

In the Yankee version of the story, three Union prisoners tried to escape by prying off part of the roof. They were shot during their attempt, turning the cell into a bloody mess. For a long time after the end of the war, the roof came off the room in the same spot at least once a year. This went on for a considerable length of time until one owner made major repairs and ended the phenomenon—for now.

As to which story is correct, it's difficult to day. First of all, the source for both stories is a man named Vernon Giffin who wrote the first version in his book *The Witch of Hooker Hollow and More Folklore,* although he had reported the second version to Dr. Ruth Musick some years earlier. It's possible that Mr. Giffin got more detailed information when he was writing his book than he did when he first heard the story. Certainly the fact that the Union occupied Keyser for a much longer period than the Confederacy adds weight to the Rebel version of the story. But the fact that the prisoners tried to escape by prying the roof off points to the Yankee version. If the roof were structurally weakened by the escape attempt, it would stand to reason that subsequent owners would have trouble with the roof until it was properly repaired.

There's another problem with the Rebel version of the story that some of you more knowledgeable may have noticed. The vengeful brother allegedly used a revolver to kill seven prisoners. To do so, he would have had to be an excellent shot, particularly since the most common seven-shot pistol of the day, made by Smith and

Wesson, was notorious for its poor accuracy but it may have served its purpose at close range.

Tales get exaggerated and muddled as they pass down through the generations. There are probably elements of truth in both stories, and an historic place like the Old Stone House, which served as a prison and hospital, deserves a spook or two.

Apart from its duties in the Civil War, the Old Stone House has an interesting history of its own. One of the owners, Colonel Angus McDonald, was a West Point graduate who fought for the South. While he was in the army he was stationed in Hannibal, Missouri. It was there that he married Cornelia Peake, the daughter of Dr. Humphrey Peake, who was Mark Twain's family physician. Twain (Samuel Langhorne Clemens) wrote about Dr. Peake and is said to have visited Old Stone House.

The Peake family accounts for another strange incident that happened at Old Stone House. Mrs. Ellen Peake De Camp, McDonald's sister-in-law, was visiting the family. One night she ran out of the house, screaming that she saw in a dream that her husband James was dead. Shortly thereafter, she received word that her husband had unexpectedly died at Governor's Island in New York.

The Old Stone House still stands, but its glory days are long gone. It is now an apartment house at the corner of Armstrong and Keys, out of the mainstream of Keyser town life. It appears to be well kept up, and we couldn't find out whether there still were problems with the roof.

How to Get There: *Take Route 220 to the north end of Keyser. Turn east on Route 46, which is Armstrong Street. Go to the edge of town to Keys Street. The house is down a hill on the left. It faces the railroad and the North Branch of the Potomac River, which is away from the highway.*

The Devil's Warning

Everyone knows the devil is an elusive rogue, and we spent the better part of a day tracking him down. Nevertheless, with an astounding series of lucky breaks—or divine guidance, some might say—we succeeded in finding one of his old haunts.

We began with scant information (depending on the tale): a unique story about the devil appearing at the Wagonwheel or White

Raven Inn, located about eight miles from Keyser. We also knew that the inn once stood in a valley at the foot of a mountain and that a creek ran behind it, but there are lots of valleys and mountains and creeks around Keyser. We had no idea whether the inn was still in operation, or even if it was still standing, for the youngest version of the story was at least 38 years old.

We were unable to find out any additional information at the Keyser Public Library. Now who would know something about an old roadhouse that might possibly have an unsavory reputation? The local authorities, of course, so we inquired at the police station. At first we drew a blank, but a passing deputy sheriff heard our inquiry and volunteered that he knew the Wagonwheel Inn. Although he had never heard of the story connected with it, he knew that it was still operating as a tavern in a certain town, in a valley, some 10 or 12 miles away. He told us where to go and warned us that the place could be rough—he had been there on several occasions to break up fights. But he also told us we would probably be all right if we went there in the day time, so intrepid ghost hunters that we are, we went.

We found the tavern without trouble. Although it lacked an identifying sign, there was a wagon wheel on the roof, just as the story and the sheriff had told us. Oddly, the nondescript white building seemed comparatively young and appeared to have once been a gas station. The place looked deserted. At first we doubted whether it was even open. But we were in broad daylight and everything looked peaceful, so we ventured in.

All eyes turned on the two strangers just like in the old westerns. Well, in truth, there were only six eyes—the bartender and two customers at the far end of the bar. We glanced about the dim interior, taking in the pool tables and wood panel walls decorated with sports memorabilia, and ambled forward with a casual air that hid our anxiety. How do you ask about ghosts in a place like this?

We introduced ourselves and explained what we were doing. We said that we had heard a story about the Wagonwheel Inn, and asked if we were in the right place. No, this wasn't the Wagonwheel, the bartender told us rather blandly. We concealed our incredulity, and made another cautious attempt, cautious because the young man behind the bar was clearly guarded in his speech. He volunteered nothing and showed no interest in our inquiry—reactions rarely encountered in our ghost hunting. We explained that we had been directed there (without saying who directed us) and had noticed the wagon wheel on the roof. Had this formerly been named the Wagonwheel or the White Raven? No, and besides the bar was relatively new. Had anyone there ever heard of the Wagonwheel or White Raven? No one had. Our wonderful lead was going down for the third time when another patron came in the side door. We lingered for a moment, reluctant to give up, for we instinctively felt that there must be something there. But we felt that we were overstaying our welcome.

"Would you like to hear the story?" Walt asked.

"Sure. Why not?" came the reply.

One evening in 1959, the regulars were enjoying themselves, talking over a few beers at the Wagonwheel Inn. No one remembers what the conversation was about, probably because the evening was like any other, with nothing out of the ordinary. The conversation began to lag when suddenly flames sprang up and "danced in the middle of the room," spellbinding everyone. Amidst the flames, the devil appeared and told them, "I am waiting for all of you." An instant later, devil and flames both disappeared. One man is said to have had a heart attack on the spot. Others ran outside screaming for mercy. Some claim that all of the survivors of that terrifying moment reformed themselves—giving up drinking, smoking, and cursing—and became regular churchgoers. Proof of the event could be seen, as late as 1962, in a low spot in the floor, precisely the place where the devil had stood. The owner's efforts to fix the problem proved fruitless, for the sag kept returning.

We experienced our own pregnant pause, but no flames shot from the floor. Instead, the newly arrived patron said, "Well, I'll be. My daddy used to tell that story all the time. He was there. Came home and told us all about it the night it happened."

After we got over our initial amazement, we began to question our source and he seemed perfectly in earnest. His father always maintained that it was a true personal experience. Did he know where the inn was? Did he! His cousin was shot to death by the bartender there on the same day that President Kennedy was assassinated!

The inn, located on US-50, had been a private residence for many years. We got detailed directions (including the owner's name), gave our thanks to everyone, and hit the trail again. We tried to avoid getting our hopes up, for we knew that this still could be a wild goose chase.

We passed back and forth a couple times and stopped at a store in the vicinity. The owner knew the place well, including the earlier White Raven name, and told us exactly which house it was. Easy to spot because of its distinctive architecture, the house features brownish, shingled walls and a hipped roof (the kind often seen on barns). Despite a powerful desire to stop and speak with the owner, we passed on. The yard had several "No Trespassing" signs, and we were told that the owner is keen on maintaining his privacy. We believe in respecting people's wishes in this regard. We therefore ask you likewise to refrain from intruding on his privacy.

There are several interesting points about this story. The most important is that the same story is told about the White Raven Inn, which we learned was the prior name for the Wagonwheel. This earlier story was published in the fall 1958 issue of *West Virginia Folklore*. So unless the devil put in a repeat performance, we suspect that this publication may have given rise to the 1959 story.

According to the earlier version, about 30 people were drinking at this rough roadhouse one night in 1938. Late in the evening, the devil came up through the floor and flew around the room. Every time his tail hit the wall, a cascade of sparks burst forth. After terrorizing everyone for a few minutes, he disappeared through the floor. As in the later version, most of the witnesses reformed themselves and converted to religion. But this time the devil didn't speak. The absence of warning makes this story more credible by avoiding a logical flaw: although the devil may enjoy scaring people, warning them of their fate would be "bad for business." But then the devil is the devil and who says he's logical.

But another plausible explanation occurs to us. The details—flames emerging from the floor (i.e., from the ground), flying around the room, bouncing off walls with sparks, and even the disappearance back through the floor—sound very much like ball lightning. Investigators have suggested that the piezo-electric effect (electricity generated when quartz, such as that contained in granite rock, is put under pressure) may occur deep underground and be strong enough to generate an electrical plasma above ground, where it would appear as a volatile ball of light. Ball lightning is also generated in thunderstorms, and eyewitnesses have reported that these "blobs" of electricity sometimes exhibit behavior that seems intelligent and can be very destructive. Too bad we don't know what the weather was when the devil made his appearance. Given the late hour and the fact that most of the witnesses had probably had a drink or two, this strange and rare natural phenomenon could easily have been mistaken for an appearance by Beelzebub himself. It certainly would give the most confirmed tippler pause to think.

Against the natural explanation, and the folklorists who don't need or want any explanation, we offer one disquieting detail. We found a remarkable coincidence connected with the White Raven name. Whitecrow is a mythical being of the Blackfoot Indians. Whether or not there is a connection, the coincidence is startling.

How to Get There: The former Wagonwheel/White Raven Inn stands on US-50, two miles west of the junction with Route 972. It is on the southeast, or New Creek, side of the road.

HARDY COUNTY

The Cole Mountain Lights

As you drive through the quiet, picturesque village of Moorefield with its splendid Victorian houses, you wouldn't suspect that it is home to one of the more unusual phenomena in haunted West Virginia, the Cole Mountain Lights. There usually is a tragic story associated with ghost lights, and the Cole Mountain Lights are no exception. Given the history of Hardy County, this story does not go back to the Civil War as you might expect, but it predates the war. It is the story of a loyal slave searching for his master.

Charles Jones was a large landowner in the area who liked to hunt. One night, he took his pack of hounds and went coon hunting up on Cole Mountain. He also took with him his most trustworthy slave, whose name unfortunately is not mentioned in any of the tales. The slave was described as being a good friend to Jones as well as a loyal servant who often accompanied him on these nocturnal ventures.

The hounds started to bay, as though they'd treed a coon. Jones and his slave ran towards the noise. The slave, being younger and more fit than Jones, was in the lead. But when he reached the hounds, he turned to find that his master had disappeared.

The faithful slave searched through the night but could find no trace of Jones. The neighbors organized a more massive search but could find no trace of the missing hunter. After a week they gave up the search as hopeless, but not so the faithful servant. Every night he went up on the mountain and looked for his vanished friend. Folks who lived around Moorefield said that they could see the yellow glow of his lantern as he carried out his fruitless quest.

On the one-year anniversary of Jone's disappearance, his faithful servant vanished as well. But strangely enough, the citizens of Moorefield said they could still see his lantern, although the color had slowly changed from yellow to red.

It is interesting to note that the Brown Mountain Lights in North Carolina have spawned a similar local legend, about a servant seeking his master who was mysteriously lost on the mountain. It's possible that the people living around Moorefield heard the story and adopted a localized version of it to account for the mysterious lights. It's equally possible that the people living around Brown Mountain heard the Moorefield story and adopted it as their own. And it also might be possible that two similar disappearances occurred and the stories aren't related to each other, at all. (For a more detailed discussion of the ghost light phenomenon, see the Introduction.) But whether or not the story explaining the existence of the lights is true or derived from another tale, the ghost light is still there glowing eerily in the night.

Many people around Moorefield still see the light today. Charles Allen, a former teacher at the Moorefield High School, saw the light from a distance. He thought it was the reflection of the moon shining on a stream. But according to other witnesses, the light appears on a part of the mountain where there is no stream.

Besides, a number of people have met the light up close and personal. And true to its origins, it seems to have a fondness for coon hunters. Several years ago two men from Maryland were up on the mountain hunting when something scared off their dogs. Then a strange red light appeared a short distance in front of them. The light approached the now nervous hunters slowly and then began to pick up speed and let out a weird scream. One of the men fired three shots at the light, but with no effect. The now petrified men threw down their weapons and ran off the mountain with the light following in hot pursuit. The light vanished when they reached the bottom of the slope. Perhaps the good and faithful servant got tired of looking for his master and threw a tantrum. Getting shot at might tend to do that to a person, even the ghost of a dead one. Or perhaps the light was a manifestation of old Jones himself, chasing out-of-state interlopers out of his private hunting preserve.

Hunters aren't the only ones who have had strange encounters with the light. A young man and his date decided to park on the mountain one night. Suddenly, a red light appeared in his car window. Thinking some of his friends were playing a little joke on him, the lad threw open the car door and leaped out, fists at the ready. But there was nothing there except the light, hovering in mid-air. He stood there, not daring to move as the light came closer as if to take a look at him. Then, as though satisfied with what it sensed, the light vanished. The young lady's reactions were not recorded.

According to the librarian at the Moorefield Library, the light is now being seen in the vicinity of a crossroads known as Walnut Bottom. It can be reached by paved roads although we wouldn't recommend taking a large recreational vehicle. There's no good point of view because the road runs parallel to the slope.

We've commented on the similarities between the Cole Mountain Lights and the Brown Mountain Lights. Our research revealed that people generally don't have close encounters with the Brown Mountain Lights. Further, the Brown Mountain Lights don't chase people and don't make any noise. Maybe the Cole Mountain Lights are ghost lights with an attitude?

Somewhere in this area, a long time ago, Charles Jones and his faithful friend and servant slipped through a crack in reality and were never seen again. Drive through the shadow-filled hollows in the oblique autumn sun and you will feel as we did. If there's not a ghost here, there should be.

How to Get There: *Take Route 220 south of Moorefield to Taylor. Turn right on CR-13 to Fisher. Go through Fisher and take the right fork onto CR-10 to Kessel. Turn right on CR-10-5 and this will take you straight to Walnut Bottom. There are no signs identifying Walnut Bottom, but when the road turns to gravel, you're there.*

Charles Sager (Never) Sleeps Here

For some reason, West Virginia state park rangers are more at ease with the ghosts in their parks than the federal rangers are with theirs. We found the state park rangers uniformly helpful, even though they usually disclaimed any belief in the ghosts. A case in point is Lost River State Park, where the ghost of a murdered man allegedly haunts the historic Lee Cabin. Instead of burying this

Front view of the Lee Cabin at Lost River State Park, where Charles Sager's ghost allegedly walks.

gruesome legacy, the park embraces it with humor, claiming in a tour handout that the cabin lights won't come on until you call for Charles Sager's ghost to turn them on. When tourists dutifully call out the name, the lights do in fact come on—courtesy of a ranger's helping hand.

Lost River State Park is named for the nearby river that disappears down a sinkhole and travels underground before emerging as Cacapon River. It lies on a portion of 17,000 acres that were acquired in 1796 by Henry "Light Horse Harry" Lee (1756-1818), the Revolutionary War hero and father of Robert E. Lee. Although the park literature claims that Henry Lee built the Lee Cabin and four others in 1800, this is undocumented and unlikely in view of Lee's personal circumstance (a busy life and substantial debt). Henry Lee sold the land in 1809.

Charles Carter Lee, Robert's older brother, began reacquiring his father's former land in 1832. He wanted to build a boarding house, or hotel, on the property to cash in on the growing fad of "taking the waters" at mineral springs. There is a potent sulfur-impregnated spring, and you can smell its pungent odor when you visit the springhouse a short distance from the Lee Cabin. From the early 19th century through the early 20th century, such springs were considered beneficial in treating a variety of diseases, and the upper classes flocked to them for their summer vacations.

Although work on his hotel did not begin until 1848, Carter's correspondence indicates that he had already built a cabin at the site—probably the present Lee Cabin—by 1843. The hotel had its ups and downs, however, and the property passed out of the Lee family in 1879. After an extensive renovation in 1897, the hotel became a fashionable resort, with bowling alleys, tennis courts, and even telephones.

All of which sets the stage for the story of poor Charles Sager, a livestock trader from Mt. Jackson, Virginia. Sometime after the Lee Cabin was built, presumably in the late 1830s or early 1840s, Sager drove his cattle over the mountains to Moorefield, where he sold them. As he returned home via the Moorefield Mountain Road (today's CR-12), highwaymen ambushed and robbed him near the site of the present park entrance.

For reasons lost to history, the thieves dragged him to the Lee Cabin, which, like most summer retreats, was often unoccupied. Perhaps the thieves thought he would tell them where more money was hidden, or perhaps the attack was an act of revenge rather than a robbery. In any case, they brutally stabbed him to death and left his body in the far corner of the left-hand room on the second floor. The blood poured from Sager's body, pooled in the corner, and dripped down the walls to the floor below. The bloodstains on the floors and walls resisted all efforts to clean them. Even more frightening were the chilling screams that emanated from the cabin on warm nights, disrupting the happy festivities at the nearby hotel. As if cursed by the tragedy, the resort came to a sad end when the hotel burned down in 1910.

We went to inspect Lee Cabin with much anticipation. Stories about indelible bloodstains are classic and this site offered a rare opportunity to investigate a remarkably specific claim. Restored by the Civilian Conservation Corps in 1940, the cabin sits in a picturesque mountain glen. It consists of two floors (over a cellar) and a porch. One room on each side on both floors flanks a central staircase. The cabin has no attic, so the vault of the roof is exposed on the upper floor. The present fireplace was added during the restoration.

We were glad to learn that the walls were original, but a little downcast to hear that they had been whitewashed. Then we noticed some stains in the corners, and our pulse quickened for a moment. Alas, after checking all the rooms, we concluded that we had found only water stains. There have been no recent reports of screams emanating from the cabin on warm summer nights. So if you decide to camp at Lost River and hear a scream in the middle of the night, that seems to come from the Lee Cabin, not to worry. It's just poor old Charlie Sager, bemoaning his fate.

How to Get There: From Route 259 in Mathias, turn onto CR-12. Follow signs to Lee Cabin. Park at the lot for the swimming pool, on the left. Across the road from the Bathhouse, the trail leads about 100 yards to Lee Sulfur Springs and Lee Cabin, which is on the right just beyond the spring.

Grant County

The Maysville Market Haunt

Sometimes when you start off hunting one ghost, you wind up with something completely different. It happened to us on several occasions during our quest. We were hunting down the story of a 19th-century peddler who was done in by a local farmer. The ghost was first encountered some 25 years after the peddler vanished by a young man on his way to see his girl. As he was going along he heard something that sounded like blood gurgling in a man's throat. He shined his light on the spot where the death rattle seemed to be coming from and the noise stopped. Then he heard a noise he said sounded like a flock of crows taking off.

Five years later, men were plowing the same field when they hit a sandstone rock, which was not common to the area. The rock made a hollow sound when they hit it so they decided to lift it up to see what was underneath. When they lifted the rock, they discovered a powder-like substance in the shape of a human skeleton. Frightened and dismayed, the men hurriedly put the stone back into place and covered it with dirt. Since that time, people going past the spot have allegedly heard the gurgling sound.

We knew that identifying this site would be tough, but we decided to give it a try. Sometimes stories like this one slip from collective memory and off into the abyss of time. We drove up Route 42 from Petersburg on a Sunday afternoon thinking that if we couldn't find the peddler's grave, at least we could see some pretty scenery.

When we got to Maysville, no one was around. We knew that we'd have to talk to someone in town if we were to have any shot at all at verifying the story. When we got to the north end of town, we noticed that the Maysville Market was open. This was a bit of luck because many small country stores in West Virginia close on Sunday.

We stopped and introduced ourselves to Sharon Kiplinger and Mary Hoverville, who worked and ran the market, and asked if they knew anything about our phantom peddler. They said they didn't, but if we were interested in ghosts, the Maysville Market was the site of strange doings.

The Maysville Market, where snacks and spooks go together.

First of all, they said there were noises upstairs that sounded like footsteps, when no one was there. Downstairs in the store, things seem to get rearranged by invisible hands. The lights like to go off and on by themselves, even when the circuits are closed. Finally, a telephone that was disconnected and unplugged, rang. Unfortunately, no one answered it so we don't know who was on the other end.

Neither Sharon nor Mary could account for the phenomena, for they knew of no deaths or violent incidents associated with the store building. They did say that the building is over 100 years old, which is evidenced by the old cedar paneling inside.

So what can account for the strange happenings at the Maysville Market? The story told by Sharon and Mary is a typical haunting, one could almost say, average and run of the mill. Most haunted places are not filled with apparitions that gush blood and scream off into the night. Instead, small incidents make reality seem slightly out of phase. Footsteps are heard when no one is there. Things are moved around, "lost" and then "found" in an obvious place. Lights seem to act on their own volition, blinking on and off at odd times. All of these things have possible physical explanations. But if you've ever lived in a haunted house, you know something doesn't feel quite right, and it's extremely disconcerting. (I'm speaking from personal experience—WJG.)

So if you find yourself going through Maysville, stop at the Maysville Market at the corner of Route 42 and Water Street. Gas up the car, get a snack, and buy a souvenir. Mary or Sharon will be glad to help you and maybe even talk about the ghost. And if the phone rings and you notice it's unplugged, don't answer. It may be the phantom peddler of Maysville wondering why no one has been by his grave recently.

How to Get There: Take Route 42, south from US-50 or north from US-220, to Maysville. The market stands on the corner of Route 42 and Water Street.

RANDOLPH COUNTY

Hidden in Halliehurst

More than any house we have visited, Halliehurst, in Elkins, looks like it *should* be haunted. Modeled after a Rhineland castle admired by Hallie Davis Elkins, the original owner's wife,

Halliehurst is the largest shingled structure in West Virginia. Add to this distinction its sprawling porches, slate roofs, turrets, stained-glass windows, "walk-in" fireplaces, and gorgeous interior woodwork and you have a truly exceptional house, a delight to visit even if it had no ghosts. As such it deserves its place on the National Register of Historic Places.

Halliehurst porch including the turret and tower.

Construction of the mansion began in 1890 and ultimately cost about $300,000, an astronomical sum for the time. In bad repair by the mid-1980s, the house was fortunately saved from demolition and restored. According to one of the restoration carpenters, who graciously gave us a guided tour of the house, most of the original woodwork remains intact. All that was necessary was cleaning and some minor repairs. We also learned that Halliehurst has exotic features aside from its ghosts, for its walls conceal secret passages, a hidden room, and a tunnel that linked it to the neighboring Graceland mansion. Unfortunately, the tunnel caved in during the construction of the student union building which stands between the two structures.

Who was responsible for this amazing edifice? Halliehurst was built by Stephen B. Elkins (1841-1911), a leading industrialist and politician who had served as Secretary of War under President Benjamin Harrison and as a U.S. Senator for the last 16 years of his life. With his business partner, U.S. Senator Henry Gassaway Davis, Elkins brought the railroad into the eastern mountains and made a fortune shipping out timber and coal. The connection between the partners was especially close because Elkins married Davis' daughter Hallie in 1877. Hallie holds the curious distinction of being the only woman who was a daughter, wife, and mother of U.S. senators. In 1904, the partners founded Davis and Elkins College on donated land south of town. After the original college had been destroyed by fire, Hallie deeded the Elkins estate to the college in 1923 with the provision that the college campus would move to the estate grounds.

Halliehurst has hosted such national figures as Presidents Benjamin Harrison and Grover Cleveland and failed presidential candidate James G. Blaine, but no one has ever reported seeing their ghosts, perhaps because they would put us to sleep with boredom. After becoming part of the college, Halliehurst served as the college president's residence. In the 1950s and early '60s, it was turned into a women's dormitory. Then it was closed and fell into disrepair. By the late '60s, ivy and weeds enveloped the house, giving it an even spookier atmosphere. Its haunted reputation grew at this time, and local teens used to dare each other to explore the house. One of them, Susie Schoonover, now works in the administrative offices in Halliehurst and told us of a ghostly incident that she knew from her own experience.

In the autumn of 1969 or 1970, Susie and some friends undertook the challenge of venturing into the house. Even without ghosts this would take some courage, because the structure was in a dangerous state of disrepair. For example, a large hole gaped in the middle of the third floor. Going around the hole, the teens explored the rest of the third floor. In the room that now houses the Darby collection of prehistoric artifacts, a door formerly opened onto a balcony. Eager for a view from the balcony, one of Susie's friends opened the door and stepped out—almost into eternity! The balcony was gone! But just as he stepped through, he felt an invisible hand catch him by the collar and pull him back.

This isn't the only time something like this has happened in the old house. One day a drama student in one of the towers tripped and began to fall down the stairs. The tumble might well have killed him, but an invisible helping hand pushed him back.

In a 1979 article in the Davis & Elkins College magazine, *Forward*, Dr. Cassandra Whyte, then assistant director of the Counseling Center located on the second floor of the house, confirmed this helpful pattern of ghostly activity. She said, "There have been many documented cases involving ghosts at Halliehurst. But almost all of these cases have been very positive, usually involving incidents where something harmful was prevented."

There are other stories that aren't quite so positive and may show a nasty side of the Halliehurst haunts. Ron Sposato, one of the photographers for the 1979 *Forward* article, fell down some stairs while shooting the story. Sposato couldn't understand why he had fallen, but his colleague, photographer Bob Wrobleski, said it looked as though Ron had been pushed. In another case, a girl claimed something tried to push her over the railing of the tower, but her boy friend caught her just in time, saving her life.

But most of the time, the Halliehurst spooks are heard or felt, but not seen. In fact, the three most common ghostly phenomena at Halliehurst are weird noises; eerie feelings or a sense of unease; and cold spots, which many witnesses have felt even on hot summer days. Although published articles and rumors make vague claims that apparitions have been seen, we have found only one specific incident, which itself is somewhat ambiguous. A female student, who was derided by her friends as "mental" and "always wanting attention," once fled screaming from the parlor on a sunny afternoon. She swore that Hallie's ghost had appeared and ordered her out of the building.

There are other stories involving Hallie's ghost, although not in visible form. One dates from the time when the mansion served as the women's dormitory. Two Chi Omega sorority sisters who had a suite in the dorm decided that they would do something to show disdain for the ghost. So they opened the door to Hallie's old room, mockingly called out, "We hope we didn't disturb you, Hallie," and then closed the door. Even before they could giggle over their stunt, the door reopened. Their initial surprise instantly turned to fear, for the room stood empty. Then, in another moment, the door "slammed in their faces."

Hallie's ghost may also be responsible for an incident recalled by night watchman Shirley Ervin. One night in the mid-1970s, he and his son were lounging in the first-floor conference room at about 2 a.m. when they heard the sound of women's voices. The voices floated up the basement stairs and grew louder, as if the women were coming from the basement to the first floor. Ervin and his son were surprised and puzzled, because they had followed their nightly routine and thoroughly checked the house to make sure no students were hiding in it after hours, as they sometimes liked to do. The two sprang up and burst into the hallway, fully expecting to nab the culprits. Instead they were bewildered, for no one was there. As Ervin recalled, "When we came out of the room, we couldn't find anyone. We searched the building, but found nothing."

As for Halliehurst's mysterious cold spots, consider a doubly witnessed dramatic example that happened to Pastor Randall F. Peters, a Lutheran minister. In the late '70s, he and two students spent an evening in the mansion, during the first full moon of the spring. Pastor Peters brought his bagpipes to test the folk tradition that the devil hates bagpipe music. He was walking through the first floor conference room, playing his pipes, when he hit a cold spot that sent chills through him. Startled, he fled from the room. Regrouping with the students, Pastor Peters recovered his courage and decided to venture into the room again. This time one of the students accompanied him. They walked down opposite sides of the conference table and discovered that the cold spot had moved to the other side of the table, where the student now felt it. Peters said it was so distinctly defined that you could move in and out of it, and feel its presence in one particular place. So maybe Hallie doesn't like to be mistaken for the devil, or maybe she, like Old Scratch, also hates the pipes.

Perhaps the oddest story told about Halliehurst is this one. While on his way to class, a student felt an unseen presence in one of the second-floor rooms. He tried to leave but found that he could no longer move his feet. After a few minutes the frightened student found he could move, so he hurried off to class. There he discovered that his classmates had been talking about Halliehurst's ghosts and about the particular room in which he had been immobilized, all at the very moment when he stood transfixed! This extraordinary incident is especially interesting because it resembles nightmares in which we find ourselves paralyzed in the face of some unknown horror.

This incident raises several questions. Did his classmates subconsciously and clairvoyantly know the stuck student's predicament? Did their discussion provide the psychic energy that caused the paralysis? Or did a supernatural presence coordinate the events to create its own horrible irony? If this is the case, the spook at Halliehurst clearly has a nasty imagination.

Recent reports of the Halliehurst ghosts are scant, perhaps because the building is generally unoccupied in the late evening. The only specific case we have found occurred a few years ago. We were told that a flower arrangement in the private bathroom located on the second floor, disappeared for four days and then reappeared in the same place. This is, of course, a standard poltergeist-like phenomenon, but it is also a standard hoaxer phenomenon. Nevertheless, we were told that the circumstances made a practical joke quite inconceivable.

The creepiest story about Halliehurst doesn't concern its spectral inhabitants, but rather what the workers found in the basement at the time of the mansion's restoration. Our guide led us down into the damp, crypt-like, underbelly of the manse, a privilege rarely accorded to tourists. We ducked under pipes and low beams as we explored the rock-walled labyrinth. Finally, we came to a small room off the main passage. Our guide told us that because of its size and construction—insulated with sawdust to keep out the dampness—the room most likely served as a wine cellar. During the restoration, however, our guide and his companions found no wine. Instead they found a coffin! Not just some modern coffin, either, but an archaic wooden coffin complete with *wooden nails*.

We felt both aghast and pleased by what we were hearing. Visions of Dracula's coffin lying in his basement sprang instantly to mind. The wooden nails seemed especially significant, because iron traditionally has talismanic power against evil. "What was in it?" we asked with keen anticipation.

Our guide admitted that no one wanted to touch the coffin, so they got a mop and used the end of the handle to push open the loose lid. An empty interior mocked them. "Probably just a prop for a sorority ritual, or for a student prank," we rationalized.

Probably. But then again, who knows what evil lurks...

How to Get There: *From US-219 (Randolph Avenue) in Elkins, turn onto Sycamore Street at the equestrian statue. Bear left onto Campus Drive. Halliehurst stands on the left side, about half the distance back to Randolph Avenue.*

The Werewolf Hitchhiker

Late at night, in the deep darkness of the country, unblemished by city lights, you see a forlorn young woman sitting on a stone by the road. Who would fail to stop and offer help in such circumstances? So you stop and offer her a ride. She asks for a ride to her home in Elkins and you readily agree, although you're a little puzzled. What was a young girl doing out all alone on a dark country road? She's silent on the drive. When you reach the address she has given, you stop and she gets out. Then she just vanishes, in front of your eyes. You just stand there, shaken to the core of your being. You can't believe it. People just don't vanish into thin air.

Slowly you recover from the shock. You go up to the house and knock on the door. An older lady answers. You tell her the story, even though you feel like a fool. She replies in a kindly voice that you're not the first person that this has happened to. It seems that her daughter was killed in a car accident at the very spot you picked her up. During the 1940s more than one motorist lived through this scenario as they drove on US-33 about five miles west of Elkins.

Of course, this is a variant of the standard phantom hitchhiker story, a staple of modern ghostly lore. In *The Evidence for Phantom Hitchhikers*, a definitive study of these tales, Michael Goss found that very little good evidence exists for the existence of these and that the location of the haunting is often quite vague, with phantoms frequently haunting vast stretches of a particular road.

The US-33 phantom hitchhiker doesn't follow Goss' theory. We can fix her location with some precision. According to the stories the woman sits on a stone *next to a bridge* at a place called *Dead Man's Curve, between Elkins and Bellington*. All we had to do was find a stone, next to a bridge on Dead Man's Curve between Elkins and Bellington. What could be simpler? Well, despite all the obstacles, we think we've located the spot.

It didn't look promising at first. No one we talked to had heard of Dead Man's Curve, and there are no significant curves by bridges on US-33 between Elkins and Bellington. Then we learned that the route of US-33 was altered several decades ago. The phantom hitchhiker stories refer to old US-33, which is today CR-151, a two-lane road that intersects US-33 at Harding, about five miles west of Elkins. So we drove the route and found a spot that matches the story superbly.

The road crosses the Tygart Valley River on a bridge at Norton and then goes up a sharp curve to the left. Anyone driving the opposite direction, coming down the hill too fast, will learn too late where Dead Man's Curve is. The capper is that a cliff rises beside the road on the west end of the bridge and provides the fallen stone on which the hitchhiker sits.

So where's the werewolf we promised? No, the young lady doesn't turn into a wolf on the night of a full moon and start lunging and snapping at people. But she may not be the only thing that haunts old US-33.

As was our habit, we always told people at the motel where we stayed, what we were up to. Sometimes we'd get a helpful hint or two, and sometimes we'd hit pay dirt. We heard a remarkable story from Vicki Cunningham, a manager at the Days Inn in Elkins. She told us that she and her husband were driving on CR-151 one snowy winter night a few years ago when they were startled by a fleeting encounter. Between Jimtown and Norton, they saw a man walking beside the road. This surprised them because the hour was late and the weather was bad. Then they got a profound shock, for as they passed, the man looked straight at them. "He had the face of a dog." Wolves, of course, are members of the canine family, so this looks very much like a modern werewolf sighting. What is really interesting about this story is that it's located within a mile of the phantom hitchhiker's rock, yet when we received this story, we had not yet located the site! Moreover the werewolf was walking beside the road, just as a hitchhiker would do. Not that anyone with three ounces of gray matter would give it a ride.

A phantom hitchhiker with a precise location, a curve whose name carries the memory of death, and a pedestrian werewolf: this is a truly spooky stretch of road. Take a look for yourself. But don't pick up any hitchhikers, especially if the moon is full.

How to Get There: From Elkins, take US-33 west to Harding. Go left on CR-151. Turn right and cross the bridge over the Tygart Valley River at Norton. The phantom probably sits on a stone at the foot of the cliff near the west end of the bridge.

The Ghosts at Rich Mountain

Rich Mountain is a lonely place, perhaps one of the loneliest places we visited in the course of our research. You get to Rich Mountain by driving up one of those cranky West Virginia mountain roads—narrow, gravel roads that twist and turn and try to shake you off the back of the mountain. And what you find when you get there is a gravel parking lot, some fields, lots of woods, a power line that flies over the mountain and a stone monument surrounded by a wrought iron fence.

On July 10, 1861, Union troops under General George McClellan fought a sharp battle with Confederate forces commanded by General Robert S. Garnett. McClellan's victory at Rich Mountain would propel him into the command of the Army of the Potomac, while Garnett's defeat would put him in the grave.

As you look around you might wonder why anyone would fight a battle in such an isolated spot. This part of West Virginia was strategically important during the Civil War. If the Confederates held this area they could threaten the Baltimore and Ohio Railroad, the chief Federal communications link with the west.

A tombstone for a house.

The campaign started on June 30, 1861, when Union forces routed around 1,000 ill-trained Virginia volunteers at Philippi. Then General Garnett, commanding Confederate troops in western Virginia, divided his forces, putting some on the road to Wheeling at Laurel Mountain and moving 1,300 men under Lt. Colonel John Pegram to fortify positions on Rich Mountain. From here Pegram could control the Staunton to Parkersburg Turnpike, a strategic highway. Pegram heavily fortified the area commanding the turnpike, naming the position Camp Garnett in honor of his commander.

McClellan took three brigades to attack Pegram's position at Camp Garnett. When he saw how strongly fortified Pegram's troops were, he was reluctant to make a frontal attack. So he decided to send 2,000 troops under General W. S. Rosecrans around Pegram's flank to take him in the rear.

David Hart, a 22-year-old whose father owned the farm at the summit, volunteered to guide the troops up the mountain and around the flank. After ten hours of hard marching over rocks and through the brush in the middle of a rainstorm, Rosecrans arrived at the top only to discover that Pegram had detached several hundred troops and a cannon to defend his rear.

Despite the inexperience of his troops, Rosecrans attacked the Rebel positions and took them by surprise. After two hours of heavy fighting, the Confederate line was broken. Pegram abandoned his position and escaped during the night. The next morning, Rosecrans occupied the now abandoned Camp Garnett, and the battle was won.

Imagine David Hart's surprise when the battle he thought would take place down the mountain, took place in his front yard, which was right next to the battlefield. The Hart home served as a hospital. Compared to some of the later battles of the Civil War, Rich Mountain was a small affair with relatively few casualties. But big or small, the suffering was the same, and maybe this traumatic wrench from innocence sparked off the unusual haunting of the Hart house.

In 1867, Lewis Kittle and Daniel Courfreight boarded with Mr. Hart while they worked as coal miners. From the very first night they moved into the room, they heard weird, continuous noises. One night, when Kittle was in the room alone, he was awakened by an unusual cold. A dim light seemed to outline the furniture in the room. Uneasy, Kittle got out of bed and moved near the door. To his surprise, eight Confederate soldiers materialized out of thin air. They approached Kittle's bed and lifted something from it. It turned out to be the body of a handsome young man dressed in gray trousers. The eight specters carried their burden out the door and vanished.

The shaken Kittle asked around and found that several other men who had rented the room had the same bizarre experience. There also was a report that a soldier had been shot in the haunted room.

A few nights later, the whole thing happened again, only this time both men were present. The cold and the light entered the room. The men hastily got out of the bed and were pushed out of the way by the ghosts as the same macabre scene was reenacted. These nocturnal visits became so frequent that the men got used to them. According to Ruth Ann Musick, who collected this tale, when the light appeared the men would wrap themselves up in their blankets and say, "Here come those damn Rebels again."

Just what transpired in the Hart house isn't clear. We found no other stories about the place, or about Rich Mountain for that matter. But it doesn't mean that all is quiet there. The old Hart house is no more. It burned down in 1940 and was never rebuilt. A picture taken in 1884 shows a good size farmhouse with a barn and outbuilding. Now all that is left is a stone marker surrounded by a wrought iron fence. It's like a tombstone for a house.

Rich Mountain doesn't have that sullen feeling that many battlefields have. We were there in early summer, near the time when the battle was fought. It was peaceful and pleasant and the scenery was most delightful. The only danger we encountered was from the poison ivy that covered the rocks where many soldiers had carved their names.

But for some reason our camera malfunctioned and we got only one good picture at Rich Mountain. The rest were partially or totally fogged over. Malfunctions of this sort are common at haunted sites. The Devils Den at Gettysburg battlefield is especially noted for this. According to David Hart's memoirs, a dozen or so "Indiana boys" are buried in the rocks. So what fogged our film? The nearby power line? A fault in the camera? The Indiana boys saying "Hi"?

Does the funeral party still march even though the house is gone? No one has said, but then how many people are up on this deserted mountain in the wee hours of the morning? We'd like to think they found some peace at last. But who knows? Rich Mountain is a lonely place.

How to Get There: From US-33 at Harding, about five miles west of Elkins, take CR-151 south. Turn right and cross the bridge over the Tygart River at Norton. Almost immediately bear left onto CR-53. Pass Coalton, and turn left on a road marked "Mabie" (this is CR-37-8, but it has no route sign on it). Pass through Mabie, and then turn left onto a road marked by a Rich Mountain battlefield sign. Follow this road to the crest of the mountain to reach the site of the Hart house. The unpaved road is rough for several miles.

POCAHONTAS COUNTY

The Ghosts of Droop Mountain

It was a beautiful day in late summer when we visited Droop Mountain. As with so many of the places we visited, it was difficult to believe that this quiet and peaceful place had been the site of the biggest Civil War battle in West Virginia. But as we stood next to where the observation tower used to be, looking out over the Greenbrier Valley as fat cumulus clouds played tag with the sun, it was easy to see why people thought this place was haunted. In fact, there are so many tales of ghosts and unexplainable events that the mountain might more appropriately be called Spook Mountain.

But before we get to the haunts, a little background will put the hauntings into context. The battle of Droop Mountain took place on November 6, 1863. The Union forces led by General William Averell were trying to drive the Confederates out of the Greenbrier Valley and, in the process, destroy the Virginia and Tennessee Railroad at the southern end of the new state. This would relieve the pressure on the Union forces that had suffered a staggering defeat at the battle of Chickamauga in September.

Facing Averell's 4,000 Federals were 1,700 men under the command of General John Echols. Echols placed his small army on the high ground at Droop Mountain, between Lewisburg and the quick-moving Union forces. Here the advantage of occupying the high ground helped reduce the Yankees' advantage in numbers. After a sharp and bloody fight, Averell managed to turn Echols' flank, but Echols withdrew from the field with most of his army intact.

The Ranger Station at Droop Mountain, the site of many unexplained occurences.

One of the real tragedies of Droop Mountain is that large groups of West Virginians fought each other, with brother against brother, neighbor against neighbor and friend against friend. There were 119 Union and 275 Rebel casualties. Most of the dead are buried all over the mountain, although there is a small cemetery behind the park offices.

This bloody little battle has spawned a swarm of ghost tales. James Gay Jones collected some of them and put us on the trail. Park superintendent Mike Smith was extremely helpful to us, even though he said he had had no personal experiences with the supernatural and was a bit of a skeptic on the whole matter of ghosts. The folks at the Greenbrier Historical Society also proved to be a great help, letting us copy choice items out of their ghost file.

The Snedegar Poltergeist

The hauntings around Droop Mountain started soon after the battle was over. In 1865, Betty and Nancy Snedegar, two little girls who lived in the area, went off to pick berries on Droop Mountain. What they got was a lot more than dessert for that night's supper. The girls found two muskets, which had undoubtedly been lost in the battle. When they picked up the weapons and started taking them home, some unknown or unseen persons started throwing rocks at them. Both girls raced home like the wind. Later, when they went out to do the milking, more rocks and clubs were thrown at them. They took shelter in the house, and the house was pelted with rocks. Rocks came down the chimney, and some reports said that stones and rocks came through the walls but left no holes. Then, according to other reports, the sheep skin rugs on the floor started to "rare up."

The girls collected the rocks and began to throw them into a large sinkhole next to the house. To their astonishment, as soon as they threw a rock into the sinkhole, it would come flying back out. These poltergeist-type activities continued until the guns were returned to their original place. Only then did they stop, and to the best of our knowledge, never happened again.

The old Snedegar place still exists but we didn't visit it because it is located two miles off the road and it is quite difficult to get to it. Superintendent Smith has visited the place and said that when he threw rocks down the sinkhole they didn't come back out.

This isn't surprising because the spirits were allegedly laid well over 100 years ago. Despite this, Smith candidly admitted that he feels uneasy when he visits the place. He says the area is "creepy," and that he felt like someone was watching him the whole time he was there. So if you're hiking around the woods on Droop Mountain, and you spot a rusty old musket sticking out of the ground, it might be more prudent if you just left it alone and went on your way.

The Ghostly Regiment

The next report of ghostly activity took place in 1914, well before the time Droop Mountain became a state park. Mr. A. W. Albert claimed to have spotted a regiment of soldiers on the battlefield. (The report did not say whether they were Yankees or Rebels.) The troops were marching two by two, and each man had a musket on his shoulder. Unfortunately we could find no further details on this truly astonishing sighting.

The Headless Specter

Does a headless specter haunt Droop Mountain? If so, seeing it seems to run in the Edgar Walton family. The first sighting occurred in the 1920s. Edgar Walton lived at the old Sunrise Schoolhouse, which is about a quarter of a mile from the entrance of the park. One day he and a friend were walking near Spring Creek Mountain when they decided to stop, rest and build a fire. Both men were startled by the sudden appearance of a headless apparition that may have been a soldier. The apparition drifted along to the middle of a gate and disappeared, leaving the two startled men to wonder just what it was they had seen.

After a 50-year hiatus, the headless spook appeared again in 1977, this time to Mrs. Clenston Delaney, the daughter of Edgar Walton. Mrs. Delaney, her husband and her sister were cutting wood at about the same spot her father had his encounter with the unknown. All three of then saw a gray-uniformed, headless ghost pass them while making a low moaning sound. Then it disappeared, they said, leaving them frightened and shaking.

It's interesting to note that one of the casualties at Droop Mountain was 2nd Lieutenant Joseph W. Daniels, Battery B, 1st West Virginia Light Artillery. Daniels had his head shot off by a Rebel shell.

It is important to note that just because a ghost has no head, doesn't mean that the person lost his or her head in life. Not all apparitions are complete individuals, so appearing headless could be misleading. The fact that it appeared some 50 years after its first appearance to the members of the same family may mean that this particular ghost has ties to that family. Or maybe the ghosts just had an acute attack of "what the heck" and decided to try its luck with the Delaneys.

But this headless ghost isn't the only one around Droop. According to a lady named Anna Atkins, who grew up in the area, a headless ghost plagued the people around Droop Mountain during the later part of the 19th century. During the battle, a cavalryman cut off an infantryman's head and threw it into a nearby pond. Although the gravediggers searched for the head, it was never found, so the headless body was buried beside the road in front of the Gerald Brown House.

Taking umbrage at its missing head, the headless spook took to stopping teams of horses that passed by his grave, no doubt to attract attention to his plight. He would grab the horses by the bridle and not let them go until dawn, much to the consternation of the teamsters. One night, the driver of a double team had his horses stopped all of a sudden. Despite all of his urgings, the beasts would not move.

Then he spotted the ghost, holding the bridle of the lead team. First he asked the ghost to kindly let go of the bridle. It didn't. Seeing that the soft approach was getting him no place, he sprang to the back of one of the horses and proceeded to beat the ghost with his whip. The horses bolted and hurled off down the mountain while the driver clung to the horse's mane to avoid falling off and being trampled. Fortunately, the horses were halted a ways down the road. But the ghost never stopped horses at this spot again. Maybe it stalked off in high dudgeon and went to bother the Walton clan.

The CCC Boys and the Spooks

In 1935, Camp Price, part of the Civilian Conservation Corps (CCC) was established on Droop Mountain. Johnson J. Heuey, one of the 220 enrollees at the camp, related this story in an interview in *Wonderful West Virginia* magazine. Camp Price could be a lonely and spooky place at night. Along with the fogs and the mist, the cries of owls and screams of bobcats added to its aura of mystery. Some people said they could hear the sound of marching feet outside the camp on moonless nights. Others would be challenged by ghostly cries of "Who goes there?" as they sneaked back into camp after visiting the local girls. Were these campfire ghost tales and practical jokes played by bored CCC boys on their more gullible friends? Perhaps. But consider Johnnie Keen's story before you rush to judgment.

Droop Mountain's Phantom Cavalry

In 1941, a hard-working lumber truck driver named Johnnie Keen was making his way home down US-219. It was 2:30 a.m. Keen, who had been working since 3:30 the previous morning, said he was tired but alert. Keen was coming down the long straight stretch at the foot of Droop Mountain. At the curve near the Brown house, eight to twelve people riding horses appeared in the truck's headlights. In Keen's own words, "I really tried out the pair of brakes on that truck. It was a heavy duty two ton."

After the truck skidded to a halt, Keen got out of the cab to give the riders a piece of his mind. Driving a truck was hazardous enough without trail riders popping out in front of you in the middle of the night. But as he moved towards them, they turned left and vanished out of the glow of the lights, leaving the thunderstruck driver staring at nothing. According to Keen the riders were wearing khaki-colored pants, blue jackets and coats similar to those worn by army officers or chauffeurs. The front horse of the group was white while the others were darker colored. They all carried saddlebags as though they were cavalry out on patrol. (This story was taken from a written account prepared by Mr. Keen before his death in 1988.)

The troop has been seen again, this time in the daylight. According to Superintendent Mike Smith, one afternoon a man was driving over Droop Mountain when he spotted seven mounted soldiers. At first the man thought they were part of a reenactment group, but as he got closer to them, they didn't move. Finally, the horsemen turned and disappeared into the side of the mountain. Six of the horsemen rode dark-colored horses. Their leader was mounted on a steed of dapple-gray.

Sometimes this phantom troop chooses to remain invisible. When they stay invisible, they seem to take great delight in charging around the park. According to James Gay Jones, one day the faint sound of a bugle was heard coming from the northwest part of the park. Soon the clatter of approaching horses could be heard but they couldn't be seen. They rode by the park office headed south.

Napoleon Holbrook was the park superintendent from 1946 to 1949. One day, his son was playing in the road in front of the park office when he heard a horse approaching. The lad looked up and saw nothing. As the sound came nearer and nearer, the boy became frightened and ran inside the office. (More will be heard of the Holbrook family's experiences a little later in this chapter.)

In October 1972, Clarence Murray, an engineer with the Department of Highways who lived near the park, decided to get in a little squirrel hunting. While out in the quiet of the woods, Murray thought he heard a horse pulling a wagon accompanied by jingling sounds. According to Murray, "It was close like it was going to run me over." But like so many other people, he could not see the source of the sound. Perhaps the ghostly cavalry was bringing up artillery, or maybe it was the sound of a ghostly caisson with a headless lieutenant in command.

The Holbrooks and the Clutters

Some of the Droop Mountain superintendents have lived there without noticing anything supernatural while others seem to attract spooks. The Holbrooks and the Clutters probably rate their own chapter. One morning at around 3:00, Napoleon Holbrook was awakened by a screaming sound that seemed to come from a section of the park known as the Cranberry Bog. Being very conscientious, thinking it might have been an animal in distress, Holbrook searched the area and found nothing.

A similar incident happened in 1950 to Park Superintendent William Davis and caretaker Floyd Clutter. The two men were hard at work one day, when they heard a scream of distress that seemed to come from the woods. A thorough search revealed nothing.

Napoleon Holbrook's daughter Carol had a strange encounter at age six. She thought she saw a man in a knee-length Confederate coat lying next to a tree in front of the residence. When she returned with her mother, the man was gone. Remember that the late 1940s was not a time when reenactors were common, so if Carol imagined this encounter, it was pretty clever for a six-year-old.

But the prize spook encounter of all goes to Carol's mother. One autumn day she was sitting in the back yard shelling beans. Suddenly, she noticed that the leaves in the nearby woods were moving as though someone was walking through them. Slowly it approached Mrs. Holbrook. She heard it stride down the cement sidewalk and then down into the cellar. She then grabbed the puzzled Carol and barricaded them both inside the house. With a ghost in the cellar, one wonders if this was the wisest choice. Another time the family heard someone shout the command "Halt!" from their front porch. When they checked, no one was there.

The Clutter family has had its share of weirdness at Droop Mountain. In 1970, Mrs. John Clutter, Floyd's mother, noticed a man standing behind the soldiers' graves in the small cemetery at the back of the house. He stepped behind a tree and never came out the other side. Quite naturally Mrs. Clutter wondered what happened, so she went and investigated but found no one—that she could see at any rate—there.

The Civil War cemetery at Droop Mountain, where perhaps the soldiers don't stay buried all the time.

On July 16, 1977, at 10 p.m., the Clutter family had come back from church and was sitting in the kitchen, having a snack. They heard the front door of the house open and the sound of youngsters talking. When they went to see who it was, no one was in the living room and the front door was locked.

In August of the same year, Floyd's wife was home alone watching television when someone, or something, started to knock on the outside wall near the television. She got up and looked out the window to determine the source of the racket. To her amazement she saw a hat like the one Mr. Clutter wore, float past the window, without the benefit of being on Mr. Clutter's head. She said, "It just floated off into the darkness...The porch light was on and I couldn't have imagined it." A spook with a sense of humor? Maybe it was the same one that liked to have fun with the CCC boys. Or maybe it was one of the CCC boys.

The Clutters' time at the park was further spiced up by occasional loud knocks on the door with, of course, no one being there. Phantom cars would pull up and car doors would slam, and of course there were no cars either. The Clutters, who seem to be very nice and tolerant people, said that the ghosts were polite since the knockings and bangings always came in the daytime.

The Gray Ghost...Horse

The ghosts of Droop Mountain have been active up into the 1990s. Just ask Ron Nelson, a reenactor belonging to the 17th Virginia Cavalry, Company F, better known as the Night Hawks. Nelson arrived on Droop Mountain one Friday night in late October. Nelson and his friend, Joe Hoff, were trying to find toilet facilities. Nelson, his needs becoming more desperate after his long drive, hurried ahead of his friend to find the men's room.

To see his way through the dark night, Nelson was shining his flashlight into the woods. Suddenly the light shown on a dapple-gray horse with its front legs slightly apart and stiff, as though it had been reigned to a stop. Then, in Nelson's own words, "The neck was arched as thought someone was pulling up on the reins, but I couldn't see any reins or bridle or saddle for that matter. The horse was looking directly at me and both eyes seemed to glow a bright yellow. They seemed to penetrate through me."

Nelson called out to Hoff and shined the light on the horse for him to see. Nelson said he could sense something on the horse's back. There seemed to be a gray mist that hovered about two feet above the horse's head. The horse continued to stare at Nelson with those glowing eyes. After about 20 seconds, Nelson set about his original purpose for being in the woods.

The next morning Nelson found out that the only horse in the area of the camp was a chestnut dray horse that was used to pull a wagon. It slowly dawned on him that he may have seen a ghost. He and his friend tried to duplicate the glowing eyes with their own horses and flashlights, but failed. Any hunter will tell you that some animals' eyes will reflect light shown in them, but the light source generally has to be higher than the eyes. So was it a real horse, or not?

Before we leave the gray ghost horse, another possibility, albeit a distant one, suggests itself. Terry Lowry's book *The Last Sleep,* a history of the Droop Mountain battle that contains an excellent chapter on the Droop ghosts, has a picture of a tree in the nearby hamlet of Mill Point called the Lee Tree (not to be confused with Lee's Tree on Sewell Mountain). On September 15, 1861, General Robert E. Lee camped beneath this tree on his way to Sewell Mountain. While at Sewell Mountain, he first saw Traveler, his famous gray horse. Now West Virginia didn't treat Robert E. Lee very kindly, and his time spent there was far from successful. In fact Lee never returned to this part of West Virginia, until perhaps now. Does Robert E. Lee's ghost, mounted upon his favorite steed, go back to the sites of his failures, mulling over what went wrong? Probably not, but it's great fun to think so.

Strange things seem to happen up on Droop Mountain on foggy, rainy nights, particularly in the fall. Do suggestible people become enraptured by the mood and the ethereal beauty and see things that aren't really there? Or does a spectral patrol of spook cavalry still pursue a mission, the purpose of which has been ground to dust by the great wheel of history? Come to Droop Mountain. Maybe you'll find an answer.

How to Get There: *From US-219, 27 miles north of Lewisburg and 15 miles south of Marlinton, turn onto CR-22 (Caesar Mountain Road). A sign for the battlefield marks the turn. A parking area next to the park office, museum and cemetery lies about half a mile ahead.*

MOUNTAINEER COUNTRY

CHAPTER THREE

Marion County

The Rivesville Headless Horseman

It's a dark and stormy mountain night, with lightning arcing across the sky and thunder echoing up and down the hollows. Now your decision to take scenic US-19 from Morgantown to Fairmont doesn't seem the wisest choice you've ever made. Through the rain and mist, and blowing leaves and branches, you slowly creep down the winding road, the double yellow line in the middle, your tenuous link to reality. You clutch the wheel and peer forward as you come down a hill somewhere between Rivesville and Arnettsville and cross an unremarkable little stream called Pharaoh's Run.

Suddenly, from out of the mist and rain, a large black horse and rider appear in front of your car. You jam on the brakes and skid to a stop. What kind of a maniac would be out riding a horse in the middle of the road on a night like this? The lightning flashes and you see to your horror that the rider has no head. In the glow of your car's headlights, you can now see that blood and gore cover the headless body and drip onto the saddle. The horse snorts and rears up. In the howl of the wind you hear pitiful moans and groans. The rider turns towards you and raises its arms in supplication or defiance, you can't be sure. There's another great flash of lightning and the horse and rider vanish.

Shaken, you speed off down the road to Rivesville disregarding the weather and the night. You pull into the nearest gas station and tell your story to the people there feeling scared and foolish at the same time. They say that what happened to you has happened to others before you over the years. You've just met the Rivesville Headless Horseman.

Nobody knows why this ghastly apparition haunts that stretch of US-19, nor do they know who he is. He's been seen from time to time by foxhunters and travelers, but only on stormy nights. Some say he's the ghost of a man, murdered in some long forgotten mountain feud or the victim of a robber, and not a casualty of battle. Witnesses say that the decapitation looks like it was done with a sword rather than some after-death mutilation. The fact that the phantom is mounted on a horse may indicate that the origin of the haunting lies in the Civil War, particularly since there is no local gruesome crime to go with the story.

Although the Fairmont area was not the site of any major Civil War battles, there was a skirmish fought there on April 29, 1863. A column of Confederate cavalry under General William E. (Grumble) Jones was sweeping through the northern part of West Virginia in conjunction with a second column under the command of General John B. Imboden. The objective of this raid was to destroy as much of the Baltimore and Ohio Railroad as possible and to collect as many horses and cattle as they could to feed the chronically short Confederate Army. They also hoped to shake the faith of the pro-Union inhabitants of the area.

Fairmont was an important target for Grumble Jones because the B&O built a long wrought-iron bridge across the Monongahela there. Fairmont was also the home of the governor of the Restored State of Virginia, Francis H. Pierpont, a staunch unionist, and this would strike a blow at Union pride. (The Restored State of Virginia claimed to be the real government of Virginia as opposed to the Confederate state government in Richmond. The western counties seceded to form West Virginia, which was different from Restored Virginia.)

Three companies of Federal State Guards commanded by Major Festus Parrish defended Fairmont. The outnumbered Unionists could not keep the Rebels out of Fairmont and the bridge from being destroyed. While the usual sniping and bushwhacking by both sides took place, many accounts say that the raiders may have lost as many as 60 men that day, many of whom were buried in unmarked graves.

There's one story about an old woman named Granny Smith who lived near the head of Pharaoh's Run. She heard Grumble Jones's troopers ride by at night and cheered them on for Jeff Davis and the Confederacy. One of the troopers rode close, bent down and kissed her on the cheek. Granny Smith said that the man was "young, beardless and handsome."

A Private Leeds, who fit this description, was shot in the chest and died from his wounds when the column was ambushed at a place called Coal Run Hollow. Does Private Leeds, seek out Granny Smith to tell her of his fate?

It's also interesting to note that Pharaoh's Run crosses US-19 twice. There is a cemetery near the bridge closest to Rivesville.

Could this be the ghost's abode during fair weather? Is one of the bodies buried there minus its head?

In some respects, Rivesville's Headless Horseman reminds us of another headless horseman, who haunted the Catskill Mountains in New York and was made famous by Washington Irving. Maybe the Rivesville Headless Horseman can't cross water either. A restless fragment from the Civil War, a murder victim seeking justice, an accident victim seeking all his parts or a poor soul doomed to haunt a small stretch of secondary road for some sin buried in the mists of time? No one knows and will probably never know. And so the Rivesville Headless Horseman will take his place among the troop of headless phantoms that haunt the West Virginia hills.

How to Get There: US-19 goes left just before the bridge at Anne Green's house at Rivesville. Go 4.4 miles down 19 until you come to William Smith Road. Route 19 crosses Pharaoh's Run just after this intersection. A hill and a cemetery on the left side of the road lie between this point and the next crossing of Pharaoh's Run, 0.8 miles away. The road is excellent and there are places to turn around. (If your name is Ichabod Crane, we'd strongly advise you to avoid this stretch of road during a storm.)

Morgan's Premonition

It was 1779, the middle of the American Revolution. On the Virginia frontier, battles between the Virginian colonists on one hand and the Shawnee and their allies on the other raged in bloody fashion. The Shawnee and the Mingo raided isolated cabins and murdered and kidnapped the inhabitants. The Long Knives (Virginia Militia) retaliated in kind, and blood flowed freely on the frontier throughout 1777 (called Bloody 7s by some) and 1778.

The frontiersmen constructed a series of wooden forts and blockhouses to which they would flee at the first sign of danger. The militia patrolled the woods, looking for possible signs of raiders. If the settlers were lucky, their first warning came in the form of a knock on the door by militia members called the Express. It was their job to warn the pioneers of an impending Indian raid to give them time to flee to the local fort. If the settlers were unlucky, their first warning was a Shawnee war whoop or the thunk of an arrow striking flesh.

Early in April 1779, a man named David Morgan received a warning of disaster that didn't come from the Express. It came from someone or something else. David Morgan was described by contemporary sources as a "man of advanced years." In the autumn of 1778, this 60-year-old relative of General Daniel Morgan, one of the heroes of the Battle of Saratoga, had "forted up" at Prickett's Fort, across the Monongahela from his cabin. He and his family remained at the fort through the winter and into the spring.

During the spring, the Virginians decided that the threat from the Shawnee and their allies had subsided. Morgan, who was suffering from one of the fevers common at the time, decided that since the weather was good, he would send his 16-year-old son Stephen and his 14-year-old daughter Sarah, back to the farm to take care of stock that had been left behind.

After the children went to do their chores, Morgan lay down to sleep. While he was asleep, he dreamed that he saw two Indians creep out of the woods and scalp his children. Morgan awoke with alarm. He immediately set out for his homestead, hoping against hope that he was not too late.

Much to his relief he saw that Stephen and Sarah had taken care of the animals and had stayed behind to prepare a garden for the spring. As Morgan watched, he saw two Indians observing his children from the edge of the woods. As the Indians made for the children, Morgan shouted a warning and told the kids to get back to the fort. The two Indians noticed Morgan and ran toward him, obviously intending to do him in first.

First Morgan tried to escape by running, but he was no match for the two young warriors. Then he took cover and his pursuers did the same. Morgan cocked his rifle, took aim and fired. He hit one of the men, who crawled off into the woods and later committed suicide to avoid capture. His second pursuer fired and missed. Then both men went after each other with tomahawks. But old David Morgan was a hard-bitten frontiersman. He had been a good wrestler in his youth, and he finally threw down his opponent and stabbed him. Morgan then broke away and made his way back to Prickett's Fort to raise the alarm. He returned with a party of men who trailed the wounded Indian who had staggered into the woods. Despite his pleas for mercy, they killed him.

Some skeptics have criticized this story because they contend that the cattle would have been taken into the stockade in such dangerous times. While this is true, the Shawnee menace had abated considerably after the autumn of 1778. The fort, no doubt, would be low on forage, and since Morgan's cabin was less than three miles from the fort, it's possible he moved his stock back for this reason. We know from other sources that cattle were routinely pastured outside the stockade and that Josiah Prickett's son was killed while bringing a cow in from pasture one afternoon. Or maybe the children went over to their cabin for another reason entirely.

DAVID MORGAN

Near this spot, 1779, David Morgan killed two Indians, of whose attack on his two children he had been warned in a strange dream. Morgan lived on a farm on the Monongahela River between Paw Paw and Prickett Creeks.

Highway marker commemorating Morgan's Premonition, located on the banks of the Monongahela near Rivesville.

In a more somber historical note, Willis de Hass reports in his book *History of Early Settlement and Indian Wars of West Virginia,* that the dead Indians were scalped and flayed and that their skins were tanned and made into shot pouches, belts and razor straps, but that David Morgan took no part in this. This type of mutilation was common on both sides. These were wars where no quarter was asked or given. Babies were brained, captives were tortured, women and children were kidnapped and cabins and lodges were burned. It was truly total war.

There's a beautiful stretch along Highway 19 where there is an historical marker commemorating Morgan's premonition. Parked along the side of the road in this peaceful spot, it was hard to think of the violence that happened here so long ago. Tales of the Indian wars are full of stories of premonitions and forewarnings but none so famous as this one.

How to Get There: *The historical marker ("David Morgan") stands beside US-19 south of Rivesville.*

Barrackville Boogies

Barrackville is a nice mountain town that's nestled in the valleys of southern Marion County, where Buffalo Creek and Finches Run meet. But hiding beneath all this domestic tranquility is some mighty strange stuff. For Barrackville may be the home of a very early UFO and a spectral canine that would even give the Humane Society pause to think.

The Flaming Arrow

Today, almost every strange thing seen in the sky is called a UFO, or alien spacecraft. But this was not always so. Before 1947 such aerial phantoms were thought to be mystery airplanes, operated by foreign enemies for nefarious purposes. Even earlier in the century and in the late 19th century, people reported seeing airships, flown by a secretive inventor from a Jules Verne story, or, the always popular, foreign power up to no good. Before this, people didn't really know what to make of strange lights in the sky and wrote them off as some unknown natural phenomenon or even a portent from the heavens.

Thus we find it refreshing to find an aerial apparition story that resembles reports from the Middle Ages and earlier. These reports normally didn't contain an elaborate explanation for the cause of the lights but were reported as straight fact. The report of the flaming arrow seen over the years at Barrackville resembles these early tales.

There is one big problem with this story. Many of its elements don't make historical sense. To ghost hunters this could have two meanings. One is that the story is totally bogus. The second is that the story is so out of whack that it couldn't possibly have been made up, because most people making up a story want it to make sense. The story of Billy Ice and the flaming arrow does have elements of truth in it. And it's too darn good a story to pass up.

The story goes like this. Indians captured a five-year-old boy from a farm in Barrackville during the Civil War. That evening, everyone in the settlement saw a "flaming arrow" in the sky. They naturally connected the arrow to the Indians, but the meaning of the event left them baffled. The specter seemed like a supernatural warning, but what good is a warning *after* the event? Once every year the flaming arrow appeared in the sky above Barrackville on the anniversary of the tragedy (the date of which is frustratingly not preserved in the story). Oddly, not even the return of the kidnapped boy 20 years later put an end to this aerial sign, which continued to appear until at least 1950. Even "Indian Bill," as the boy was dubbed, could not explain it.

This is something more than an imaginative folk tale, because Indians really did kidnap young William "Indian Billy" Ice (1725-1830) from his pioneer parents' farm. And he really did return to civilization about 20 years later. He is especially remembered in the Barrackville area because the western part of the town, including the cemetery where he is buried, lies on 500 acres of land that he patented. A headstone erected by the Ice Family Association in 1929 now marks his grave. We suspect that the rude footstone was the original headstone, as it bears Indian Billy's initials and death date (unusual for a footstone).

But Billy Ice could not have been kidnapped by Indians during the Civil War. If his footstone is to be believed, he'd been dead for 30 years. Billy would have been five years old in 1730, long before the Barrackville area was settled. He must have been abducted farther east.

So what is this flaming arrow? Probably not a meteor but something slower, giving settlers time to call their neighbors out to look at the startling sight (remember we are told that *everyone* saw it). This sounds more like a comet, but comets don't appear every year on schedule, and they are generally seen for several weeks at a time.

The flaming arrow of Barrackville was last seen in 1950. Conceivably it could be appearing still, only today it would be called a UFO. It may be significant that 1950 is only three years after the start of the modern UFO era. Or perhaps this phenomenon was always a UFO, and the "flaming arrow" was a misinterpretation. Maybe the ET has gone home.

But it's the regular appearance of this phenomenon that makes it interesting. Most natural phenomena don't keep a regular schedule. This regularity gently pushes it towards the realm of the supernatural.

Nice Doggies!:

There's an earthbound ghost that balances Barrackville's strange aerial phenomenon: a ghost dog. But not even the most ardent dog-lover would care to meet this canine.

Shortly before the Civil War, a Methodist preacher named Henry P. Leeper lived in a small house on Finches Run, just north of Barrackville. While out walking one day, he encountered a heavy, thick-legged dog standing on a large, flat rock beside the path. Bristling and flashing its teeth, the dog seemed ready to attack. Henry stomped his foot and shouted, "Git out!" but the dog stood its ground, tensing for the attack. Desperate to protect himself, Henry bent down and picked up a rock. When he stood up to throw it, however, he was amazed to find that the dog had vanished! Rushing home, he found his wife and a neighbor woman talking in the yard. When he told them his story, the neighbor laughed and said, "You've seen Mr. Straight's dog!" She then proceeded to tell him the tale behind the vicious apparition.

There are *two* different explanations for this haunting. Leeper's son, Thomas, who related his father's experience in 1949, said the neighbor told his father that the dog had once attacked Mr. Straight's three-year-old. Mrs. Straight, rushed outside, gave the dog a powerful kick, and rescued her child, but not before the child had been badly bitten. Two drunken men passing by saw the incident and became enraged. They caught the dog and beat it to death. Then they took the dog to the large, flat rock and cut it up with their knives. More than a dozen people subsequently saw the dog's ghost on the rock, usually at the same time in the evening.

There is a second explanation that says Reverend Leeper ran afoul of the vengeful spirit of one of Clem Robbinson's foxhounds. Clem Robbinson had a frightful temper. One day when one of his fox hounds got side-tracked chasing a rabbit, Clem got so angry he clubbed the dog till its head came off. As in the other story, he killed the dog by a large, flat rock. Thereafter, people would see a headless dog run down the hill, cross the creek, and disappear up the other side by the rock, which came to be known as Dog Rock.

There is evidence that the Robbinson (or Robinson) family resided in the area, because CR-21, north of Barrackville, is called Robinson Hollow Road. In addition, a Robinson Run flows just north of CR-21. So perhaps this is the hound that threatened to savage Reverend Leeper.

One ghost or two ghosts, headless or otherwise? This is not a nice doggy.

How to Get There: William "Indian Billy" Ice lies in Ice Cemetery in Barrackville. From US-250, take CR-21 to Barrackville. Turn left just in front of Bain and Moon Heating and Air Conditioning company. The cemetery stands at the top of the hill. William's marker stands on the right, near the front of the cemetery.

The hollow that the dog haunts is most likely the one traversed by Strait's Run Road. From US-250, take CR-21 to Barrackville. Continue on the road north of town. Strait's Run Road (CR-30), a narrow unpaved road, forks to the right about a mile north of Barrackville.

Fairmont's Headless Ghost

Hollywood fills us with false expectations. We expect ramshackle Victorian houses filled with cobwebs and specters, weedy cemeteries haunted by the walking dead, and boggy forests where mists conceal monsters. But frankly, haunted sites are rarely spooky looking—at least in the daytime. But the site of Fairmont's old B&O Railroad depot is an exception. This place has an air of evil decay about it, even in the daytime. We strongly advise that no one visit it at night, not due to any supernatural threat, but because of the real danger of being mugged. There are things worse than ghosts that lurk in the darkness.

We parked beside the old, closed cast-iron bridge, a rusting hulk over the Monongahela River, and walked down a pitted, dead-end road. Traveling one block from the bustle of downtown Fairmont had plunged us into a lonely industrial wasteland, hidden by the hillside. On the right stood a tall, dark, dilapidated building, a perfect set for a horror movie. Originally it housed a hotel that served the railroad trade.

On our left, the railroad tracks angle in, cutting off the road just beyond the pilings of the current Route 310 bridge. The depot once stood in the clearing here, but after passenger traffic ceased it was abandoned for many years and was recently torn down. Debris litters the site, and wooden beams, presumably from the depot, still lie rotting in large stacks.

Railroads are dangerous places. People die quick, grim deaths if they're not careful, and quick, grim deaths often result in ghosts. The Fairmont depot is no exception to this rule. In the old days, a chain hung from a pole over the track just before the station. When the chain hit the incoming train, it signaled the engineer to begin slowing for the depot stop. One day around 1915, a brakeman working on top of a car forgot about the chain and was decapitated.

Although the chain was removed, people soon began to see the worker's ghost looking for his head along the track at dusk. They told of a headless man carrying a lantern, who crosses the tracks and then disappears.

Site of the old depot at Fairmont.

Unlike many similar tales, this one has a remarkable pedigree from an original witness named Joe Board. Initially a skeptic, Board himself saw the apparition one evening and told the story to his daughter, Idris Adams of Fairmont. She in turn passed the story on to Gary Schoonover of Elkins, who gave it to folklorist Ruth Ann Musick in 1958.

As we noted in the introduction under ghost lights, such railroad "ghosts" may actually be a mysterious electrical phenomenon induced by the railroad tracks. Because the tracks here still exist (and remain in use), it is quite possible that this ghostly light continues to appear occasionally. We have no recent reports, however, and must once again warn you of the potential danger of this isolated location, especially at night.

How to Get There: *The depot site lies beside and below the Route 310 bridge in Fairmont. From the east on Route 310 (Jefferson St.), turn right onto Adams Street, and then turn right onto Madison Street and descend the hill. At the bottom, park by the old, closed bridge and walk down the dead-end road on the right, which leads beneath the Route 310 bridge. The depot once stood in the clearing just beyond the* *bridge. The multistory, dilapidated building on the right was the hotel that served the railroad.*

The Atheist's Revenge

Becoming a ghost and joining the realm of the supernatural must be a terrible and surprising fate for an atheist, for it undercuts much of his argument. No wonder that a lonely atheist miner named Anderson, shunned by his God-fearing fellows, turned into such an angry, vengeful, persistent ghost.

Anderson worked in the Big Vein section of the Carolina Mine, located in the town of Carolina, in Marion County's coal-mining district. One day in the 1890s, he was killed in a gas explosion. While hauling out his body, one miner callously gloated, "An atheist has met his retribution." No sooner had he spoken than a horrible cry shattered the silence and echoed weirdly through the deep, dark passages of the mine. Then the gloating miner and his fellows alike heard Anderson's voice vow eternal revenge. Terrified, the men loaded the mule hauling the coal car, but the mule refused to budge. In frenzy they fled desperately on foot to the elevator and back to the surface.

Tiring of the taunts of skeptics who had not been down "in the hole" when Anderson spoke, some miners gathered up the courage to return. They took two more mules, perhaps thinking that the weight was too great for the stubborn single mule. The mule, the coal car, and Anderson's body were there, just as they had left them. They hitched up the extra mules, but all the prodding, pushing, pulling, cajoling, and cursing in the world could not move those mules. Then someone remembered a bit of old country lore: the mules were frozen in place because they could see the ghost. The miners went back for another mule—a blind one—which then led the rest out of the mine.

Anderson's curse went to work immediately. First, the coal vein had caught fire in the explosion, so the company closed down the mine, which remained deserted for the next 20 years. When the mine reopened, the local miners, remembering the vengeful ghost, refused to work there. Consequently, outsiders were brought in. This did little good, however, for upon them fell a plague of tunnel collapses, gas explosions and at least one devastating flood. This sounded like a spook with an attitude and was one story we hoped to hunt down. So we went off to Carolina.

Sitting in a bowl of high hills with just one road in or out, Carolina is a perfect setting for a Stephen King novel. Indeed, it is a small, pleasant, well-kept community, with nothing spooky about it, which just happens to have an extraordinary legacy of a haunting in its midst. Located in a large, fenced area on one side of Main Street, three of the original mine buildings have been recently refurbished to form the Carolina Business Center, a family enterprise. The mine had been long since closed and the main shaft filled in. As you look through the gate you'll see the rectangular building on the left, once used to store dynamite. Look to the right and there's another rectangular building that was the mine's main boiler room. Standing to the left of the boiler building and extending behind the dynamite building, you'll see a long, low structure that's now divided into offices and storage areas. When the mine was operating, this building held the machine shops, and trains would roll into it, like planes into a hanger, to be repaired.

When we arrived in Carolina one Sunday afternoon in late summer, we didn't think that we would be able to do more than locate the mine site. We never imagined that Carolina would prove one of our richest locations. Since we had little to go on, we did what most ghost hunters do in this situation. We smiled our most sincere smiles and introduced ourselves to a young couple sitting out on their porch. Much to our delight, they didn't look at us as though we were crazy and told us that old-timers told them that numerous accidents at the mine had led to its closing and that everybody in town knew that the mine was supposedly haunted. Furthermore, they had heard many stories from local people who claimed to have had spooky experiences at the site. When we asked their name, so that we might credit them, we were stunned to learn that it was *Anderson!* But to our dismay, these Andersons have no connection to the Anderson in the legend, because they are comparative newcomers to Carolina, having moved there only nine years before. But still the coincidence boded well for our search.

So we went to the site of the old mine. As we were snapping pictures, this lady came and asked why. As it turns out, she was Trudy Lemley, one of the co-owners of the Carolina Business Center. After we explained our project she graciously invited us in for some much-needed ice tea. We then spent a delightful couple hours learning a little of the history and lore of the Carolina Mine.

Trudy and her husband Terry founded Carolina Business Center in the hope of attracting enterprises to the town, thereby improving its sagging economy. So they rent space in the center to various small businesses, and Trudy operates a wood shop there. When they bought the property in 1993, it was weedy as a jungle and full of junked cars and old tires. They have succeeded most impressively in cleaning it up and repairing the buildings, which all date between 1919 and 1941. The previous owner of the property, Hamilton Electronics, operated a glass-cutting plant there. Workers from that plant also talked of ghostly events, though the haunt seems to have been less active during their tenure.

The Consolidation Coal Company opened the mine in 1916 and operated it until 1941, when Bethlehem Mine Corporation took over. Although we have been unable to find information about the earlier mine at the site, the 1916 date nicely fits the legend's time-frame, in which 20 years passed between the Anderson incident in the 1890s and the reopening of the mine.

The mine shut down permanently in 1949 because of the large number of accidents that occurred there. Although the mine contained a lot of methane gas, it suffered few if any explosions (contrary to the legend). The accidents were cave-ins and other odd incidents, such as the death of its best horse, Mut. Mut weighed 2,200 pounds and could pull a coal car by himself and was a beloved wonder among the miners. One day Mut was placed in the elevator cage at the bottom of the shaft. But someone forgot to secure his position. According to Trudy, "...when the cageman brought him up the shaft, he got caught in the arch of the main heading and broke his neck." In time, the miners blamed the ghost for Mut's misfortune.

The mine's main shaft led to the Pittsburgh Vein (called the Big Vein in the Anderson story), 510 feet below the surface. Strange sounds often rose out of the shaft but whether they were natural or ghostly, no one could tell. No one can remember any person or animal ever falling down the shaft. It was filled in for safety reasons when the mine closed. But the shaft wouldn't stay filled in. Guy Ice, Jr., Trudy's father, first filled the shaft with dirt, but soon after, the shaft reappeared! Trudy told us that "the stoppings in the main headings in the shaft had broken loose because of the build-up of water, and all the dirt had washed away." They put new stoppings in and the shaft was successfully refilled and has stayed refilled. The site of this shaft is in the grass just to the left of the boiler building.

Even though the mine is closed and the shaft is filled, this haunting continues to produce frightening phenomena. According to the testimony of witnesses, all the buildings have had inexplicable power outages and strange sounds but the haunting seems to focus on the dynamite storage building and the boiler building.

Haunted boiler building at the Carolina Business Center.

The dynamite storage building, which stands beside another filled-in shaft, was formerly very dry. If dynamite gets damp it can become quite unstable. Now, however, the site has become quite damp for some inexplicable reason. A woman named Freda, who worked there a few years ago, often heard someone going up and

Haunted dynamite storage room at the Carolina Business Center, where we saw the light.

down the steel stairs that are inside the building. She always went to investigate, always with the same result. In the doorway dividing the rooms, the oilcloth that substituted for a door would be swinging, as if someone had just passed. But when she looked, of course, no one was there. The tread of ghostly footsteps failed to frighten her, however. She often spoke to the ghost, though without any reported effect. She explained her lack of fear to her son Bobby, who also worked at the site by saying, "Don't be afraid of the dead; be afraid of the living." Bobby, unconvinced, refused to work there at night.

In contrast to the placid stair-climber, a ghost of a more malicious nature haunts the boiler building. Just before the Lemleys purchased the site, a couple from Parkersburg operated a custom lumber business, Pioneer Hardwood, from the boiler building. They and their employee, Jerry, experienced many weird events there.

Pioneer Hardwood stayed on as renters after the Lemleys began renovations. At that time, Jerry began to accuse Terry of working in the building during the night and using his radio, because every morning Jerry found the station had been changed. Further, objects would be moved from their usual places so Jerry was certain Terry was using his tools.

The accusations were unfounded for Terry stayed away from Pioneer Hardwood. It seems extremely unlikely that any night visitor could have sneaked in to play a prank. A high fence, topped with barbed wire, surrounds the site, and the gate is padlocked at night. Moreover, at that time the Lemleys didn't even have a key to the boiler building, a fact that Jerry didn't know. Then one day a power saw turned on by itself in front of a terrified Jerry. Power tools with a mind of their own would shake up the most stouthearted woodworker, and Jerry left.

The Parkersburg people left and the Lemleys took over the operation. Trudy moved her own wood shop into the long building and hired Chad, another former employee of Pioneer Hardwood. Now that she had an employee, Trudy hoped that she could occasionally take some time off to take care of personal business. When she explained this to Chad, however, she found that the prospect unnerved him. According to Trudy, "He refused to work there alone—even in the daytime—and soon after got another job."

Then Trudy Lemley made us a startling offer. She asked if we wanted to spend the night in the main office. At that time we weren't really prepared to do a spook stakeout. Although we had a camera, we didn't have a tape recorder and some good flashlights, minimal equipment for any ghost hunt. We agreed to come back. So late one misty October evening we came back armed with cameras, a tape recorder and assorted equipment, to confront Anderson's ghost or whoever or whatever was haunting the Carolina Business Center.

We decided we didn't need to spend the whole night there. If Anderson didn't appear by one o'clock or so, he probably wouldn't. Nor did we wish to drive back to our motel through the dense fog, which begins to seriously thicken after midnight. Since any self-respecting ghost should put in an appearance by midnight, we decided that we would stay until about 1:00 a.m.

After touring the cold, largely empty boiler building—undeniably a spooky-looking place—we chose the comfort of the Lemley's office kitchen for our vigil. We're ghost hunters, not masochists. We figured if the ghost really wanted to make a point, he'd know where to find us. And neither of us wanted to be stumbling around a lumber filled room, possibly in the dark, filled with self-starting power tools with an attitude. We may be intrepid, but we're not crazy.

We settled in around the kitchen table, played tapes, talked ghosts, and drank coffee. After we had been there an hour or two, Walt noticed, through the office window, a diffuse, round, red light coming from the windows of the dynamite building. The weird light moved steadily to the right for several yards and then blinked out. "Did you see that?" Walt asked. I hadn't, so he described it.

We felt a little excited. Was this it? Had he seen a ghost? But being experienced spook hunters we didn't jump to any conclusions. We immediately went out to investigate. The night air was already chilly and damp, and fog was forming in places. We walked over to the dynamite building and tried to peer in the window (the building was locked), but our flashlights were too weak to penetrate very far. We contented ourselves with looking around outside. Of course, we found nothing, not even a whiff of swamp gas (one of the many explanations for UFOs) to explain the eerie light.

Back in the office, we kept watch, hoping the light would appear again. We were soon rewarded for the light reappeared, in the same place, doing the same things. This time, however, we noticed that it coincided with a passing car on the road outside the business center compound. Was there a connection? There had to be, and yet it seemed physically impossible. The car and the light were in the same general direction, but we knew that the light could not be penetrating the building, even through a window, because the angles were all wrong.

Another car went by and it happened again. But by careful observation we soon solved the mystery. The tail lights of the cars were reflecting off the windows of the office and then off the windows in the dynamite building. Because of this remarkable double-reflection, the lights didn't look like tail lights but rather a dull red glow. Coincidentally, Carolina has another, similar optical illusion that has enhanced its haunted reputation. Trudy told us, "The new sodium light by the old Catholic Church reflects a pink-red light off the windows, giving a strange glowing effect. Many people have commented on this unusual illusion. When they drive by at night, they think the place is on fire."

Sadly the optical illusion was the highlight of our vigil. We saw nothing more and heard nothing but the occasional barking of the business center guard dog and unearthly yowling of a couple of bobcats. We challenged the ghost to appear, not always a wise thing to do, but it didn't. From midnight to 12:30, we ran a tape recorder on record in the hope of picking up some electronic voice phenomena known as spirit voices. (In the 1960s and '70s, many people claimed success in recording ghostly sounds and messages that were not otherwise audible, especially in haunted locations. Parapsychologists call this "electronic voice phenomena.") When we played back the tape at home, we heard nothing but our own fidgeting and coughing.

The spookiest part of the evening was the slow ride through the fog, back to Fairmont. We challenged the supernatural and in righteous indignation, it ignored us. We could envision Anderson's ghost, skulking in a long abandoned tunnel muttering, "Order me around, will they? I'll show them!" And maybe this is a good thing, because Anderson's ghost doesn't sound like anything you'd want to mess around with.

How to Get There: From US-19, west of Fairmont, take Route 218 north. Turn left onto CR-52, which becomes Main Street in Carolina. The Carolina Business Center stands in a fenced compound on the left side of the street.

Some More Coal Mine Ghosts

There's an old West Virginia folk song that urges young men to "Seek not your fortunes down in the mines." The song makes this plea with good reason. While coal has been a major source of West Virginia's wealth, underground coal mining was and still is, despite many updated safety regulations, a dirty and dangerous occupation. There's always the danger of explosion, either of methane gas or the coal dust itself. Then there are cave-ins, runaway mine cars and any number of underground catastrophes that could snatch life away in an instant or leave an entombed miner gasping for breath, listening in vain for a rescue that could come too late. And there was always the hidden danger of black lung or other diseases that could slowly steal away the life of the strongest miner.

Naturally, West Virginia mine disasters have produced more than their share of ghostly tales and spooks. But the problem with using haunted mine stories in this type of guidebook is that the average non-miner would never get to visit the haunted spots. This is further complicated by the fact that many of the haunted mines are closed and sealed up. So we can guide you to the pithead, but all you'd really see are abandoned buildings or overgrown fields. But a book about West Virginia hauntings that stinted on mine ghosts would be a poor effort indeed. So we've decided to include a couple of the more interesting ones even though we can't direct you to the exact site of the hauntings.

On December 6, 1907, an explosion tore apart the main shafts of the Number 6 and Number 8 mines of the Fairmont Coal Company in Monongah. The explosion killed 362 of the 367 miners at work that day and was the worst mine disaster in West Virginia history. After investigating the tragedy, authorities believed that the explosion was caused when coal cars broke loose from their couplings and crashed at the bottom of the shaft. The crash ignited the coal dust and the whole mine blew up.

Not only humans died in this catastrophe but their animal helpers did as well. In those days mine horses were used to haul the coal through the mine tunnels. The explosion caught 12 of the poor beasts at the junction of two tunnels and they were fused into a solid mass of flesh and hooves by the force of the blast. Rather than carry the dead animals to the surface, the miners pushed them into a side tunnel and they were sealed up.

Eventually the mine was cleaned up, reopened, and a new batch of miners resumed their dangerous trade. But the old mine horses didn't seem to know that they were dead. Once in a while, when mine crews would stop for lunch breaks, they could hear the sounds of galloping horses coming down the tunnel right at them. The sounds of the horses would pass by the startled men before fading off into the distance. Although many miners heard the horses, no one ever saw them. No one knew why a little bit of the life essence of these beasts lingered on long after their grisly deaths.

A second tale comes from the Grant Town Mine. Six miners were killed when a tunnel in the South Main section caved in on them during a blasting operation. The bodies of the six men were never recovered. Grant Town used an underground electric railroad to haul coal out and take miners to and from their work. One day, long after the accident, the train operator saw two red lanterns near the section where the cave-in took place. This was the usual signal from miners who wanted a ride. The operator stopped the train and opened the gates of the man-trip (passenger) cars. He then went on his way to the end of the line. Imagine his shock when no miners got out of the man-trip. He raced back to check and found two red lanterns in the car. Oddest of all, the red lanterns were a type that the company hadn't used since the cave-in.

But this wasn't the last time that the spooks with red lanterns would be heard from. A few weeks later, Mack Retton and Stanley Minlovitz were working the midnight shift, in the battery shack, charging batteries. They heard someone moving outside the shack. Wondering if it was the foreman coming to make sure they were on the job, they opened the door and looked out.

What they saw chilled them to the bone. Six figures carrying red lanterns walked past them towards the South Main Section. The last one said "Hi, Stan" in Polish. Stan was a friend of one of the miners who died.

Soon the miners wouldn't go near the section. So the company made up a route around it and sealed the section off with three yards of cement. But even after this, miners said that they could hear cries, coming through the cement from the haunted section.

The Grant Town and the Monongah mines are no more. A power plant has been built over the Grant Town Mine and all that's left of Monongah 6 and 8 is a weed grown field off a bad dirt road. This raises an interesting question. Do invisible mine horses still clatter down abandoned tunnels, even if there is no one down there to hear them? Do six red lanterns bob up and down in the sealed off tunnel at Grant Town and the cries of the doomed men go unheard? Do ghosts need us, the living, to function, or do they have a quasi-existence of their own?

Another interesting fact turned up in our investigation of coal mine ghosts. According to material gathered by Jay Robert Nash in a book about various disasters entitled *Darkest Hours,* there were twice as many coal mine disasters in the month of March in West Virginia than in the next closest month, which was January. Twelve major disasters happened in March. Whether this is some statistical anomaly or there is some sort of physical reason, we don't know. So perhaps Julius Caesar isn't the only one that should beware of the Ides of March. If you go down in the mines in March, be careful.

How to Get There: Monongah Mine: from US-19 in Monongah, turn down the hill at Monongah Middle School. At the stop sign, a hard right is a one-way road leading back up to US-19. A soft right leads onto a heavily residential, dirt road. This leads to the vicinity of the Monongah Mine in about one mile, but the mine is completely closed and filled in, and there is nothing to see. This dirt road and the mine site overlook West Fork River.

Grant Town Mine: from US-19 near Rivesville, take CR-17 northwest about six miles to reach Grant Town. The power plant that was built over the mine lies on the right side of the road at the town.

The Coffin Riders

Occasionally we come up with stories that seemingly refer to the same phenomenon but are totally different tales. Good examples of this are the tales of two very different spooks who supposedly haunt places very close to one another. They are the coffin-riding ghosts that appeared in the Monongah, Eldora, and Boothsville areas. The thing that links these stories is the spooks' method of locomotion, namely coffins. This is why these tales are interesting and this is the reason we've included them.

In April and May of 1863, Confederate generals William E. Jones and John D. Imboden led a cavalry raid on a wide circuit through West Virginia. Behind them they left not only destruction but also ghost stories, several of which we've included in this volume.

Jones' raid went through Fairmont, where he destroyed the iron B&O Railroad bridge over the Monongahela River. (See the Rivesville Headless Horseman for details.) According to legend, some Confederates killed during the raid are buried in nearby Monongah. One of them was killed after being taken prisoner when a Union captain recognized him as the man who had killed his brother. Disregarding the customs of war and burning with vengeance, he shot the Confederate prisoner in the head, killing him. This act of revenge would come back to haunt the captain in a most disturbing way.

After the war, the captain settled in Monongah and fell in love with a girl who lived in Watson (a Fairmont suburb on the south side of West Fork River). On his first trip to visit her, he passed through a dark, uninhabited hollow that lies below the cemetery where the prisoner he had killed was buried. The captain heard the terrifyingly familiar rebel yell, looked up the hill, and saw the dead Confederate mounted on his coffin, charging towards him. The captain took to his heels and outran the ghost, which chased him to the edge of the ravine.

The captain must have been very much in love, because he continued his visits for months, always outpacing the coffin rider, who never left the ravine. Then his luck ran out. One night when he failed to return, his friends found him in the hollow, dead from a shot to the head. When they took out the bullet they found that it was "old and previously used." So his friends dug up the Confederate corpse. To their astonishment they found that the bullet in the corpse's head had disappeared, and that the corpse held a smoking revolver. Thus the ravine picked up the name Coffin Hollow.

Of all the stories we have collected, this is one of the hokiest. When you read a ghost story that sounds like the script from a bad television show, you tend to disregard it as being an obvious fabrication. So why include this obvious piece of fiction at all? Because, independent of this particular story, Coffin Hollow has a reputation as a genuinely evil place, haunted by ghostly screams.

We discovered this when, as usual, we were asking direction from local people. One teenager was well acquainted with the story, which she discounted even as she admitted the place was spooky. She told us that local teens like to visit the hollow and try to scare one another there. Further confirmation came from a middle-aged man in a store. He had never heard of the Coffin Hollow story or name but he knew the place as Ghost Hollow, as did most people in town. We later learned of an incident that undoubtedly enhanced the hollow's horrific reputation. Trudy Lemley, of Carolina, told us that about six years ago a man killed his girl friend and dumped her body in Coffin Hollow. Perhaps this dark, overgrown hollow attracted the killer because it is hidden from any habitation. Or perhaps, like Hawk's Nest (see The *Genius Loci* of Hawk's Nest), Coffin Hollow exerts an evil influence. So if you decide to go to Coffin Hollow, don't linger.

Our second coffin-riding tale comes from Mrs. Hess Bender of Bobtown, who experienced the haunting shortly after the Civil War. While returning home one evening, she was shocked to see a man riding a coffin float up from the ground, sail across the road at eye-level, and disappear over the bank of Booth's Creek. Thoroughly shaken, Mrs. Bender turned around and went back to Boothsville to spend the night with her friends, the Smiths. When she told them her improbable tale, they concluded that she had seen the ghost of a stranger from Pennsylvania who allegedly was murdered near the spot. The man's expensive fur hat, punctured on one side by a bullet hole, had been found some time before by a local hatter named Sam Cooper. If Mrs. Bender had been the only one to see this bizarre vision it could have been readily dismissed as a hoax or hallucination. But other witnesses, including local resident Isaac Koon and two other women from Bobtown, reported seeing the coffin rider—always in the same place in the early evening.

A new road was built apparently bypassing the haunted site. But in 1874 or 75, three boys—Tom Rhea, Barney Whaling, and Will Barnes—who hailed from Monongah and Rhea Chapel, had a rather unpleasant encounter with the coffin rider. They were on their way home from a baseball game in Boothsville. As they passed the haunted spot Tom wished the ghost would appear so he could "whistle him to dance."

Well, sometimes when you call on the supernatural you get your wish. Sure enough the coffin rider arose from the side of the road. Catching sight of the ghost, Tom's horse reared up and took a great leap before dashing off with a shaken Tom clinging to its back. Barney and Will lingered long enough to watch the apparition follow its usual routine, crossing the road and disappearing down the bank, and then they too left as fast as they could. The trio supposedly came back the next day and measured the leap Tom's horse made at 19 feet.

The present road to Boothsville closely parallels Booths Creek. You can't really tell where the old road was, but we suspect it ran down the opposite side of the creek from today's road. Bobtown, a community too small to appear on modern maps, lies near the junction of US-250 and the Boothsville Road. Despite these uncertainties, the location of the haunting is well known locally. One Boothsville informant, Robin, knew the ghost rode a coffin without knowing the specifics of the story. He also said that the haunting continues.

Although Boothsville is the hamlet associated with the haunting in the story, the location is actually more than a mile away, in the community of Eldora. The coffin rider haunts the far side of the creek crossing on Hoglick Road, an unpaved road that splits from the Boothsville road at Eldora. The dark, tree-lined creek features high, steep banks and dense foliage. It is especially notable that the haunted side is uninhabited and undeveloped.

We think the first tale may be derived from the second. The second story has more of the ring of truth to it. The locations are close, and perhaps two different tales of murder picked up the same detail.

An intriguing enigma lies at the heart of the coffin rider story. If this is the ghost of a murdered man whose body was never found — where did the coffin come from? Is this some sort of spectral riddle or is the spook simply trying to tell people, "Hey! I need one of these to rest in peace!" Or maybe the coffin rider isn't the murdered man at all. A true puzzle from beyond the grave.

How to Get There:

Coffin Hollow: From US-19 in Monongah, turn down the hill at Monongah Middle School. At the stop sign, turn left and cross the bridge over West Fork River. Pass the town hall, which has a historical marker commemorating the Monongah disaster. Cross the bridge over Booths Creek and go up and down a long hill (Bridge St.). Cross another bridge over Booths Creek and turn left onto CR-56 at the stop sign. This is 1.2 miles from US-19. The hollow to the left along the road is Coffin Hollow. (For those who wish to contemplate this ghostly place, there is room for one car to pull off on the right shoulder.) The road quickly turns up hill to the right and leaves the hollow. A left at the next stop sign and a right on Mary Lou Retton Dr. brings one out on US-250 in 2.3 more miles.

Booths Creek-Eldora: From exit 132 on I-79, take US-250 south. Almost immediately turn right onto CR-250-3. At Eldora, turn right onto CR-27-6 (Hoglick Road). This shortly crosses Booth's Creek at the site of the haunting. There is room to pull off the road a little beyond the crossing.

The Ghosts of Prickett's Fort

This story starts out like so many others. We came to Prickett's Fort on a beautiful autumn day to look for a ghost. We don't find it. Instead, we find several other haunts that we didn't turn up in our original research. Once again serendipity strikes, this time repeatedly, and we stumble into a veritable plethora of ghost lore.

The story that originally pointed us to Prickett's appeared in the Fall-Winter 1965 issue of *West Virginia Folklore*. It concerned the ghost of a man named Tom Evans and went back to the early days in West Virginia that some call the dark and bloody time. But first, let's set the scene.

In 1774, a group of settlers led by a man named Jacob Greathouse massacred a small group of Mingo Indians at Yellow Creek, in the Ohio Valley. This was not a particularly bright thing to do for the group had included relatives of the Mingo leader, Logan. Until this time, Logan had been a good friend to the settlers, often helping them and counseling peace with them. After hearing of the deaths of most of his family, Logan vowed vengeance and set the frontier alight with the flames of revenge. Poor Tom Evans got caught up in the middle of the fight.

Evans was killed by the Mingos, who cut off his left hand. (The mutilation of corpses was quite common in these frontier fracases—on the part of both sides.) It's conceivable that Evans took part in the Yellow Creek massacre or that the Mingos thought he did. Evans' body was buried in a cemetery near Prickett's Fort, where his wife and children settled down to try and make the best of their ruined lives.

Then one dark night, the family was awaked by the screams of a man who sounded just like Tom. They hurried to Evans' grave and found a skeletal left hand next to the marker. To their surprise and horror, they found Tom's wedding ring on the third finger of the hand. The talk around Prickett's Fort was that the Mingos heard the screaming of the ghost and, fearing that the hand was possessed by an evil spirit, attempted to return it to its owner.

The stockade of recreated Prickett's Fort.

We carefully searched the graveyard near the fort but found no Evans buried there. This isn't surprising because the older tombstones tend to deteriorate over time, and many of the graves were marked with field rocks with no carving upon them. We decided to check out the historical interpreters at the fort but none of them knew anything about Tom Evans. But we did meet Thoma Barrow, who told us several other stories that were every bit as good as Tom Evans's screaming hand and were more up to date.

The area was first settled in 1759 by Jacob Prickett and his 10 children. Because of their continual skirmishing with the Indians, the pioneers built a series of forts and blockhouses where they could hole up when the Indians were on the warpath. Shawnee and Mingo raiding parties were often small groups who preferred attack by stealth and ambush to a direct frontal assault. They were not equipped for siege warfare nor were they skilled at it. Thus a simple blockhouse, often no more than a fortified cabin, often meant the difference between life and a gruesome death on the West Virginia frontier.

Prickett's Fort was one of the largest forts on the frontier and in use for 20 of the 25 years that it stood. The fort was constructed on a small rise overlooking the confluence of Prickett's Creek and the Monongahela River. The site offered a high vantage point important for defense and lay near a transportation route. The fort consisted of blockhouses, cabins, a meetinghouse, a storehouse and a stockade fence. The blockhouses were designed so that those inside could fire down at any enemy gathered around the lower story. Between 80 and 100 families, plus as much of their livestock as they had time to bring, would "fort up" at Prickett's until the danger had past.

The current complex at Prickett's Fort is a recreation of the fort as it was in 1774. It was built by the Prickett's Fort Memorial Foundation in 1976 for our national Bicentennial. It probably is not

The back of the Prickett homestead looking out toward the haunted walk.

built on the exact site of the original fort because no one knows exactly where that was.

Also on the site, just south of the fort, stands the Job Prickett house, built by the great grandson of Captain Jacob Prickett. The house was built on the site of Jacob Prickett's original cabin and is constructed of bricks that were handmade on the spot. It contains Victorian furnishings, many of which belonged to the Prickett family. And if the tales told about it are true, it is full of ghosts who may or may not belong to the Prickett family.

The family abandoned the Prickett house sometime after World War II. During the 1960s and 1970s the local kids, who considered the house to be haunted, used to prove their bravery by going upstairs in the dilapidated old house and waving out of the window. They claimed that they could see lights in the windows at night when no one was there. They also reported seeing a light, moving from the graveyard, which is just over the hill, to the house.

This is not unusual, for the members of the Prickett family also reported seeing lights from time to time when they lived at the house. For example, during World War II, Madelaine Prickett Hood was sitting on her porch swing on a soft evening in June or July. She was looking at the garden when she saw a halo of light form over the roof of the well house. Startled, she walked to the end of the porch to see if she could determine the source of this strange phenomenon.

Since it was the time of the new moon, she knew it couldn't be moon glow. She was familiar with foxfire, the phosphorescent glow on rotting wood, and she knew it wasn't that. There were no other lights on in the house, and no other lights showing. The glow lasted about 20 minutes and then slowly faded away. Madelaine had a feeling that her husband was in trouble or terrible danger. He contracted lung disease and died shortly after the end of the war.

The other "light" that haunted the Pricketts usually appeared in October. According to one account from Madelaine and her mother-in-law, Maw Maw Hood, the light, which resembled a man carrying a lantern, went from the barn, then crossed the road and went up the hill to the cemetery. There was no sign, sound or shadow of a person, and both women reported that the light moved too slowly to be a will-o-the-wisp (phosphorescent lights that generally hover over swampy or boggy ground). The light has been reported by generations of Pricketts and probably was the same light as the one seen by the local children. No one has seen this light in recent times.

Weird things at the Prickett place are not confined to the grounds. According to the interpreters and other people who have worked in the place, strange things happen in the house as well. People working in this house by themselves become uncomfortable, feeling that they are not alone. One day, several people were working upstairs when they heard footsteps coming up the stairs. They waited to see who was paying them a visit but no one came in. When they checked the stairs, no one was there. When the footsteps happened again, they decided to ignore them, which is probably the wisest thing you can do when the supernatural intrudes on your life.

Then one day there was the kitchen door that kept slamming itself, over and over again. Perhaps it was being closed by the same mysterious hands that rearrange the tea and coffeepots in the kitchen. No one ever witnesses them being moved, which is probably a good thing, but pots and pans are shuffled nonetheless. Is one of the departed Prickett ladies dissatisfied with the arrangement, or just bored?

One day in June of 1997, a heart-shaped water puddle appeared under a rocking chair in the living room. The staff was astonished because it hadn't rained in quite some time and it wasn't a cooking spill. The staff mopped the puddle up and went about their business. It seems that the spooks at the Prickett house are not only persistent, but creative as well, for the puddle reappeared the next day in exactly the same spot. The staff said that the water was muddy. So they cleaned it up again and it has yet to reappear. Did some long forgotten Prickett die at sea, or in a steamboat accident or perhaps a flood? And did he or she return to the old homestead to let everyone know all is well? Maybe.

Then there's the mysterious shadow that walks back and forth across the back porch but vanishes when someone checks. One day in 1992, three or four interpreters were standing in the front parlor with both the front and back doors open. All of them saw a shadow walk by, but when they went to check, of course, no one, that they could see at any rate, was there. This was before the barn was reconstructed, so no earthly prankster could have been hiding there. This has happened to several other individuals working alone in the house. Needless to say, it disturbed them greatly.

Enough of the house! How about the rest of the grounds? There's an area behind the stockade where music festivals are staged and shows are held. Reenactors like to camp in this area, but maybe after reading this, they won't. Some say that the field was the site of a common grave for Indians but no evidence has turned up to support this. Nevertheless, people have had strange things happen to them in this area.

Take the case of the night watchman, someone you'd think would be quite used to dark and lonely places and the moaning of the wind. It was a dark, damp and dank night with no moon. After the fort was closed to visitors, the watchman was making his rounds. Out in the darkness he could hear movement and felt something closing in on him. He was too frightened to get out of the car. He'd been at the fort many nights before, but had never experienced anything quite like this.

But the watchman wasn't alone in having these feelings. Other people who have camped on the site say that they've had their tent poles moved by unseen forces and have heard heavy movement around their tents. In 1995, one reenactor was camped watching a music festival. He was sitting with his back to the fort. Suddenly he felt a sharp tap on his shoulder. Thinking it was one of his companions he turned around, but no one was there.

There is a story that may account for these strange happenings. In September 1775, Isaac Prickett, the 16-year-old son of Jacob Prickett, went out with Mrs. Susan Ox to bring in the cattle. The two were attacked by marauding Shawnee who were attracted by the sound of the cowbell. Young Isaac was killed and scalped within sight of the fort. Mrs. Ox was abducted and never heard of again. Maybe she's come back and just wants us to know. Or maybe she and her cattle are still being pursued across the ghostly landscape by a band of phantom Shawnee warriors.

Finally, strange things happen in the reconstructed meetinghouse at the fort. Greg Bowers, the gunsmith, told us that one day he heard a clattering noise come from the empty meeting hall. A wool carder that had been lying on a bench at the end of the hall was now lying in the middle of the floor, about seven feet away from where it originally rested. It was impossible for the carder to fall off the bench and land in that position. It had to have been thrown or placed there.

Ghosts in a new building? Read on. The Christmas celebration is a big thing at Prickett's Fort. In 1993, Thoma Barrow, our chief informant on spooky doings at Prickett's, had her picture taken with another lady, next to the fireplace in the meeting hall. When the picture was developed it showed smoke in the form of a face with a mustache and a beard. It turns out that the meeting hall was constructed of logs taken from old hill cabins that were demolished. Perhaps something was included other than the logs.

So go to Prickett's Fort and look around. Have Thoma tell you a story. Visit the gift shop. Watch Greg make a musket. Take a tour of Job Prickett's house. Look around the old graveyard. Maybe Susan Ox will tap you on the shoulder. Or maybe you'll see the shadow on the back porch or hear the phantom footsteps, or in the evening, watch the light bob towards the cemetery. Probably you won't see anything unusual at all...probably. But you'll certainly have a good time taking a trip back into history.

How to Get There: From I-79, take exit 139 and follow the Prickett's Fort signs.

The Hoult Water Monster

Does West Virginia have its own version of the Loch Ness Monster? Perhaps. Both the Indians and the pioneers told tales of a strange creature that allegedly haunted the Ohio and Monongahela Rivers. The Iroquois called it the Ogua or Agua (which is Spanish for water). Early settlers described the beast as an amphibious creature that lived under the water in the daytime and came out on land at night to hunt for deer. The Ogua would attack a deer from ambush, entangle its victim in its 15-foot-long tail, then drag its helpless prey into the river and drown it. Then the Ogua ate its meal in the river.

One story is recorded in a letter available in the manuscript collection at West Virginia University. Writing to his parents, a young man living in Fort Harmar, along the Ohio, told of a man in the Fort Harmar area who came upon an Ogua just as it snared a deer. He ran back to the fort, got some others, and they proceeded to club the beast to death. This Ogua apparently didn't follow the rules and consume its kill under water and thus paid the ultimate price. The Ogua weighed 444 pounds, resembled a turtle in shape and had two heads. These creatures allegedly lived in mud holes next to the deep parts of the river.

Other people claim that Chief Hiawatha, the Mohawk who united the Five Nations of the Iroquois, concocted the story out of his nightmares in order to frighten off white settlers. This seems to be an iffy proposition since Hiawatha united the Five Nations long before there were very many white settlers. This is not to say that some clever Shawnee or Delaware didn't make up the tale as a kind of psychological warfare against the pioneers or that woodsmen's tall tales didn't give life to an Indian legend.

Bearing these traditional tales in mind, consider what allegedly happened to two early pioneer families that settled around Hoult. The James Taylor and John Nichols families moved into the area around 1745. They constructed a double cabin over a prehistoric "cracked stone pavilion, made solid with mortar, and composed of mussel shells." On October 22, 1746, Nichols's 12-year-old son William was fishing on the Monongahela. Suddenly he fell in—or was pulled in. Hearing his desperate cries for help, his father and brother arrived to see him go under for the last time.

Their rescue attempts proved futile. William's body was never recovered. Tradition has it that William was carried away by a creature that looked like a turtle and was as big as a bear. The next day, James Taylor allegedly found a huge bone jammed between some rocks. The bone was seven feet long and curved like a man's rib. Everyone thought that it came from the beast. (It's possible that this was the fossilized rib of a mastodon, an extinct animal that Taylor probably knew little if anything about.)

A few days later Nichols's teenage daughter was awakened by the sound of a huge hairy creature rubbing itself against the side of the building. Peering out through some chinks in the wall, she saw a large, shaggy shape bigger than a sow. She then screamed and everyone awoke. Shortly thereafter, both families packed up and moved back east of the Alleghenies.

A tall tale? An Indian myth? A story concocted by the British to keep Americans from moving west of the Alleghenies? Or was it a story made up to cover a darker deed, perhaps even murder? It does seem to be a rather fantastic tale. But there are several solid sources for the story. A 19th-century collector of oral history and folklore named Adam O. Heck interviewed several people about it. The Reverend Henry Morgan believed it and had heard it from his father, who got the story from William Nichols, a nephew of John Nichols. Another source, John Mahon, got the story from his father, who knew James Taylor. Finally, the double cabin built on the prehistoric stone floor did exist and was known locally as the Indian Fort.

If you're still skeptical, and you have every reason to be, consider this. American alligators sometimes subdue their prey by lashing it with their tails. They like to seize their prey from the shore, and then roll it in the water until it drowns. Then they tuck their victims in a hole under a mud bank and come back and eat them later. This is probably an alligator version of a well-done steak.

The Monongahela next to Hoult is now quiet and peaceful. If anything lurks in its muddy waters, it dodges coal barges and motorboats. And if you stand on the shore next to the coal dock, and feel a bit of trepidation as you look out over the still waters, and then feel a cool breeze, don't be concerned. That's just the ghost of Chief Hiawatha, laughing that his little joke is still catching nervous settlers.

How to Get There: *From I-79, take exit 139. Pass the road to Prickett's Fort and turn right on Suncrest. Bear left at the fork by Philip Lighting. In about 1.6 miles, the road passes close to the river in the vicinity of Hoult. Do not attempt to park, as this is a coal-mining road and the land on both sides is marked "no trespassing."*

The Ghosts of Benton's Ferry and Vinegar Hill

The Benton's Ferry Ghost Lights

The Tygart Valley is one of the places first settled when the pioneers made their way across the Allegheny Mountains. Then it was rough and unsettled country, but now it's a vacation land where you can fish, boat, hike or just find a place to relax and take in the beauty. It's also the home of one of the most extraordinary ghost light cases we have ever heard of. Benton's Ferry is located on Tygart Valley River, a little above Fairmont. People said that on dark nights a dozen pairs of bright lights were seen at Benton's Ferry. Marching in a line, they floated down Copper Hollow from Linn Cemetery, crossed the river, and disappeared up Kettle Run, a narrow gully that climbed Vinegar Hill. The sound of a "mournful chanting" often accompanied this weird spectacle.

The Linn Cemetery, where murdered slaves march in a ghostly procession.

The story told to explain these lights is about a tragic incident from the Civil War. Abolitionists often conducted slaves down Kettle Run to an old log house known as The Log, which was part of the

117

Underground Railroad. Here they would wait until it was safe, and then cross over to Copper Hollow and northward towards freedom.

One night, however, some raiders killed a dozen slaves awaiting safe passage at Kettle Run. They cut off the slaves' heads and put them in a kettle (thus giving the name to the gully), which they deposited on the riverbank as a warning to the family living in The Log. Undaunted, that family took the kettle of heads on its journey to freedom, across the river and up Copper Hollow to Linn Cemetery, where they buried it. But the heads could not rest, and they were often seen by the lights of their eyes, backtracking the route in search of their bodies.

Oddly enough, this ghostly procession could be seen only from one small window in The Log, which still stood when this story was recorded in the 1959. Unfortunately The Log lost this magic window when it was remodeled, sometime before 1959, and so the lights can no longer be seen.

We visited Linn Cemetery and found that the sign on its entrance claims the cemetery was established in 1880. This might seem like a fatal blow to the story, but we discovered that the site was certainly used as a cemetery much earlier, for one broken gravestone says, "Thomas Westle [missing letter], Died 1852." A few other stones there are comparably old but unreadable.

It's unusual to have several ghost lights cross a river, and this makes this haunt quite interesting. Leaving aside the folk tale elaboration, it sounds to us like a case of real ghost lights that may or may not be extinct. Ghost lights usually continue until the landscape is altered in some way to disrupt them (as in the removal of railroad tracks). Did the construction of modern houses in the area disrupt these lights, or do people today pay so little attention that they fail to see what may be a rare phenomenon?

The Flattened Spook of Vinegar Hill

If you stand at Benton's Ferry you'll see a ridge that parallels the river. It's called Vinegar Hill and it allegedly is the home of a specter that most people would prefer not to meet.

Many years ago some brothers, who lived on top of the ridge near Vincent Cemetery, made cider and sold it to a large inn used by the railroad men and cattlemen who passed through Fairmont. While making a delivery one stormy night, one of the brothers met with an accident as he maneuvered a wagonload of barrels down the steep road to the river. Frightened by the lightning, his old mule stopped short, throwing him and a barrel off the wagon to the ground. As luck would have it, the heavy barrel pinned his leg, and he could do nothing to free himself. His brothers finally heard his cries for help though he would soon wish otherwise. The brothers were drunk from sampling cider all day and not thinking very clearly. Instead of lifting the barrel up, the brothers simply gave the barrel a push. It rolled forward over the whole length of their prone sibling, crushing him to death.

If you visit the road on a dark, stormy night, you may see two spots like eyes appear. Then a white mist forms around them to produce "a huge flat man" who beckons to you. If you dare to follow, he will lead you—staggering, falling, dancing, and screaming—to the top of the hill. There you'll hear the sound of hundreds of rolling barrels and the ghost will cackle and disappear.

Although Vincents still live on Vinegar Hill, we have been unable to locate Vincent Cemetery, which is probably a small family cemetery on private land. The inn mentioned in the story may well be the hotel by the haunted railroad depot in Fairmont (see Fairmont's Headless Ghost).

We are also uncertain about the location of the road in this story, but it seems very likely that it is the narrow, steep dirt road that climbs Vinegar Hill from near Kettle Run. This is really the only road that fits the story. With a deep ditch on the right and a steep cliff on the left, this one-lane road is extremely dangerous, however. We advise against driving on it, lest you become the new resident ghost!

How to Get There:

To get to Linn Cemetery: From exit 133 on I-79, take Pleasant Valley Road to Benton's Ferry. Turn left on Serene Drive and right on Riverview Lane. The cemetery lies on the right at the top of the hill. Total distance is about 1.3 miles.

To get to Kettle Run: Go south on US-250 from Fairmont. As it ascends the hill at Hillview, take the fork to the left between the Ford and Buick dealerships. Then turn left and go downhill to the river. No signs mark either spot. You will reach the closed Benton's Ferry Bridge in half a mile from US-250. The road narrows as it passes between expensive modern houses built for boating enthusiasts. Kettle Run, today merely a deep, narrow drainage ditch, crosses the road at a point eight-

tenths of a mile from US-250. There is no place to park. You must either turn around in a driveway or take the dangerous road up Vinegar Hill (which we advise against; see above).

HARRISON COUNTY

The Cunningham Massacre

This next tale is a good example of what ghost hunters have to contend with. The facts are so garbled that the ghosts may be the truest part of this story. This tale is a testament to the power of folklore to confuse and obscure a real historical event.

According to the story, John and Sara Cunningham were a pioneer couple living on Cunningham Run, about three miles northwest of Shinnston. In 1813, John and his eldest son Aaron went to a local meeting to prepare the defense of the area, as the War of 1812 was raging not all that far away. While they were gone, Indians raided their homes and massacred Sara, John's six other children, and Aaron's wife, Sally. Overcome by grief, John jumped to his death in a gorge. On the anniversary of the massacre, one can see the wraiths of John and Sara chasing their children over the hills at Indian Rock. The children run away because they blame their parents for not defending them. Good story, lousy history.

Here's what really happened. The massacre did take place, but 28 years earlier. John and Sara were named Thomas and Phoebe, Aaron and Sally were named Edward and Sara, and the number of children killed was four. Here is the true story, as told by Thomas and Phoebe's granddaughter.

Thomas and Phoebe, both 19 years old, married in 1780. They settled on a branch of Bingamon Creek now called Cunningham Run, in a house nearly adjoining that of Thomas's brother, Edward. Though a tiny woman, Phoebe already had four children at the time of the massacre: Henry, 4; Lydia, 3; Walter, 2; and Thomas, 6 months.

Thomas, the elder, was on a trading visit east of the mountains. One August day in 1785, six Indians raided his cabin. One warrior entered the cabin, surprising Phoebe and the children at their noon meal. In an instant, he tomahawked Walter in the head. The uproar attracted Edward's attention, and he exchanged shots with the Indian in the house and wounded another outside. The Indian inside then dragged Phoebe and the children kicking and screaming to his companions outside. Here they tomahawked and scalped Henry, and hatcheted Lydia in the head. Finding that Lydia was still barely alive, they dashed her to death against a tree. (This practice was commonly called braining babies.)

After setting fire to the house, some of the Shawnee carried off Phoebe and her infant and dragged off their wounded companion on a litter. Others stayed behind, hiding in the woods, shooting at Edward and his son as they tried to extinguish the fire. Edward and his family soon abandoned the houses, which the Indians burned during the night. A search party the next day failed to find the Indians, who had taken Phoebe over the mountain to a rock shelter on Little Indian Run (near present-day Oakdale), two miles northwest of the farm. A day or two after the raid, they tomahawked the infant in Phoebe's arms.

After spending three years as a captive, Phoebe was ransomed at the Maumee Rapids conference near Perrysburgh, Ohio, in autumn 1788, and was eventually reunited with Thomas at their old home site. They had eight more children together and settled in Ritchie County in 1807. Thomas became the first Methodist minister in the area and died in 1826. Thereafter, Phoebe lived with a daughter in Calhoun County until her death at age 84 in 1845.

And what of the ghosts? According to Withers's *Chronicles of Border Warfare*, one spooky event actually preceded the massacre: "On the day before the capture, a little bird came into Mrs. Cunningham's cabin and fluttered around the room. Ever afterwards she grew frightened whenever a bird would enter her house. The fear that such an occurrence would bring bad luck to a household was an old and widely held superstition."

We spoke with Laura Floyd, a Cunningham descendent, and Glenn Sturm, Jr., a Cunningham in-law who lives by the massacre site. Both of them knew the detailed history of the massacre, but had never heard the ghost story. Nor have they experienced any ghostly phenomena at the site. They did confirm the existence of Indian Rock, located on private land on the hillside, out of sight of the road. If the story has been forgotten in the vicinity, it may be because the

Cunninghams all left the area, and have returned there only in the last 10 to 15 years.

Beside the road at Cunningham Run, an inscribed stone erected by the family in 1956, marks the massacre site. It reads: "Site of the community's first settlers, Thomas and Edward Cunningham, whose homes were burned by the Indians, August 1785 and Mrs. Thomas Cunningham captured and her children slain." The site lies in a broad pastoral valley whose beauty belies its bloody history. One might well see agonized ghosts scurrying over the gentle hills here, but let us hope the children do not blame their parents.

The Cunningham Massacre Memorial.

How to Get There: *From US-19 in Shinnston, take CR-3 to Peora. Turn left onto CR-8. After 0.9 mile, the road crosses Cunningham Run. On the right, beside the road just after the crossing, stands the monolith that commemorates the Cunningham massacre.*

MOUNTAIN LAKES

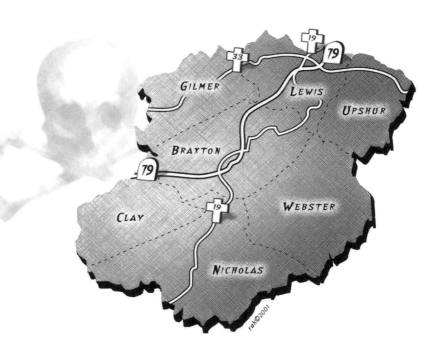

CHAPTER
FOUR

GILMER COUNTY

The Old School Spirit

Ghosts seem to like institutions of higher learning. Maybe it's because the populations of these places are like them, transient and ephemeral. Or maybe college students, with their inquiring minds, are more receptive to trans-dimensional contact. Or maybe there are a lot more old buildings and dim hallways for ghosts to skulk in.

Nestled in the hills above the little city of Glenville, Glenville State College is no exception. For many years, Glenville State's resident ghost has been startling students, caretakers and faculty by moving chairs around in the classrooms, tapping on the plumbing, banging on waste paper baskets, mindlessly opening and closing doors and turning the lights off and on. And like so many of the haunts we've looked at, Glenville State's ghost is seldom seen but often heard.

The haunting is blamed on a poor woman named Lou Lin, who in 1918 had the bad luck to be beaten to death in her own house. Her murderer or murderers were never caught. Sometime after the murder, her home was purchased by the college, demolished, and a women's dormitory named Verona Maple Hall was built on the site. Later a building named Clark Hall was built between Verona Maple

Clark Hall at Glenville State College, home to a bygone spook.

Hall and the cemetery that adjoins the campus. These two buildings were the center of the hauntings.

The more skeptical among you are probably thinking, "A girls' dorm filled with impressionable coeds built on the site of an unsolved murder next to a cemetery and a college filled with young men looking for ways to let off steam." You may be right, but before you leap to any conclusions, consider these stories collected by Dr. James Gay Jones, who for many years was a history professor at Glenville State.

Late one night a student was working in the basement of Clark Hall. Suddenly his concentration was shattered by a noise that sounded like it came from upstairs. Thinking he was the only one in the building, he went to investigate.

Before he started climbing the stairs, he reached out to flip the light switch, but the lights came on before he could touch the switch. "Aha!" he thought. "Someone upstairs has turned the lights on." So he climbed the stairs and opened the door at the top of the landing.

Just as he opened the door, the lights went out and left him standing in the dark. As he looked down the hall he thought he saw, silhouetted in the eerie red glow cast by the exit sign at the end of the hall, something that looked the size of a small black bear. The thing seemed to be swaying back and forth. By this time the young man prudently decided to leave, so he began to back up slowly, groping for the light switch. Suddenly, the lights came on by themselves and the object, whatever it was, had disappeared. If this were a single, isolated incident, one might suspect a prank or perhaps an hallucination bought on by overwork. But it wasn't.

On another occasion, students passing Clark Hall noticed the draperies in one of the classrooms open and close. They hurried to inform the night watchman who had just finished locking and securing the building. So the watchman agreed to check Clark Hall once more, but he found nothing. The students who were watching all the building exits saw no one leave.

Then there was the time a young couple strolled past the cemetery shortly after midnight. To their horror they saw what they described as a "dense gray mass" rise from the corner of the cemetery and come toward them. The young man began quoting from the scriptures and the mist suddenly vanished.

The cemetery next to Clark Hall, where the students saw the gray mist.

College hijinks or a tormented soul seeking justice or maybe something entirely different? Dr. Jones feels that it may have been the ghost of Lou Lin passing through Verona Maple and Clark Halls on her way to the cemetery. He may be right. We all know what strange things can happen in cemeteries—particularly at night.

A few years ago, Verona Maple Hall was torn down to meet the demands of progress. The students, who by this time seem to have grown rather fond of the spook, performed a formal procession of welcome, transferring the ghost from Verona Maple to Clark Hall. Dr. Jones reports that the students that took part in the ceremony were "serious and discrete in their demeanor."

We walked through the Upper Campus on a balmy Sunday in early autumn, strolled through the cemetery and took pictures of Clark Hall. The peace and tranquility belied the tragedy that took place there so many years ago. We saw no strange, ethereal beings and heard no weird noises. But then we were just visitors. We really didn't belong there and were just passing through. But who knows what you might hear or see if you visit Clark Hall, especially after dark.

How to Get There: *From I-79, get off at exit 79 and take Route 5 west. Near Glenville, just after Route 5 forks to the left (away from US-33) bear left onto Linn Street. Pass the Health and Physical Education building. Clark Hall is inset at the end of the parking lot beside this building. The cemetery lies southeast of Clark Hall.*

BRAXTON COUNTY

The Flatwoods Monster

The hills around the small town of Flatwoods are home to some pretty strange doings. One of the strangest of all was encountered one late summer night by a group of young boys and one of their mothers. The incident would catapult Flatwoods into national consciousness for a brief time in 1952 and leave a lasting impression on the people living there, down till today.

The Flatwoods Monster case caused a brief national sensation in 1952, because it was the most bizarre and best-witnessed UFO event up to its time. It was the first "high strangeness" case. High strangeness cases feature details too peculiar or strange to logically be alien visitors from outer space. These cases tend to be dismissed by those who favor this theory.

Upon examination, most high strangeness cases exhibit strong supernatural elements, and the Flatwoods Monster episode is no exception. Even its name, the Flatwoods Monster, embodies the folk wisdom that this apparition is a monster and not a visitor from another planet.

We start the tale with an undisputed fact. A green fireball (a flaming meteor) flashed over five eastern states—including Pennsylvania, Maryland, West Virginia, and Tennessee—at 7:15 p.m. on Friday, September 12, 1952. At about that time Neal Nunley (14), Theodore May, (12), Edward Don May (13), Theodore Neal (12), Tommy Hyer (12), Ronald Shaver (10), and Eugene T. Lemon (17) were playing football by the grade school in Flatwoods. At a pause in their game they noticed a strange object in the sky. They said it was round, "silver like," and about the size of an outhouse, and that it gave off "sheets of flame" that lighted up the ground. They first saw the object when it passed *around* a hill, something physically impossible for a meteor. Then it crossed the sky, almost grazing the trees, and dropped abruptly behind the crest of Fisher's Hill, which rises on the opposite side of US-19 from the football field. Theodore May said, "Look, boys—there's a flying saucer!" Neal Nunley suggested it was a meteor and that they should go and look for it.

The boys set out to find the "meteor." They crossed US-19 and followed a twisting dirt road up Fisher's Hill. Rising about 400 feet above the surrounding country, the hill contained a pasture for the Bailey Fisher farm, with some scrub woods on the northwest side and scattered trees near the top.

One of the last houses on the road, a very small structure built of cinder blocks, belonged to the May family. The May boys left their football and told their mother Kathleen what they had seen. Ronald Shaver took up the UFO idea, exclaiming, "A flying saucer has landed on the hill, and we're going to look at it!"

Kathleen, a 32-year-old beautician replied, "Boys, you're crazy." Their earnestness intrigued her, however, so she decided to go with them. She had Lemon, a friend who had been visiting the family, get a flashlight.

The party took Lemon's large dog and set out up the gently climbing road, which was little more than a wagon track at this point. They saw a glowing (or flashing) orange light coming from near the top of the rounded hill, but it soon disappeared. Trekking nearly half a mile, they passed through Fisher's gate, which they dutifully rewired shut behind them, and came to an old, abandoned gate. Here Lemon's dog ran ahead, began barking frantically, then turned tail and streaked homeward, bypassing the group. Then they were surrounded by a strange mist. It had a sickening odor and burned their eyes, nostrils, and throats. Most versions of the story make it sound like they intrepidly pushed on through this mist, but we think that the rest of the events occurred in the next few seconds.

Lemon had been panning his flashlight to the right of them, where open pasture is located on a small shelf that lies parallel to, and slightly below, the road. Then they heard a "bump, bump, bump" sound up ahead and saw two glowing lights that looked like eyes. At this point, Lemon turned his light on the eyes, and the object "flared up." (What the phrase "flared up" actually means is unclear from any of the descriptions.) To their astonishment they saw, under an oak in a small clump of scrub, a figure, vaguely manlike, standing more than ten feet tall. (We know the figure's height because the top of its head almost reached a branch measured at 12 feet from the ground). While the bottom of the creature was hidden by the bushes, the rest of the body was a nondescript green "skirt" about four feet wide. Perched on top was a round, blood-red head with no features except two orange-glowing eyes. A black shield or cowl, resembling the ace of spades, surrounded its head. (Should you be so inclined, you can buy a statue of the Flatwoods Monster at the bookstore in Sutton.)

The entity, only five to eight feet away, slowly drifted towards them while making a "sizzling" sound. Lemon fainted. The others fled in panic down the hill, dragging the unfortunate Lemon with them. They didn't stop running until they reached the May house. There, Mrs. May was so shaken by the experience that she vomited off and on until midnight.

Someone called a few neighbors, as well as A. Lee Stewart of the *Braxton County Democrat*, a newspaper in Sutton. Soon an armed party including Stewart gathered to investigate. After considerable coaxing, they managed to persuade Lemon to guide them back up the hill. Stewart later wrote that Lemon "just shook and shook like he was scared to death," but he finally agreed to take them up the hill. When the party reached the spot where the creature had been it was gone. Darkness prevented a closer examination so nothing was discovered. But Stewart reported that he could still smell the mysterious odor near the ground.

The spot where the Flatwoods Monster appeared.

The next morning Stewart returned to the hill, where he allegedly discovered a pair of "skid marks," two parallel tracks where the grass was flattened. They ran down the slope about ten feet, perpendicular to the path. The tracks each measured about a foot wide and stood eight to ten feet apart. At the bottom of the tracks, an area about ten feet wide was trampled.

A third, almost forgotten investigation shortly after the incident was conducted by National Guard Captain Dale Leavitt, who made a report to the Chief of the National Guard Bureau. Leavitt undertook this investigation because Lemon was a member of Company G, 150th Infantry of the National Guard. Leavitt described Lemon as "a very intelligent person. He is a good soldier, learns quickly, and seems in no way impaired mentally." Leavitt concluded that "these people saw something, just what is unknown," adding that "their fright was genuine, and it was a difficult task to persuade Gene T. Lemon to accompany a posse of shotgun-armed farmers and police back to the scene the same night the incident took place."

Stewart gave a similar assessment, saying, "I know all these people. And I tried every way to tear this story down. But they all told the same story and they all stuck to it. I've never seen people more in fright."

Ivan T. Sanderson, a famous zoologist and journalist who wrote on UFOs and other strange phenomena, conducted the most extensive investigation of the Flatwoods Monster. He was handicapped by two factors. First, he never spoke with Kathleen May and Eugene Lemon because he arrived on the same day that May, Lemon, and Stewart were in New York for an appearance on the television show *We the People*. Since Mrs. May and Lemon were the two oldest witnesses, and less prone to flights of fancy and perhaps more observant, this is a serious omission. Second, Sanderson began his investigation a week after the incident, thus relying on memories that may have been weakened by forgetfulness and distorted by the publicity of the event.

Sanderson's work helped clarify what happened by discounting several alleged details. He notes that he could not find the "skid marks" that Stewart wrote about and that none of the boys could point them out. Similarly, he concluded that the "grease" found on the hill undoubtedly was the sap of a local plant called "tar grass." He also emphasized that the boys uniformly affirmed that the entity had no arms, contrary to some early reports.

Unfortunately, Sanderson's report also adds a detail that has greatly skewed the interpretation of this event down through the years. He claims that the group sighted a glowing tear-drop-shaped "object," about the size of the May outhouse, a short distance below the entity. Most researchers have thought that this was the creature's space ship.

If the group really sighted such an object, why isn't it mentioned in any of the early reports? Early reports may add phony details, but they don't normally omit a sensational detail. Furthermore, this detail is inconsistent with how the story was originally told: the whole thrust of that story was that they had seen nothing on the hill until the mist and the entity startled them. Since the mysterious object only emerges a week after the incident, we believe that the witnesses, unwittingly but honestly, added this detail because they came to believe that the creature they had encountered was an alien from outer space, and thus had to have a space ship.

Unlike other investigators, Sanderson looked into some collateral stories as well. At about the same time that the monster appeared on Fisher's Hill, Woodrow Eagle was driving on Route 4 on his way to Sutton. Near Sugar Creek, about three miles southwest of Gassaway, or 10 miles southwest of Flatwoods, he saw a flaming object crash into a steep wooded hill. Thinking that it might be an airplane, he drove to a gas station where he phoned the Sutton sheriff. Despite the call, no one investigated until Sanderson came along. Similar objects reportedly fell near Frametown and west of Charleston, the latter producing a rain of ashes. It seems most likely that all of these incidents were caused by remnants of the meteor falling to earth.

Sanderson's investigative report, completed in December 1952, was largely incorporated into his book, *Uninvited Visitors*. Not included in that book was his highly accurate map of the scene and his "appraisal of the witnesses." Sanderson said that the witnesses' "stories were entirely consistent throughout," although he also noted that "violent arguments broke out among them over details." After interviewing them one at a time and together, he concluded, "They appeared not only honest, but extraordinarily sensible."

Some additional reports give more UFO-like descriptions of objects seen in Braxton County the same night as the Flatwoods event. All of these are vague and unconfirmed and have no value. The strangest of these claims, not reported until 1975, comes from George and Edith Snitowski of Queens, New York.

Like Woodrow Eagle, they were driving between Frametown and Gassaway at the time of the Flatwoods event. Suddenly their car lost all power. While George checked the battery, they began to smell something like a combination of burning sulfur and ether which caused their baby to cough. George went to find out where the smell was coming from. Climbing a small rise on the left side of the road, he saw a large sphere hovering near the ground and giving off a violet light about 60 yards down slope. When he tried to move closer, thousands of needlelike vibrations seemed to prick his whole body. He became nauseated and staggered back to the car, pursued by a floating creature about 8 or 9 feet tall with a big head, bloated body and long spindly arms, almost a comic book version of the Flatwoods Monster. George reached the car safely and got in. The family crouched down in terror as the creature inspected the car's hood with its spindly arm. In another moment the creature floated back to its spaceship and flew away. According to writer James Gay Jones, the next morning a gas station attendant pointed out a strange mark on his car, "a V-shaped brown spot" that was apparently burned into the hood.

Our own investigation of the Flatwoods site shows that even after 46 years it is sometimes possible to discover new facts. We located the present landowner, Mr. L. T. Davis, who allowed us to walk up the hill over the same route the witnesses took on that frightful evening. We were astonished to find that the site has hardly changed since 1952. We know this because everything there appears on Sanderson's unpublished map. The vegetation is the same, the Fisher gate is still there, the remains of the other gate are noticeable, the old road is still followable, and nothing at all has been built on the hill after all these years. We were even able to find the spot where the entity allegedly stood. Although the large old oak is gone, new shoots and small trees are growing up at the spot. We also noticed that the plants on the shelf just below the ridge are significantly different from those on the rest of the hill. This is the area where the UFO was allegedly seen on the ground, and suggests that there may be a connection. On the other hand different plants may grow there because that area of the hill gets more run-off water. The surprising lack of development on the hill—which is not farmed or used for pasture anymore—gave us the strong impression that the hill is shunned because of its reputation.

We also learned from Mr. Davis a remarkable, previously unreported fact. He told us that the May house burned down within six months after the incident and that the family moved away. When he bought the land, Mr. Davis built a storage building on the cinder block foundation of the May house, which he pointed out to us. It would be easy to dismiss the fire as a coincidence, but such misfortunes often occur to witnesses in high strangeness UFO cases and evil hauntings. Indeed, we also learned that many of the original witnesses had been dogged by misfortune and all had left the area.

In assessing this case, we believe it probably is a haunting rather than as an encounter with space aliens. The fireball was probably just that, a large meteor that broke up, with pieces falling from Flatwoods to Charleston. The boys, ascending the hill with the expectation of seeing something extraordinary, were in a receptive frame of mind. Did some supernatural influence play upon that receptivity? The odorous mist, recalling Satanic brimstone; the entity's menacing quality, ghostly floating, and glowing eyes (a traditional characteristic of Celtic and other supernatural monsters); and the fear that instantly overwhelmed the witnesses all suggest a supernatural origin for the event. It is even possible that the Flatwoods Monster is related to Mothman, for they both seem to haunt the same general area and have similar characteristics, such as no arms and glowing eyes.

Another element for a supernatural interpretation comes from Gray Barker, one of early investigators of the Flatwoods Monster. He claimed that the area was rife with Wampus Cat stories. Because it resembles a large cougar, the Wampus Cat might be regarded as folkloric evidence for the survival of cougars in the Appalachians. There are many reports of eastern cougars up and down the mountain range.

But no cougar or panther ever acted like a Wampus Cat. Not only could the Wampus Cat appear and disappear at will, but Barker claimed that in some old accounts it transformed itself into something like a flying saucer. Some residents of the area reportedly regard the Wampus Cat as a Satanic manifestation. Unfortunately, we don't place much confidence in Barker as a source for this information, because he later became well known as a hoaxer. The prospect that the Flatwoods Monster is a hillbilly version of the Cheshire Cat from *Alice in Wonderland* doesn't strike us as being plausible.

Alternatively, the Flatwoods Monster story could be a case of mass hysteria. Skeptics have suggested that the entity's eyes were just the eyes of a possum or owl in a tree, and the sensation of being overcome by a sickening odor is the very hallmark of many other mass hysteria cases. The mass hysteria explanation leaves a lot to be desired, since it is no less mysterious than UFOs or monsters and it's illogical to attempt to explain one enigma with another. For all we know, mass hysteria might be a natural response to a supernatural event.

A final pertinent fact would go a long way toward explaining why Fisher's Hill might be haunted. According to John Sutton's *History of Braxton County*, some of the buildings in Flatwoods were constructed on top of the earliest pioneer graveyard. What became of the interred remains is not said. Were they moved to Fisher's Hill? Are the dead crying out their anguish that their eternal resting-places have been disturbed?

How to Get There: From I-79, get off at exit 67 and take US-19 north. Upon entering the village of Flatwoods, look to the hill on the right, beyond the Value-Priced Quality Cars lot. About a half mile up this hill is the location of the Flatwoods Monster encounter. The site is on private land, and the road to it is gated. Do not trespass.

The Phantom Wagon of US-19

US-19 is an old road that winds and wiggles its way through the heart of West Virginia, from Bluefield in the south to Morgantown in the north. It was the main road until the construction of Interstates 77 and 79. Many strange things have happened along its twisted length, but nothing more strange than the phantom wagon, seen from time to time near the little town of Flatwoods, the home of the famous Flatwoods Monster.

For many years, local people have reported seeing a pioneer wagon pulled by four white horses on bright moonlit nights. The wagon is driven by a young man in his thirties. Seated next to him is a blond female in a long, white dress. Some witnesses report that the wagon is full of tools and other things that pioneers would take along to settle. The wagon gets up the hill and then disappears.

It would be tempting to dismiss this story as one of the many folk tales that has come out of backcountry West Virginia. It contains many folkloric elements. For example, the wagon is drawn by four white horses, symbols of death in West Virginia folklore. The woman is dressed in white, hardly what you would wear to cross this rough and rugged country.

However, Nancy Roberts in her book *Appalachian Ghosts* tells a frightening tale of a sinister encounter with the ghostly couple by a modern-day truck driver named Craig Tolliver. Tolliver was hauling 22 tons of steel girders when he pulled over the crest of a hill on US-19 near Flatwoods. The hill was known to be a dangerous one and had claimed the lives of several drivers. To his dismay, he saw in his lane a wagon drawn by four horses. He blew his horn and jammed on the brakes. Even though he was in low gear from his climb up the hill, he couldn't stop. His brakes began to smolder but

The sign outside of Flatwoods along US-19, where the Phantom Wagon is reported to travel.

still the wagon did not move out of the way. Tolliver knew he couldn't go around the wagon because the weight of his load would send him over the embankment to certain death. So he braced for the impact that he knew was to come. Just before his rig touched the back of the wagon, the wagon disappeared. The thoroughly shaken Tolliver looked in the rear-view mirror where the crumpled wreck should have been and saw nothing but an empty road, shining in the moonlight.

Tolliver knew he had to take a break so he stopped at the next truck stop. Feeling that he had to talk to someone about his strange experience, he told his tale to an elderly gentleman who happened to be one of the local citizens. The man said that he had heard the story of the phantom wagon since his childhood and that he had seen the wagon one night in his youth, when he was coming home from visiting his girl. He was walking over the hill when he saw the wagon pulled by four white horses with shiny black harnesses. The woman in white's blond hair hung down to her waist. He walked faster to try and catch up with the wagon but, before he could hail it, the wagon vanished.

The man told Tolliver that his grandfather said that a young couple had decided to settle near Flatwoods, but before they could reach their campsite near Hacker's Creek, they were murdered by Indians who left their mutilated bodies at the side of the trail. Ever since that time, when the moon is bright, the wagon is seen at the top of the hill where it sometimes causes bad accidents.

This story is extremely interesting because full apparitions such as the phantom wagon are not very common. Neither are apparitions that seemingly try to cause harm. Most ghosts don't even seem to know that the observer is around, and if they do interact with the living, they play mindless tricks or in some instances are even helpful. And like many ghost stories, this one has some inconsistencies.

The idea that these phantoms may be the ghosts of pioneers doesn't ring true. Now it is true that many early settlers were slaughtered by the Indians and slaughtered the Indians in return, but typical pioneers didn't possess wagons drawn by four white horses. If they had wagons they were usually pulled by workhorses or oxen. This is particularly true of the early West Virginia pioneers. This sounds more like the rig of a wealthy 19th-century farmer.

Secondly, Hacker's Creek was the site of an early pioneer settlement, but it's located up in Barbour County near Philippi, not near Flatwoods. Interestingly enough, Hacker's Creek is the site of the massacre of a family named Wagonner. Not that there's any connection but it's one of the interesting things that pop up when you poke around the paranormal. Besides, Hacker's Creek may be the name of some local stream either in the past or that's too small to appear on any map.

Now this does not mean that there is no apparition on US-19. It just means that the explanation for it doesn't seem to fit very well. It is interesting to note that, according to Sutton's *History of Braxton County,* there had been settlers in the Flatwoods area since the time of the Revolutionary War, although the town of Flatwoods was not established until 1880, when the railroad came through. However, some of its earliest buildings were built over a pioneer graveyard. Maybe the disturbance of old bones set loose these phantoms with an attitude as well as the Flatwoods Monster.

But maybe we can offer an even more prosaic explanation for the haunting. We have traveled about 7,000 miles, all over West Virginia, to write this book. We've driven on modern turnpikes and roads little better than trails. When traffic was heavy or road conditions were particularly bad, we would joke that the road demons were out.

The road demons make coal trucks come around blind curves in the middle of the road on narrow mountain roads. They put huge potholes and road debris in places you wouldn't expect them. They got us lost in cities and the backcountry. They tried to push us into rivers and had us meet buses on one-lane bridges. But their favorite trick was to put us behind a slow-moving logging truck on a steep and curvy road where passing was impossible, all the time whispering in our ears, "Get by this guy! You can pass him!" How many have answered that particular call and have ended upside down in the holler with gasoline dripping on them?

Well maybe road demons are just a figment of our sometimes-twisted imaginations. Or maybe they really exist. They may be responsible for the legion of phantom hitchhikers, headless horsemen, ghost cars and other paranormal impedimenta that haunt West Virginia's highways and byways. And maybe, just maybe, they take the form of a wagon pulled by four white horses, driven by a young man and a woman dressed in white, that comes out on certain moonlit nights and scares drivers off the road near Flatwoods.

But two road warriors such as us would never let the road demons deter us from getting a good story, and neither should you. So if you're near Flatwoods some moonlit summer night and you want to go searching for the phantom wagon, do it! Just remember to drive carefully.

How to Get There: *From I-79, get off at exit 67 and take US-19 north, reaching Flatwoods in less than a mile. We believe the haunting is somewhere north of the village.*

NICHOLAS COUNTY

The Ghosts in the Valley

Do the bonds of friendship between an man and his dog go beyond the grave? Here is the story of one such relationship, cut short by war, that seems to have breached the walls of death and may exist even until today.

In 1862, the Civil War in West Virginia had degenerated into small battles and skirmishes between Confederate partisan rangers on one hand and small units of the Union Army and local militia units called the Home Guards on the other. One of the chief bones of contention was the control of the Baltimore and Ohio Railroad, the Union's east-west lifeline. One of the many partisan groups whose target was the railroad were the Moccasin Rangers, led by a man named Perry Connolly. In 1861, the Moccasin Rangers gained a reputation for fierceness and brutality and were sought by Union forces all over the central and western parts of the state. (Connolly's two brothers, James and Cornelius, fought for the Union in the 9th and 10th West Virginia Infantry Regiments. This is a fine example of how deep the divisions were caused by the Civil War.)

One unusual thing about the Moccasin Rangers was that a young and pretty mountain woman named Nancy (Peggy) Hart was a full-fledged member of the troop. Many units of both armies had female camp followers, but the sources we consulted made it clear that Nancy was not a camp follower but an "ordained, full time member" of the troop who could, "be sweet and guileless as the flowers in May but in reality was a fearless woman as deadly as a copperhead snake."

Perry Connolly relied on Nancy Hart, and this Civil War version of Bonny and Clyde raised havoc around Parkersburg. Then they moved operations to Braxton, Webster, Nicholas and Summers counties. In late December 1861, Federal units almost wiped out the Moccasin Rangers at their camp in Welsh Glade in Webster County. Connolly was wounded in the first volley but continued to fight on until he was beaten to death with gun butts. While many of the survivors joined William Lothar (Mudwall) Jackson's cavalry, Nancy Hart was forced to hide out in Nicholas County.

A unit of the 9th West Virginia Infantry under the command of Lieutenant Colonel William C. Starr captured her and a female companion. They were taken to Summersville, where 60 men of the 9th West Virginia were stationed in an attempt to keep guerrillas under control. (The 9th West Virginia Volunteer Infantry was composed of refugees from parts of western Virginia controlled by the Confederates. These men were usually driven from their homes by the Rebels. The regiment served in the Kanawha and Shenandoah regions and particularly distinguished itself at the Battle of Cloyds Mountain.)

Nancy Hart was held in an attic room over the company headquarters. During the day the door was open so that the guards could keep a careful eye on the two women. The guards were forbidden to enter the room, but conversation with the prisoners was not forbidden.

One day Jeremiah Haymond of Company F was on guard outside the door. This was the last time he'd mount guard, for soon he was dead, killed by none other than Nancy Hart, who used her sweet, innocent, mountain girl routine to convince Haymond to hand her his musket. One source says that Hart wanted to convince Haymond that she could shoulder it as well as she shouldered the rifle at home that kept the stew pot filled with large and small game.

However she got the musket, she turned it on the hapless Haymond and shot him dead. She ran to the stables and stole Colonel Starr's horse and fled from town riding bareback. About a week later, she guided a battalion of Jackson's Cavalry into the town by a back road. Here, they surrounded the headquarters and captured Summersville without much resistance.

Not all of the soldiers were caught in the trap, and many of them headed for Gauley Bridge where their headquarters unit was located. One frightened group decided to make its way down the Peters Creek Valley. Unfortunately one of their number had been shot in the chest, and the rest of the men had to take turns carrying him.

The wound was serious and painful and the man kept crying out in his agony. His comrades were afraid that the Rebels were right on their trail, for all of them knew that when straggling infantry met up with enemy cavalry, the end result was surrender or bloody death for the infantry. They were afraid that the moaning of their comrade would give away their position to the Rebels. The man was bleeding badly, and they all knew that unless he got help quickly he would die. So they stopped and held a hurried meeting to decide what to do.

They concluded that their friend was close to death and that he couldn't continue on. They did not want to leave him to be captured or so helpless that he would be devoured by wild animals. None of his comrades could work up the heart to kill him, so they decided on the unusual course of burying him alive.

They hurriedly dug a shallow grave and placed the unfortunate soldier in it. Some sources say the soldier was conscious and realized what was happening. They filled it in and covered it with leaves so it wouldn't be discovered by the enemy. One can only guess at the thoughts that went through the young man's mind as dirt and leaves hit his face and body. How abandoned and alone he must have felt. Deserted by his comrades to die alone in wilderness. Abandoned by all but one, his faithful dog.

As the men finished their grisly work and prepared to resume their flight, they noticed that the wounded soldier's dog lay down on the grave and refused to leave. Despite all their callings and pleadings, the dog stood by his master's grave, whining and howling. Fearing that the dog would give them away, the soldiers shot the dog, threw its body into the brambles and fled towards Gauley Bridge. The sad and ironic part is that the Confederate troops were not pursuing this group, but heading out of town in the opposite direction.

Since that time, travelers in the Peters Creek Valley have reported seeing the ghosts of the Yankee soldier and his faithful dog walking through the woods. They say that the soldier moves slowly with his hand clasped to his chest. He walks as though he's in great pain. His dog walks behind him, whining and whimpering, echoing his master's agony. The ghost has been seen by so many people that Peters Creek Valley has been called Haunted Valley by some. The ghosts walk any time between dusk and dawn.

And what of Nancy Hart, the young woman who was ultimately responsible for all of this? There's not a lot of detail as to what happened to her after her escape. She joined up with Captain George Downs' company of Moccasin Rangers and fell in love with a man named Joshua Douglas. She married him and they moved to the Greenbrier Valley. She lived in the mountains until she died and now lies buried on Manning's Knob in the Monongahela National Forest.

How to Get There: *From US-19, take Route 39 into Summersville. As Route 39 leaves Summersville to the northwest, it descends along Peters Creek.*

THE NEW RIVER GREENBRIER VALLEY

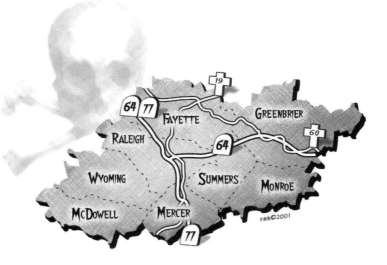

CHAPTER FIVE

Fayette County

Footsteps in the Air?

Modern civilization may have created a problem for ghosts by dispossessing them from their haunts. When we knock down old buildings, do we leave old ghosts without a home? Do they go away, or do they continue to haunt the new building or the empty lot? What if they haunted an upper floor, where none now exists? Do they walk in the air above our heads, no longer seen or heard by the people below?

The haunting of the old city hall in Montgomery, Fayette County, raises these questions. Built before World War I, the brick building housed the police and volunteer fire departments as well as the city bureaucracy. It had no ghost, however, until the latter part of its history. In the late 1970s, some policemen on the midnight shift heard the sound of footsteps creaking the wooden floorboards above them. This was odd because they knew no one was there. The steps crossed the room to a kitchen, and then came the sound of running water, rushing down the drainpipe that ran through one corner of the police station. Then the footsteps returned to the other side of the room.

Instantly, one of the patrolmen recognized the sounds. It was the old Fireman-in-Charge of the midnight shift, who walked every night from his office to the kitchen to get a pill for his indigestion. Trouble was, he had died some ten years before, and the fire department's midnight shift had been ended. The offices above were locked and deserted all night.

Soon other policemen, sometimes two or three at a time, heard the ghost. Caught between his natural skepticism and the evidence of his senses, one policeman decided to put his training in action to get some hard evidence of the ghost's existence. One night he went upstairs, made sure the offices were deserted, and tightly shut off both faucets. Then he wiped the sink dry, lined it with dry paper towels, and locked up the offices.

The ghost was undaunted. About two or three o'clock in the morning, the officer heard the familiar creaking of the floorboards above and then the sound of the water running down the drain. He catapulted out of his chair and bounded up the stairs. He quickly unlocked the door only to find the office empty. No one could have slipped in and out. Nevertheless, when the patrolman examined the sink, he found the towels soaking wet!

The ghost might have acquired a greater reputation except for urban renewal. Soon after the ghost was first heard, the old city hall was demolished. Today a one-story Go-Mart stands on the site. And what of the ghost? Does he still hover above the grocery, silently treading ethereal floorboards in an eternal search to calm his churning innards? Who can say?

How to Get There: Montgomery lies on Route 61. The Go-Mart stands on the corner of Lee Street and 3rd Avenue.

The Colonel at the Glen Ferris Inn

Nestled in the Kanawha River valley, overlooking the Kanawha Falls, the Glen Ferris Inn exudes a sense of peace and tranquility. In the autumn, the mountains on the opposite shore take on a festive hue. The food is good, the rooms are comfortable, the scenery is beautiful, and if you like outdoor sports, recreational activities abound. You can go white-water rafting, or hiking or just sit and watch the river if you don't feel particularly energetic. And when it comes time to go, you might feel reluctant to leave. Indeed, some guests from Civil War times liked the inn so much, that they have yet to leave.

The inn started life in 1839 as Stockton's Inn, a place that catered to the stage coach trade. This was before the time of the railroads, and the rapids in the river made water transportation an adventure. During the Civil War, the inn was fired on as it became a bone of contention between Union and Confederate forces fighting for the control of the strategic Kanawha Valley. Gauley Bridge, just a few miles down US-60 became the headquarters of the Union Army under General Rosecrans and was destroyed and rebuilt on several occasions. Camp Reynolds, which was located not too far across the river, was the temporary home of two future presidents, Rutherford B. Hayes and William McKinley. At one point during the war, the Federals blew up a large ammunition dump at a place called Zolls' Hollow, which rocked the inn and scattered shell fragments all over.

Throughout the war the inn served as a residence and refuge for soldiers of both sides.

After the war, the railroad came through and the stage coach traffic slowly died out. The area turned out to be rich in minerals and metals, and the Wilson Aluminum plant was built near by. The Glen Ferris site was selected because aluminum smelting requires large amounts of electricity, which was generated by a turbine at the falls.

The Union Carbide Corporation stepped in and purchased the inn as an adjunct to the aluminum plant. It was they who added the ten-room wing in 1929. The inn underwent several changes in ownership as the mill changed hands multiple times. Finally, it was purchased by a local family and renovated into the building you see today.

But what of the ghosts? Well, the main haunt seems to be a Confederate soldier, who's dressed like an officer and has a long beard. The staff has begun to call him "the Colonel." He has been seen, the top half of him at any rate, skulking in the hallway leading to the kitchen. If you have the courage to speak to him, he'll slowly fade away.

The spook is not totally morbid and even has a playful and helpful side on occasion. One time, a cook was getting something out of the walk-in cooler. When she came out with her burden, she heard the heavy door close behind her. She looked around and there was no one there. She knew that the door was so heavy that it never closed by itself. So she thanked her invisible helper and went about her work, which is probably the best thing she could do under the circumstances.

Other things happen too, but not quite so dramatic. Once in a while, in the wee hours of the morning, ghostly footsteps may be heard scampering down the hallway. Maybe it's the ghost of one of the Union Carbide crowd, late for a staff meeting. And the owner confided in us, that one calm day, the water in one of the bird baths in the garden began to slosh and froth all on its own. A very localized earthquake? Perhaps. Or maybe the Colonel has a peculiar sense of humor.

So why does the Colonel skulk around the Glen Ferris Inn? The owners don't have a clue. Remodeling and making changes in an old building reputedly can awaken long dormant haunts who seem to resent any change. And the Colonel seems to be a Confederate. Throughout the war, Rebel soldiers suffered from chronic food shortages, so maybe the Colonel wants to hang around all that good food. Or maybe someone in the preternatural world where all spooks dwell has decreed that every country inn must have a resident ghost and the Colonel was assigned to Glen Ferris.

The sideyard of the historic and haunted Glen Ferris Inn.

So visit the Glen Ferris Inn. Take part in the recreational activities or just sit in the garden and watch the river. But if you get hungry at night and decide to raid the kitchen for a midnight snack, you might get a lot more than a cold chicken leg or a sandwich. You may get to meet the Colonel.

How to Get There: The inn stands on the river side of US-60 in the town of Glen Ferris.

The *Genius Loci* of Hawk's Nest

Let's face it. Most haunts have no effect on visitors. The worst a visitor can expect is to feel disturbed or oppressed or, in the rarest cases, to experience a frightening manifestation. Hawk's Nest is different. It might kill you.

The small, beguiling Hawk's Nest State Park lies across an arm of Gauley Mountain, overlooking a large bend in the New River. It protects two large shelves of rock that afford splendid views up and down the river: Hawk's Nest, on the west, and Lover's Leap (apparently the original Hawk's Nest), on the east. The first recorded mention of Hawk's Nest is the 1751 survey of the Kanawha and New Rivers by Christopher Gist, the first white man known to have ascended to the rocks. In 1812, while on an expedition to explore the New River area, Chief Justice John Marshall climbed Hawk's Nest, which thereafter became widely known as Marshall's Pillar.

But it seems that Marshall's Pillar had a second name, Lover's Leap. According to tradition, the name comes from the standard Indian princess story—in which an Indian princess and her lover from an enemy tribe, a native Romeo and Juliet, leap together to their deaths rather than deny their love. (In one variation, the princess kills herself because a white man killed her lover.) The same story is told about dozens of other "lover's leaps" across America. All qualify as what folklorist Richard Dorson called "fakelore," a manufactured tradition, which in this case arose from the late 19th-century impulse to romanticize Indian culture.

If that was all Hawk's Nest had to offer, we wouldn't include it in this volume. But we are told that people *have* died there and *continue* to die there.

George Atkinson's *History of Kanawha County,* published in 1876, gives what is most likely the original story. A pioneer Romeo and Juliet fled Fort Union (settled in 1770 and now named Lewisburg) because the girl's parents objected to their match. While admiring the view from atop Hawk's Nest, the girl became dizzy and fell to her death. In grief, the man jumped into oblivion. Their parents supposedly found their shattered bodies there later.

While Atkinson's story may have little factual basis, it does show that the suicide tradition at Hawk's Nest reaches far back in history. Reports of later suicides at the site offer only slightly more detail. For example, a pregnant schoolteacher whose boyfriend wouldn't marry her is said to have jumped. In another case, a woman from Beckley parked her car, ran out on the rock, and leaped; no reason was ever found for her suicide. Then one day in 1925, students from New River State College (now West Virginia University Institute of Technology), in Montgomery, came to Hawk's Nest for a picnic. Amidst the festivities, a 17-year-old boy named Robert Dudley Caldwell fell to his death. Whether this incident was suicide or youthful hijinks gone tragically wrong isn't really clear.

While visiting Hawk's Nest, we tried to obtain more definite information about the suicides there. As you might expect, tourist-hungry park officials don't like talking about such matters.

Nevertheless, some park employees did confirm that the rocks are a favorite place for suicides. In recent years, they said, more seem to prefer the Hawk's Nest overlook to Lover's Leap, perhaps because it is more secluded from the lodge.

Still other tragedies have hovered around Hawk's Nest. On January 30, 1908 an explosion at the Bachman Mine, on the opposite side of the New River, killed 9 men. Death on a massive scale came to the mountain with the building of the Hawk's Nest Tunnel, which was intended to divert water for the production of electricity. During the construction, from 1930 to 1935, about 500 men died from silicosis, a lung disease cause by the high silica content of the rock's dust. At least some good came out of this tragedy, as the horrendous death toll focused national attention on the silicosis threat to miners, leading to new research on the problem.

Despite all the deaths, there are only two ghosts associated with Hawk's Nest. One old story tells of a family assaulted by a white horse that glowed like a halo. Frightened by the sudden appearance of this strange apparition, the family fled into their house. But the horse stomped down their door, rampaged through the house, and stormed out the back door. Then the horse flew into the air and ascended until it disappeared, though leaving in the sky a glow that lasted long after it had gone. An updated version of this story was told in 1952, but instead of a victimized family the phantom horse attacked some young men camping out at an old house.

White horses appear often in West Virginia ghost stories, probably as an outgrowth of the German and English traditions, in which the dream of a white horse was a death omen. In Mason County, at the mouth of the Kanawha, the white horse is a kind of angel of death so perhaps we should not be surprised to see the white horse at Hawk's Nest and the one at Parkersburg (see The Parkersburg Aerial Apparition) take to the air to become a pre-technological UFO.

There is another ghostly tradition at Lover's Leap. People say that if you stand on Lover's Leap and listen hard on a quiet evening, you may hear the echo of past tragedies—the faint sound of a body tumbling over rocks, crashing through the trees, and landing with a thump on the rocks 500 feet below. (Although we listened very hard, we heard nothing.)

Perhaps the real "ghost" at Hawk's Nest is a *genius loci*, the genii of the location. In Roman belief, this was the guardian spirit of a place, but in the older Persian tradition, such genii were fallen angels, hostile to man. A place marked by tragedy, like Hawk's Nest, was thought to be in the grip of a *genius loci*, who delighted in tempting people to their deaths. So if you find yourself standing at the brink of Lover's Leap, admiring the view, and feel an urge to stretch a little farther beyond the railing, to see over the edge of that projecting cliff—well, you've been warned!

How to Get There: Hawk's Nest State Park lies on US-60 a few miles west of Ansted. A short trail leads from the tourist lodge to Lover's Leap. Farther west, another short trail leads from the parking area by the park store to the Hawk's Nest overlook.

The Ghostly Drummer of Big Sewell Mountain

Did you ever hold a séance? Most of the time not much happens. You and your friends sit around a table, staring at a candle, feeling a little foolish, calling in vain for a contact from the other side. Well, occasionally the other side answers in frightening ways you don't expect. Just ask Emma Lou Fox and her friends about what happened that night they got bored and decided to hold a séance and conjured up the ghostly drummer of Big Sewell Mountain.

As you may have guessed, the ghostly drummer comes from the Civil War. Big Sewell Mountain is the site of one of the largest Civil War battles that was never fought. Like a baseball game, it was called on account of rain.

It was September 1861, early in the Civil War. Robert E. Lee had just been given command of all of the Confederate troops in western Virginia. The Union forces, commanded by General William S. Rosecrans, were making their way up the Kanawha Valley, which they occupied up to Gauley Bridge.

After defeating Confederate troops under General Floyd at Carnifex Ferry, the Yankee troops moved towards Lewisburg, and from there, they hoped, eventually on to Richmond. In their way stood General Robert E. Lee on the eastern summit of Big Sewell Mountain at a place called Camp Defiance. The Union eventually occupied the western summit, and before it was all over, 17,000 men on both sides would face each other across Sewell's ravines and gullies. Each side was spoiling for a fight, Rosecrans with his eyes on Lewisburg and Richmond, and Lee on the Kanawha Valley.

But there were two things both generals hadn't counted on, West Virginia weather and disease. September and October 1861 had some of the rainiest weather in the history of the state. The primitive roads were turned into quagmires of clinging mud that made the task of supplying food, clothing, shelter and ammunition almost impossible for both sides. This was particularly true for Lee's troops, who were always chronically short of everything.

Men slept in the sleet and rain without overcoats or tents. Because of the almost constant rain, they had very little chance to dry out properly. This, combined with poor food, allowed measles, typhoid, typhus and pneumonia to rage through the camps of both armies. On the Union side, only 5,200 men out of 8,000 were fit for duty. Things were even worse for the Confederates. In one Confederate regiment, the 14th North Carolina, 277 out of 750 were fit for duty. One Mississippi regiment left 50 dead on top of Big Sewell.

Both sides faced each other for over a week, each waiting for the other to attack. Both generals realized that an attack under these conditions and over such rough terrain would be suicidal for any attacking troops. General Rosecrans, fearing that his supply lines would be cut, retreated to Gauley Bridge. Confederate troops lingered until October 20 before leaving the mountain to its wild inhabitants and the dead.

When Robert E. Lee camped on top of Big Sewell, he pitched his tent under a sugar maple tree. It was here that he first saw Traveller, his famous horse. After he left, the locals christened the maple, "Lee's Tree." A wrought-iron fence was eventually built

The site of "Lee's Tree." The tree you see now is not the original.

around it to protect it, and the Lee's Tree Tavern was built near it. And it is here that the ghostly drummer beats his phantom rhythms.

Which brings us back to Emma Lou Fox and the ill-fated séance, the account of which appears in Dennis Deitz's book *The Greenbrier Ghost and Other Strange Stories*. When Emma was a teenager, she would accompany her mother to Lee's Tree Tavern, which by this time had been turned into a private residence. Emma Lou's mother would often baby-sit for the family that lived there.

One night Emma Lou and her friends decided to hold a séance. Sitting in a candle-lit room, they called the spirits from beyond. The quiet and the flickering of the candle put Emma Lou to sleep or else into a trance. She began to dream of floating in a fog and moving faster and faster towards a big building bathed in light.

Suddenly a scream snapped her back to reality. Her friend who screamed sat with her hands over her eyes, talking incoherently about the candle flame that kept growing and growing. Emma soon found herself explaining what happened to her mother, who had run down the stairs upon hearing the scream.

"Who was playing the drum?" asked her mother.

"No one," said Emma, now thoroughly frightened. Her mother had heard the rhythmic beating of a drum get louder and louder until she heard the scream.

Lee's Tree is gone now, cut down by the CCC in 1936 and sold as souvenirs by the Daughters of the Confederacy. Lee's Tree

Tavern is now a smoldering ruin, this little bit of history now ashes. But local residents say that a drummer boy was buried in an unmarked grave somewhere near Lee's Tree. And they say on those rare October

The charred remains of Lee's Tree Tavern.

nights when the wind is calm and the fog shrouds the mountaintop, you can hear the phantom drummer, calling to arms an army that hasn't existed for 139 years.

How to Get There: *From Rainelle, go west on US-60, climbing Big Sewell Mountain. Near the crest, pass an historical marker about Lee's Tree. Next pass the road to Buster's Knob (CR-60-18), on the left. Just beyond this junction, fork right onto a small road, which climbs a short distance to a level ridge. Park here beside the Lee's Tree site enclosed by a fence and marked by a sign. Beside it lie the ruins of Lee's Tree Tavern.*

McKinley's Face

This is one of the strangest stories we've uncovered in all of haunted West Virginia. It doesn't deal with ghosts or haunts, but a bizarre series of portents, curses and events that seemingly go one step beyond mere coincidence.

After the Civil War, the C&O Railroad decided to push a rail line from Covington, Virginia in the east, to Guyandotte, West Virginia on the Ohio River. Since the land was rough and mountainous, the engineers decided that the cheapest and easiest way to build the railroad was to follow the river courses. But there were few bottomlands associated with the rivers that ran through the mountains so roadbeds had to be blasted out of sheer cliff sides, particularly in the New River region.

Despite the vast economic benefits it would bring, there was considerable local opposition to the railroad. Some local people believed that when the cliff sides were blasted away, they could see silhouettes of the people in their communities on the remaining rock walls. They believed that these silhouettes foretold of the death of that person because it put a curse on them.

Now we jump ahead to September 6, 1901. The main line has long been finished and workers are now blasting out a roadbed for a spur line from Thurmond to Minden, some four miles away. About a mile down the line, workers blasted away the rock. When the dust settled they looked up and saw a face in the rock. One of the workmen said that the face looked like that of President McKinley. A second said that this was an ill omen. Less than an hour later, the telegraph office in Thurmond, informed the work crew that President William McKinley had been shot at the Pan American Exposition in Buffalo, New York by an anarchist named Leon F. Czolgosz. Three days later, thanks to the fumbling of his doctors, McKinley was dead. Was this a curse, a portent or coincidence? Read on.

Many of you may not know that William McKinley served as an enlisted man and then an officer in the 23rd Ohio Regiment, commanded by another President to be, Rutherford B. Hayes. McKinley was a quartermaster sergeant, who was decorated and brevetted to Second Lieutenant at the battle of Antietam in Maryland for serving his troops food and hot coffee while they were under fire.

The 23d Ohio spent much of the war in West Virginia. Lieutenant McKinley would have spent much time in Camp Haskell, later called Camp Reynolds located on the Kanawha River near Kanawha Falls and also time at Camp Tompkins on the New River. In the later years of the conflict, the 23rd Ohio was responsible for policing a good chunk of West Virginia and chasing the guerrillas and bushwhackers that were so common during that time period. Thus it wouldn't be surprising if, at sometime during his stay, McKinley passed near the future site of McKinley's Face. Stranger still, McKinley's assassin, Leon Czolgosz, was an immigrant, anarchist factory worker who signed his name as Nieman (a play on the German word *niemand*, "nobody") lived in Kanawha City, across the river from Charleston, and worked in a wire factory there.

McKinley's Face is truly located in the back of beyond across the New River from the tiny village of Thurmond. Thurmond wasn't always so small. In its salad days, Thurmond was the center of the New River coal industry and had a population of over 300 people.

Thurmond was specifically designed to service the railroad and at one time generated more freight tonnage than both Richmond and Cincinnati combined. It was the only town in the United States that didn't have streets, and the only way in or out was by the railroad. It had a reputation as a wide-open town. A local wag once said, "The only difference between Hell and Thurmond is that a river runs through Thurmond." It's claimed that a poker game at the New Glen Hotel lasted 14 years and stopped only when the hotel burned down. Thurmond was also the setting for the film *Matewan*.

Thurmond's a lot more peaceful than it used to be. According to the lady at the local store, there are eight full-time residents. The town is a center for white-water rafting and other outdoor activities and has a fine museum, which is open in the summer. It's also a great place to train watch because the railroad still runs through it.

McKinley's Face is still there, a bit overgrown but visible, but the spur line is no more. It's now the Thurmond-Minden Trail. You can only see the face going from Thurmond to Minden.

How to Get There: From US-19, midway between Beckley and Fayetteville, turn onto Route 16, and then onto CR-25 at Glen Jean. CR-25 is a narrow twisting road that descends about six miles along Dunloup Creek to Thurmond. Park at the first designated area on the left. Take the Thurmond-Minden Trail, which starts at the end of the lot. After about a half-mile, bear left at the fork. The right fork is the Southside Junction Connector, leading down to Thurmond. Soon after passing this fork, start looking for the Face, which juts out of the cliff on the left, about 15 feet up and just beyond the curve. It is important to visit between late autumn and early spring, as the leaves will otherwise obscure the view.

The Haunted Highway

Do phantom hitchhikers appear only when they know they are going to be picked up? We ask this question because if a phantom hitchhiker appears and you don't pick her up—the vast majority are female—then how do you know if the hitchhiker was a ghost or a real person? These phantoms do not have a ghostly appearance. Indeed, their substantiality is an integral part of the standard story. Consequently, unless they have foreknowledge of getting a ride, phantom hitchhikers could conceivably infest America's roads, mistaken as ordinary transients by those who pass them by. How would we know otherwise?

These thoughts occurred to us because after thousands of miles of driving on West Virginia roads, the first hitchhiker we saw was on a stretch of road famous for its phantom hitchhiker. He was rather scruffy looking and his luggage was a garbage bag slung over his shoulder. We didn't stop. Now had the hitchhiker been a comely young lady, who knows?

The haunted highway is the 15 miles of the West Virginia Turnpike (I-77/I-64) between Beckley and Mossy. This remarkable section of highway has had more than its share of phantom hitchhikers. And we use the plural because the phantoms are both male and female not just the traditional damsel in distress. Phantom hitchhikers are usually the most effervescent of apparitions because they almost always evaporate when closely investigated, as Michael Goss demonstrated in his classic study, *The Evidence for Phantom Hitch-hikers*. You might be tempted to dismiss these tales as hoaxes or hallucinations brought on by road fatigue, but these phantoms have been encountered by highly credible individuals, including state troopers and highway maintenance personnel. These people all swear that they've encountered something very real.

One state trooper we spoke with told us of his bizarre experience on the haunted highway. The trooper stated that he once picked up along the highway a little girl who was apparently lost. She got into the patrol car but said nothing, and he proceeded to headquarters. She remained perfectly quiet in the back seat, and when he glanced in his mirror after a few minutes he was shocked to see that she had disappeared. Was she crouching down behind the seat? He pulled over and checked, but found that she was gone! He swore he wasn't drunk, and he was perfectly serious when he told us the story.

In another case, a trooper arrested a phantom hitchhiker, because hitchhiking is illegal on the highway. Following standard procedure, the trooper handcuffed the prisoner and put him in the back seat of the patrol car. Again the hitchhiker mysteriously vanished. When the officer noticed that his prisoner had disappeared from the back seat, he checked and found no trace except for his handcuffs lying on the seat.

In the old days, these stories poured into the old Morton's Truck Stop, known as Glass House. Now demolished, this service plaza near Beckley served as a swapping center for phantom hitchhiker stories. In addition, the Glass House itself was supposedly the focus of substantial haunting, though the details are lacking.

These stories largely date to the period between 1954, when the turnpike was first opened, and the 1970s, when the state began upgrading the road to make it part of the interstate system. Our investigation, however, found that the stories remain ongoing and prolific. With the Glass House gone, the tales now flow into the new Morton's Truck Stop, near exit 74. Its manager, Vicky Allen, told us that she has heard "many crazy things" and just "shrugs it off in order to keep sane." Some years ago, mysterious noises from the basement of the new plaza badly frightened many employees. They calmed down a bit when they were told that the steam pipes in the heating system were the cause. And maybe they were.

The most intensely haunted place on the highway was the maintenance building at Nuckolls, used to store heavy equipment and as a refueling depot for the state troopers' patrol cars. It was demolished some years ago, and we can't help wondering whether its terrifying reputation, widely attested to among highway workers and state troopers, led to its destruction.

Three phenomena plagued the maintenance building. Lights in the building often turned on or off by themselves, and mysterious lights were seen floating through the building when no one was inside. According to the former maintenance supervisor, Clinton Ayers, one particular window opened and closed by itself, even when people were looking at it. The most common phenomenon—and the most unsettling—were the loud banging sounds on or within the building itself.

Sometime the sounds echoed from the walls; at other times they came from the garage doors, which sounded as though they were being slammed closed one after another. The people in the building would run outside to see what the commotion was about and find the area deserted and quiet. Scratching their heads, they would go back inside, and immediately the banging would begin again. In at least one case, a trooper fueling his car one evening heard the slamming garage doors and ran to them to see what was going on. As he told some terrified highway workers who emerged from the building, he saw nothing.

The banging proved so persistent and unnerving that the whole maintenance crew became spooked, the night watchman wanted to quit, and the troopers dreaded going there to refuel. A few people fell back on the old comfortable explanation, that the heating system caused the noises, but invariably those holding to this theory had never heard the noises for themselves. Others thought it might be a particularly persistent prankster, though none was ever seen and no one lived within several miles of the area.

One story told to us by a highway worker of 20 years experience sounds very much like a prank, although the teller, Larry, was quite convinced of its uncanny nature. One evening when Larry went back to his van to get a pipe he had forgotten, he was startled to see his lights on. Opening the door to turn them off, he found human excrement on the seat. His bafflement rested on three facts: he saw no one, his door was locked, and he did not believe that the prank could have been pulled in the short time he was away from his van. A lock picking recluse with a bizarre sense of humor or were the Nuckolls ghosts particularly nasty?

The only conventional apparition story we know from this site comes from Clinton Ayers, writing in *The Greenbrier Ghost and Other Strange Stories*. On several occasions, Ayers heard a truck approaching along some nearby railroad tracks. Looking out his window, he saw a World War I vintage army ambulance. It proceeded to leave the tracks, approach the maintenance building on the road, and then turn off onto a side-road to a nearby cemetery. To learn more, he tried running outside with a spotlight, but this proved useless, because by then the vehicle had seemingly vanished in the darkness.

Folklore collector Dennis Deitz has offered a very plausible reason for the haunting of the highway, especially in the section northwest of Beckley. From near Beckley all the way to the Kanawha River, the road closely follows Paint Creek first and then Cabin Creek. These valleys saw some of the early mine "wars," and later suffered devastation in the 1916 flood of Cabin Creek and the 1932 flood of Paint Creek, which together killed some 150 people. Deitz adds that the highway's construction disturbed many graves, especially at Glass House, where a whole cemetery was moved. Disturb the dead at your peril.

The highway's fame—or curse—has spread over the years. Far to the south of Beckley, the Bluestone Service Plaza seemed to host ghosts as well as travelers in the early 1990s. Workers on the midnight shift swore they heard chains rattling. Some were so frightened they quit their jobs. Skeptics, however, once again claimed it was just noisy steam pipes in the basement.

Less easily explained is another experience related to us by Larry. He said that he was once in the basement at the Bluestone, resetting the boiler, when a cold draft wafted by him. He might have welcomed it in that hot room had it not been so frighteningly inexplicable. Make no mistake, Larry is no gullible fool, and if he was joshing, he did it with a straight face and took the tale no further. He said that this was his only personal experience at this site, though he had heard many colleagues speak of ghostly occurrences there. When we asked about alleged aerial lights seen along the turnpike, he told us that he had never heard of any such reports. He suggested that such reports probably stem from Air Force training flights, which are always done at night in the southern part of the state.

Why should the Bluestone plaza be haunted? Larry suggested that the cause was the disturbance of the Miller cemetery during highway construction. Located at milepost 18, this family cemetery lies less than two miles from the plaza.

Whether noisy pipes or ghosts, the turnpike administrators solved the problem by remodeling all the service plazas a few years ago. In the process, they filled in all the basements. Somehow, though, we don't think these ghosts will stay buried.

It is possible that all of these tales are just fanciful folklore. But why do certain places accumulate heaps of tales while others have none? A 12th-century Scottish castle, sure, but a modern highway?

How to Get There: The site of the Nuckolls maintenance building can be reached by getting off the turnpike at exit 66 (Mahan) and taking CR-83 northwest. At Whitaker, a side road crosses the highway on a bridge. At the end of the bridge, the road forks. Park here, but don't block the road. Take the right fork down hill to the area of the Nuckolls maintenance building.
The Bluestone Service Plaza stands at exit 20 on I-77.

RALEIGH COUNTY

The Sandstone Ghost Light

There's a quiet spot where Laurel Creek empties into the New River. People come to fish or stop into Boyd's Store for a coke or a sandwich or just to enjoy the beauties of the river. This bucolic and serene area is the site of one of the most unusual ghost lights in West Virginia.

The story of the ghost light goes all the way back to the Civil War. Samuel Richmond was a staunch Union man, which was an unusual thing to be in this part of West Virginia because Summers and Raleigh counties for the most part supported the South. Although some small battles were fought in the area, the war in this part of the state consisted of guerrilla warfare involving small groups, which the Confederates called partisans and the Yankees called bushwhackers. These groups would attack Union patrols or companies of local militia called the Home Guards.

With the breakdown of law and order brought on by the war, robbery and murder were rampant. Old scores were settled and new feuds were started. Neighbor killed neighbor, and family members fought with one another in the name of Northern or Southern patriotism. Bitter seeds were sown that resulted in such famous episodes as the Hatfield and McCoy feud. Some will tell you that the bitter aftertaste of the war lingers in the hills to this day.

Samuel Richmond used his canoe to run a ferry service across this calm part of the New River. He lived in a house on the Raleigh County side of the river. In September 1865, an embittered Confederate sympathizer named Jefferson Bennett shot him as he crossed in his canoe. Richmond lived long enough to paddle the canoe back to the landing near his house and then died. And people now say that on certain nights Richmond's spirit, in the form of a light, repeats that fatal journey.

Ghost lights usually don't appear over running water. The physical conditions are not right for a light to occur. Will-o-the-wisps usually form over marshy areas not running streams. Foxfire needs decaying vegetation to occur.

So the Sandstone Ghost Light is a bit of a puzzle. Our brief survey of people living along the shore and working at the store didn't turn up anyone who had seen the light or even knew anything about it, although we must admit that our survey was far from comprehensive. They did know about the Richmond ferry service and told us that the old Richmond homestead was torn down in 1975, but that the family still lives in the area.

So if you want to relax some evening, take a drive to Sandstone and walk along the shoreline where Laurel Creek runs into the New River. Rest a while, and you just might see what remains of Samuel Richmond's spirit make that last and final journey that comes to us all.

How to Get There: From I-64 between Beckley and Lewisburg, get off at exit 138 and take Route 20 south about a mile to Sandstone. Park by Boyd's Store. The road to the left of the store has views of the

New River, where the light was seen. Do not trespass on the private land on both sides of the road.

Beckley's Haunted Theater

Old theaters seem to attract ghosts like honey attracts flies. No old theater worth its salt doesn't have stories of semi-transparent spooks in the balcony or specters lurking in musty storeroom corridors. The Soldier's Memorial Theater and Arts Center in Beckley is no exception, and if eyewitnesses are to be believed, the spooks there put on quite a show.

The main haunt at the Soldier's Memorial Theater seems to be a man in his 60s, dressed in a 1930s-style suit. One summer morning, Cecil Chaney, the executive director of the theater, was opening up the building and checking it out, to make sure no vandals or burglars had sneaked in over night. He found the building empty, so you can imagine his surprise when he saw a man walk by his office door.

The front of the Soldier's Memorial Theater in Beckley.

Chaney described the man as being opaque, in a hazy, semi-transparent sort of way. A subsequent search of the premises found no one.

But Cecil Chaney isn't the only one who saw the transparent specter. Artist Pat Meadows was working on scenery for an upcoming production when he felt someone staring at him for a long time. Annoyed, he looked up and saw the ghost sitting in the balcony. Meadows, who strikes us as being braver than most people, spoke to the apparition. "I hate it when people watch me and don't tell me," he said.

The ghost just kept staring and made no reply. So the cool Mr. Meadows returned to his work. When he looked up again, the ghost had vanished.

Other strange things have happened at the theater. On two occasions, Chaney heard children playing inside the auditorium. When he checked, surprise, the room was empty. On both occasions he checked outside the theater to make sure some weird acoustical phenomenon wasn't carrying the noise of children playing outside into the room. There were no children anywhere in the vicinity.

But the strangest thing of all happened to theater Board President Scott Worley. One night, while standing alone in the theater lobby during a performance, he heard a saxophone start to play. Concerned that some weird practical joker was attempting to sabotage the performance, Scott began a search of the building. Much to his surprise, he discovered that the phantom saxophone could be heard everywhere in the building except the auditorium where the performance was being presented. If this ghost is trying to pass on a message from beyond, it must be a dandy. It really makes you wonder just what goes on in the theater late at night, when no one is there.

The Soldier's Memorial Theater and Arts Center didn't start life as a theater. Even though it looks as old as the hills that surround Beckley, the building is really a creature of the 20th century. Let's take a quick glance at its history, and maybe we'll get a clue as to the origin of some of its haunts.

On November 15, 1931, the citizens of Beckley and surrounding towns gathered together to celebrate the laying of the cornerstone of Raleigh County's newest addition. Marching bands played and veteran's units marched by with flags waving, and the crowd gathered to watch the ceremony. Some of them climbed up on the temporary flooring that stored heavy stones to be used in the construction, so that they could get a better view of the proceedings. Just before Rev. E. Gibson Davis was to give the invocation, the flooring gave way, hurling spectators and stones to the basement floor some 12 feet below. Six people were injured and three required hospitalization.

According to an eyewitness report that we obtained from the Raleigh County Library, the steel supports holding the stone and the people bent, broke and pitched everything into the basement. The most seriously injured was a Mrs. R. P. Richardson of McAlpin, who received shoulder and hip injuries and "suffered considerable [sic] from shock." Panic was averted when the Mark Twain High School band struck up a march tune.

After things calmed down and the injured were removed, the ceremony went on. Mr. W. H. Hill, president of the Mankin Lumber Company, stated that spectators had been warned away from the flooring that collapsed. Mrs. Richardson's husband, who also suffered from an injury to his leg, stated that if any warnings were given, he hadn't heard them. The building was finished in the spring and dedicated on Memorial Day, 1932, without further incident.

In the following years the building served as the Raleigh County Courthouse until a new courthouse was built and as the county library. Later it housed the YMCA. Even today there are state offices in the basement, art center offices on the first floor, and meeting rooms on the second, so the building serves as a community center.

As is our practice, we visited the theater the weekend before Memorial Day, 1999. The building sits brooding at 200 Kanawha Street, looking more like a mausoleum than a theater or an office building. We don't spook (pardon the pun) easily, but we can personally testify that the Soldier's Memorial Theater is one of spookier places we've visited.

We arrived at the theater on a splendid Sunday afternoon but no one was there. The front door was open, and since this is a public building, we went in to look around, see if we could find anyone, and snap a few pictures. The auditorium is spacious and has great acoustics, considering the building wasn't designed as a theater. We walked around back stage and began snapping photos. Mike was setting up for a shot of the spacious balcony when we both were startled to hear someone moving around up there. Neither of us could see anyone, so we continued to take our pictures.

Later we went up and checked the balcony but found no one. It's quite possible we heard birds, or bats, or theater mice scurrying around. It's also possible someone or some thing didn't want its picture taken. We decided to come back the next day to see if we could find someone who could shed some light on this mysterious place.

When we returned the next day, the only person we could find was a young woman who was on stage, painting scenery for the next production. We asked her about the weird events at the theater. While she hadn't personally witnessed any strange phenomena, she said that other people had told tales, and she confirmed most of what was reported in the newspaper item that sent us here in the first place. She did say that many people thought the hauntings took place because the nearby high school and playground were built on the site of a Civil War graveyard. And if you've read this book all the way through, you know what happens when you disturb old bones, especially soldiers' bones, particularly Yankee soldiers' bones.

We checked out the neighborhood and found that it did play a role in the Civil War. The Samuel Keefer residence served as quarters for Rutherford B. Hayes, commander of the 23rd Ohio and future president of the United States. In 1863 it was a Union hospital. The standard of medical care not being too good back then, it probably kept the graveyard full of new residents.

We left our source to her work and decided to take another look around the building. While we stood in the lobby, we could hear women's voices coming from upstairs. We decided to check but found nothing except the piano that allegedly plays by itself from time to time. After closer investigation, we decided that the voices probably came from the offices in the basement...probably.

As we were leaving for the last time, we ran into our scenery painter. "By the way," she said, "how did you guys get in here?"

"The door was open so we just walked in," we replied.

"That's funny," she said, looking a little anxious. "I know I locked this door when I came in, and until you two came, no one else was here." No one that we could see, at any rate.

So who or what haunts the Soldier's Memorial Theater and Art Center in Beckley? A man dressed in depression-era clothes? Mr. Richardson asking us to remember his poor wife's plight or is it W. H. Hill, looking for people to warn off the temporary floor? Is there a basketball game going on from YMCA days, which will continue on throughout most of eternity, or is it a bunch of spectral kids just being kids? Does the shade of Rutherford B. Hayes come back and play saxophone solos or tinkle the ivories on odd occasions? Probably not. Hayes was a rather stuffy individual who didn't allow drinking or dancing at the White House during his term as president.

Theater management makes the best of the situation and uses these real haunts as a come-on for a haunted Halloween tour where actors dress up as monsters and spooks to provide you with a seasonal scare for a few dollars. While the commercial exploitation of a haunt might cause some raised eyebrows among the skeptics, no one has presented any reason to doubt the veracity of the witnesses or the truthfulness of the events they described. And as authors of a ghostly guide book, a decidedly commercial venture, any protest we would make along these lines would ring very hollow. So take in a performance at the Soldier's Memorial Theater, or take the ghost tour (persons under ten not admitted). But don't be surprised if that older-looking gentleman dressed in the old-fashioned clothes, suddenly vanishes during the second act.

How to Get There: From I-64, get off at exit 124. Follow Route 210 into the heart of Beckley, where it becomes Kanawha Street. The Soldier's Memorial Theater and Arts Center stands on the right, at 200 Kanawha Street, on the campus of the College of West Virginia. Parking is available in a lot beside the theater.

SUMMERS COUNTY

The Spirit of a Steel-Driving Man

John Henry he said to the Captain,
You know a man he ain't nothin but a man,
And before I let that steam drill beat me down,
I'm gonna die with my hammer in my hand.

Just outside the little town of Talcott, located on a sharp curve in Route 3, is a large statue of a very muscular black man with a hammer. The statue commemorates a man that some people say didn't exist, the legendary John Henry. Anyone who has tried to learn to play the guitar knows who John Henry is, because they've played the song immortalizing his famous duel to the

Statue of John Henry.

death with a steam drill. Now unless they're from West Virginia, most people have no idea where this contest happened. According to the legend it took place in the C&O Railroad tunnel under Big Bend Mountain. This is where John Henry made his living driving steel, and some say that his ghost still does.

Post-Civil War America was a time of great industrial expansion, with railroads being built at an astonishing rate. The C&O decided to build a rail line from Covington, Virginia to the Ohio River at Guyandotte, West Virginia. Given the rough terrain and the state of the construction arts in 1870, it's remarkable that the railroad was built at all. But it was finished in 1873, ahead of schedule.

One of the biggest obstacles the C&O had to face was Big Bend Mountain. In order to save time and money, the C&O designers developed the strategy of following the river valleys to lay their track. Unfortunately, Big Bend Mountain forces the Greenbrier River to make a 10-mile circle around its base. Ironically, the river ends up about a mile from where it started its curve. Thus the C&O decided to tunnel through the mountain, and this started John Henry on his date with destiny.

The entrance to the Big Bend Tunnel (no longer in use).

In 1870, digging tunnels was a labor-intensive activity. Since this part of the Greenbrier Valley was a sparsely settled wilderness, labor had to be imported. The biggest pool of labor was that of recently freed slaves who had trouble getting any kind of work. For many of them, this dangerous and dirty work was their first job as freemen.

During its construction, the Big Bend Tunnel claimed many lives. It is estimated that one out of ten men who worked on its construction died. The reason for this is a basic law of physics. The tunnel was being driven through wet, red shale, which has the nasty habit of collapsing after it dries out.

The attitude towards black workers was harsh. Often when an African-American man was killed in an accident, his death would go unreported so as not to alarm the other black workers. According to some reports, the bosses claimed that the dead black men had not been christened and therefore weren't entitled to a Christian burial. Thus many of them were buried beneath the debris at the eastern end of the tunnel. Perhaps it would suffice to say that while working conditions in the Big Bend Tunnel were harsh for both black and white workers, blacks had it a little harder than most.

Into this hostile environment came a man called John Henry, or did he? There is considerable doubt as to exactly who John Henry was and some claim he didn't exist at all. Some sources say that he was a 200-pound 6-foot black man who was an ex-slave. Others that he came from Jamaica. There's even one story that he was a white man from Kentucky, but this claim seems ludicrous. The C&O Railroad has no record that a man named John Henry ever worked for them. But the railroad claims that its employment records for those days were destroyed in a fire. There's also another explanation, which we'll discuss in the last part of the chapter.

Is John Henry a legend like Paul Bunyan or Pecos Bill, or did he actually exist? The feats ascribed to John Henry are not beyond the realm of human possibility as are those of Paul Bunyan. So it is probably safe to assume that John Henry, or some one very much like him, actually existed. D. Louis Chappel in his book *John Henry, A Folklore Study,* says he spoke to men who claimed they knew John Henry, and all agreed he had a duel with the steam drill. But they disagreed on what happened to him.

John Henry was a driver. In those days, tunnels were blasted through mountains by explosives. The drivers would hammer steel bits into the rock to drill holes for the placement of the explosives. Men called turners loosened the bits and turned them while other men collected the dull bits from the turners and sharpened them. They also kept the turners supplied with fresh bits.

Good drivers were held in high esteem by their fellow workers. They would often hold contests to see who could drive the bits farthest. A skilled driver could hit the bit about 90 times a minute. A typical contest lasted 15 minutes.

John Henry was considered to be the greatest driver that ever lived. Henry could use two nine-pound hammers on separate bits simultaneously. People said that he kept a steady rhythm going and going and would often sing in time with the beating of his hammers.

One day the railroad decided to test a steam-powered drill, the forerunner of today's pneumatic drills, on tunnel construction. The drivers took umbrage at this unwarranted intrusion on their dirty and dangerous domain. So they arranged a contest between John Henry, with his two nine-pound hammers, and the steam drill. The contest lasted some 35 minutes, and at the end, according to the version of the song that we learned (and there are a huge number of different versions):

> *John Henry drove that steel 15 feet,*
> *And the steam drill drove it but nine,*
> *But he tried so hard that he broke his heart,*
> *And he laid down his hammer and he died,*

But wait. Did John Henry lay down his hammer and die? Like so much surrounding this story, there are different versions of his death. One says he died of a stroke induced by his tremendous exertion. Another that he went home and died of a fever. Finally, a man named Neal Miller says that John Henry was killed in an explosion in the tunnel and buried in the fill.

However John Henry died, workers refused to go back into the tunnel because they claimed they could hear John Henry's rhythmic hammering. A foremen claimed that the sound they heard was the dripping of water from the roof of the tunnel onto the floor. Eventually, the workers all went back but not without a certain amount of trepidation. It's bad enough to work in a tunnel that could collapse at any second, without it being haunted to boot.

But rumors persisted, and in 1876 came the strange tale of a bricklayer named Alfred Owens, who was working on a project to brick in the walls of the tunnel to prevent dry slate from falling on the tracks. One day while Owens was hard at work, he heard the rhythmic pounding of a hammer. As he looked up, he saw in the tunnel opening, in the light of his headlamp, a huge figure rhythmically swinging a hammer in each hand. Owens was frozen to the spot. As the specter got nearer, Owens slipped and fell at its feet. When he looked up the ghost was gone. It is not recorded whether or not Owens continued his employment with the C&O.

Down through the years, belief in John Henry's ghost has persisted among the black communities living near the Big Bend Tunnel. In 1932 a parallel tunnel was completed, and the floor of the original tunnel was concreted. One day, while concrete was being poured in the number 3 shaft, workers came across an old hammer and drill bit. The men refused to disturb the tools because they believed they belonged to John Henry.

The old (on the right) and new Big Bend Tunnels.

However, an early version of the John Henry song, modern archeology and a clever bit of detecting by a history professor may shed some light on just who John Henry really was. According to a December 8, 1998 item in the *Washington Post,* Scott Nelson, an assistant professor of history at William and Mary, was puzzled by the last verse of a very early version of the John Henry song.

> *They took John Henry to the White House,*
> *And buried him in the san'*
> *And every locomotive come roarin by,*
> *Says there lies a steel driven man,*

Folklorists and historians didn't know what to make of the first line of this verse. Nelson knew that convict labor from Richmond Penitentiary worked on the C&O construction. Nelson searched the Internet to get a picture of Richmond Penitentiary and found one that showed a white machine shop or barracks. Further, the company that purchased the prison site from the state of Virginia discovered an unmarked graveyard while digging a drainage ditch near a former railroad bed.

A forensic examination revealed that the mass grave contained the remains of 300 people, mostly men with a scattering of women and children, both black and white. Among the skeletons were a few, very robust individuals. Finally, local newspapers of the time carried stories that reported that prison authorities were burying prisoners at the jail instead of in a decent burial ground. The Richmond City Council ended the practice in 1877.

Thus all of the pieces fell into place for Nelson. When prisoners talked about going to the White House they didn't mean the one in Washington, D.C. They meant the one in Richmond Penitentiary. They meant that someone had died and was going to be buried.

So was John Henry an ex-slave who became a slave laborer for the C&O Railroad? It was common practice back then to put convicts to work, so it's quite possible. The song also tells us how John Henry may have died. When racing the steam drill, "He broke his rib on his left han' side and his intrels [sic] fell on the groun'." What may have happened is that the hammer unexpectedly recoiled and hit John Henry in the ribs, crushing his chest and killing him. His body would have been hauled back to Richmond Penitentiary and buried with all of the rest near the White House next to the train tracks.

Does the ghost of a driver still prowl the depths of the Big Bend Tunnel, pounding away at phantom drill bits, and if so, is it the shade of a hero named John Henry? If any place in West Virginia should be haunted, by all lights the Big Bend Tunnel should be. A contemporary issue of the *Wheeling Intelligencer* stated that there were 2,000 men at work on the New River section of the railroad and that 6,000 would be employed by the end of the month. Now while this figure doesn't tell us how many men worked in constructing the Big Bend Tunnel, it certainly gives us a good idea. And if one out of ten died, then the casualty rate was similar to a mid-sized Civil War battle. For example, 78 men died at Droop Mountain, the largest Civil War battle fought in West Virginia.

Given the way some of the casualties of this battle against the mountain were treated, either being denied a Christian burial and tossed like garbage into the fill at the end of the tunnel or being hauled back to Richmond and dumped into unconsecrated ground, it's surprising that a legion of phantoms doesn't haunt the tunnel. Desecration of the dead and ill treatment of their bones seems to be one of the key ingredients to setting off a haunt. And maybe the steel-driving man is committed to drive steel for eternity so that we remember the great sacrifice and great injustices that took place here.

How to Get There: The statue of John Henry stands along Route 3, on Big Bend Mountain, a little west of Talcott. To reach the tunnel, turn onto CR-17 in Talcott, then turn onto the gravel road that parallels Route 3 and head toward the visible tunnels. Trains still use the tracks and modern tunnel, so exercise extreme caution and do not enter the tunnel. The disused tunnel, on the right, is the original. Do not enter it, as it is in dangerous disrepair.

GREENBRIER COUNTY

Zona Shue, the Ghost That Testified

One of the strangest episodes in both legal history and the history of the paranormal happened in Greenbrier County in June 1897, when Edward Trout Shue was convicted of murdering his young wife Zona by testimony that allegedly came from Zona's ghost. This is the only time that we know of in legal history, when the testimony of a dead person resulted in a conviction for murder.

Trout Shue was a strong and handsome itinerant blacksmith and stonemason with a bad reputation and an eye for the ladies. He divorced his first wife by throwing her things out of the house. She never came back. Trout's second wife was even more unfortunate. Trout was so jealous that he took her out on his stonemason jobs, and she would help him with the work. One fateful day she was helping him build a chimney by loading a bucket with rocks, which Trout would haul up to the roof where he was working. A rock accidentally fell on her head and killed her. Trout Shue also spent time in jail for horse stealing. Thus he was not what you would call a good catch.

So when Trout Shue began to court pretty 15-year-old Zona Heaster, Zona's mother Mary protested, but to no avail. Trout and Zona were married, and two months later Zona Shue was dead. Zona's body was discovered by Andy Jones, a young lad that Trout Shue had asked to help Zona with her housework. The frightened boy first ran to the blacksmith shop and told Shue what had happened, then ran for the doctor. When he and Dr. Knapp returned to the Shue residence, they discovered that Shue had moved his wife's body from the floor to the bed and had dressed her in an old-fashioned high stiff collar that was fastened around her throat with a scarf. When Dr. Knapp tried to examine Zona's head to determine the cause of death, Shue held her head and refused to let go. For some reason, the doctor did not pursue the matter.

During the days before the funeral, Shue never left his dead wife's side while others were present, and when not standing next to the coffin, would permit no one else to go near it. He also placed a folded sheet on one side of Zona's head and old clothes on the other, to keep her head in an upright position. This may all seem rather strange to modern audiences, but the embalming of bodies wasn't a common practice in many places, particularly poor rural areas.

Several days after Zona was buried, Mary Heaster claimed she was visited four times by the ghost of her daughter. In the last two of these visits, Zona's ghost related the facts of her death to her mother. The ghost said that Trout Shue flew into a rage because she had cooked no meat for supper. Then, using his strong blacksmith's hands, he began to choke her and snapped her neck.

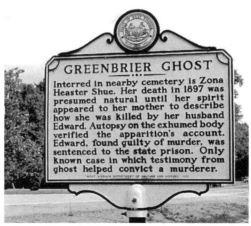

Zona Shue historical marker on US-60.

Mary Heaster told this disturbing tale to her neighbors, who were quite sympathetic but probably wrote off the alleged ghostly encounters as the dreams of a grieving mother. Finally Johnson Heaster, her brother-in-law, began to think that there might be something substantive to Mary Heaster's claims. After talking with Shue, with various family members who attended the wake and the funeral and with the witnesses at the scene of Zona's death, he took up the matter with John A. Preston, the local prosecutor.

After mulling the matter over, Preston decided the case needed further investigation. So he ordered an autopsy, something that was rarely done in the mountains where graves were treated with great respect. During the autopsy, while Trout Shue was present (another departure from modern criminal procedure) the doctor discovered that Zona's neck was broken, confirming her mother's dream. Shue was arrested and brought to trial.

Shue was defended by Dr. William Rucker and James P. D. Gardner, the first African-American attorney to practice in Greenbrier County Court. Many individuals testified to Shue's odd behavior before and during the funeral. Dr. Knapp testified that Shue refused to relinquish his hold on Zona's head so that the doctor could not examine it. The doctor also testified that the break in the neck could not have been self-inflicted, so poor Zona could not be accused of committing suicide.

Zona Shue's grave.

But the real turning point of the trial came with the testimony of Mary Heaster and her encounter with her dead daughter's ghost. Although the defense could have had Zona's testimony dismissed on the grounds that it was hearsay evidence, they undoubtedly felt that the mountain of circumstantial evidence piled up against Trout Shue might have convicted him without Zona's testimony. Thus they chose to allow it to stand so that Dr. Rucker could discredit Mary Heaster as irrational and unstable during his extensive cross-examination and thus undermine the whole thrust of the prosecution case.

But the desperate defense didn't work, and Mary Heaster stoutly stuck to her story. Shue testified one whole day in his own defense, but the more he talked, the guiltier he sounded. It was no surprise that the jury found him guilty of murder in the first degree. But because of the circumstantial nature of the evidence, the jury felt that it could not, in good conscience, recommend the death penalty. So Trout Shue was sentenced to life imprisonment. Shue was spirited out of town to avoid a mob who thought the jury had been too lenient and sent to Moundsville State Prison. He died there on March 13, 1900 from an unspecified illness. No one knows where he was buried.

As time went by and passions cooled, speculation arose about Zona's demise. Some people said that Zona died a natural death and that her mother broke her neck in the coffin in order to frame the hated Trout Shue. Given Shue's behavior around the body, this doesn't seem quite likely, and a post-mortem fracture of the neck would probably have been noticed by the doctor doing the autopsy.

The second speculation gets even more involved. Some said that Zona was pregnant with an illegitimate child and had died as the result of an abortion performed by Dr. Knapp, who had been treating her for an unspecified illness. Knapp then broke her neck to cover the matter up.

A variant of this story said that Shue murdered Zona when he discovered she was pregnant with a child that couldn't possibly have been his. Given Shue's jealous nature, this is a good motive for murder. (Rosemary Ellen Guiley, in her book *The Encyclopedia of Ghosts and Spirits,* reports that records show that Zona Shue had an illegitimate child in 1895 and that Dr. Knapp listed her cause of death as childbirth.)

Historian Katie Lechter Lyle, in her book *The Man Who Wanted Seven Wives*, also attempts to discredit Zona's ghost. In her research she found that the issue of the Greenbrier *Independent* that carried Zona Shue's death announcement also carried the story of a murder case in Australia that had been solved because people reported seeing the ghost of a murdered man sitting on a rail fence next to the horse pond in which he had been drowned. Years later, a dying man confessed that he had witnessed the murder and was threatened with death if he revealed the details. So he made up the ghost story so that the body of the murder victim could be recovered. Lyle theorized that Mrs. Heaster read the story and did the same thing to get at the ultimate cause of her daughter's death.

What the ultimate truth to this story is, no one can say. Everyone directly involved is long since dead. We've seen some of their tombstones. It's clear that Trout Shue was not exactly a candidate for husband of the year. He'd already been through two wives, one dead under peculiar circumstances, and frequently boasted he wanted to have seven wives. His strange behavior surrounding Zona's corpse and the funeral certainly seems to indicate he was trying to hide something. Was the death purposeful or accidental? Was it no meat for supper or something else more sinister? The answers lie buried deeply in the sands of time.

Did Mary Heaster use mountain cunning to bring a murderer to justice or did Zona Shue reach out from beyond the grave and reveal a hideous murder? Whatever happened, the story is an interesting one, and we'll go along with the ghost. Since Zona Shue has not made a reappearance, we'll assume she finally found justice and now rests in peace.

How to Get There: *Four sites connected with the Shue case can be visited.*

John A. Preston: *The prosecuting attorney is buried in section C-4 of the Lewisburg Cemetery, which is bounded by Church, Foster, Court and McElhenry streets. From I-64, take US-219 into Lewisburg, where it becomes Jefferson Street. Turn right onto Washington Street and then left onto Church Street. Excellent brochures and maps can be obtained at the Greenbrier Historical Society at 101 Church Street. The cemetery lies a block farther down Church Street.*

Greenbrier County Courthouse: *The Greenbrier County Courthouse, where the Shue trial was held, still stands at 200 North Court Street (that's two blocks north of Washington Street).*

Roadside Historical Marker: *An historical marker commemorating the Shue ghost stands on the west side of US-60, on the south side of the interchange with I-64 (exit 156).*

Zona Shue's Grave: *To reach Zona Shue's grave, get off I-64 at exit 156 and take US-60 west toward Rainelle. Take the first left, an unmarked road to Meadow Bluff. Turn right onto CR-25, which becomes CR-60-32 at Meadow Bluff, and continue straight ahead a couple miles. Little Sewell Mountain looms ahead, but if you start to ascend it you've gone too far. Turn left onto CR-26, a narrow dirt road, just before that ascent. CR-26 ascends steeply and almost immediately passes Soule Chapel Methodist Church on the left. Turn in here. Zona is buried in the church cemetery. Beside her are the graves of her mother, M. J. Heaster (Dec. 15, 1849 to Sept. 6, 1916), and father, J. H. Heaster (Oct. 15, 1847 to Apr. 5, 1917).*

The Angelic Army of Lewisburg

The Civil War has provided us with many strange tales of ghosts and hauntings, but perhaps one of the strangest comes from Greenbrier County just west of Lewisburg. On the first of October, 1863 at 3 p.m., hundreds of witnesses allegedly saw a phantom army appear in the sky and march off towards the west. The army marched across the sky in a column thirty or forty men wide. Individual soldiers were said to be of various sizes and, as they marched, their arms and legs moved just like soldiers marching on parade on terra firma.

Some witnesses said the "soldiers" all wore the same white uniforms, while others said the spectral parade was accompanied by blue glowing objects. The column marched across the skies over the valley and into the hills beyond, where it disappeared. The phenomenon lasted approximately one hour.

Just as the shaken people of Greenbrier were getting over their astonishment, the phantom army marched again two weeks later. Confederate pickets at a place called Bunger's Mill observed much the same phenomenon. Local residents corroborated the story and said that the strange procession lasted about an hour.

The story created a sensation across the South, and Greenbrier County was soon swarming with reporters and investigators. More similar occurrences were reported from nearby counties but none so spectacular as those witnessed in Greenbrier.

What really happened on that long ago October day is a real mystery. What people saw may have been a bizarre weather phenomenon that resulted in a cloud formation that resembled a marching army. If this is the case, it would be one of the wildest simulacra to ever occur, so this explanation doesn't seem likely. (A simulacra is an image or likeness of a person or object found in nature.)

Perhaps what occurred was a mass hallucination brought on by the stresses of the Civil War, which was becoming extremely bloody. Lewisburg itself was fought over in May of 1862 and was a place of refuge for casualties of the 1861 campaign in the Kanawha Valley. Or perhaps a series of peculiar cloud formations induced a mass hallucination.

Maybe the whole thing was a hoax, made up by some enterprising Southern editor to raise the flagging spirits of the

Confederate citizenry at a black time in its history, by hinting that God was on their side and had sent an army of his angels to watch over them. Or perhaps it was a story that was meant to be fiction that somehow took on a life of its own. This has happened repeatedly in wartime. Perhaps the most famous incident was that of the so-called Angels of Mons in World War I.

Or perhaps the army was real, an army of the dead or soon to be dead, that was headed towards the west, the symbolic destination of dead souls. And who's to say that this phantom army was from the Civil War or from any war being fought on this earth. Perhaps it was an army of specters, not of this dimension or time, marching across the sky towards a destination located somewhere around a corner in infinity.

How to Get There: *Go to Lewisburg, off I-64, in the Greenbrier River Valley, and look up.*

NORTHERN PANHANDLE

CHAPTER SIX

WETZEL COUNTY

The Jennings Gang

When the Civil War erupted in the spring of 1861, John Jennings came out strong for the Union. In his patriotic zeal he joined the 15th West Virginia Infantry. But after six months of dreary camp life interspersed with moments of danger, Jennings became homesick for his wife and five sons and four daughters. So like so many others, he deserted.

But the army didn't take kindly to Jennings' desertion. They were so upset that they sent a company of men and an officer to pursue him and bring him back. Jennings knew the country around his home like the back of his hand, and he escaped them. The U.S. government, however, would not give up. From then on, Jennings was pursued by the local militia, known as Home Guards. The Home Guards were formed to defend the local areas against attacks by Confederate guerrillas and raiders and they also chased deserters. They weren't well thought of by some people, particularly rebel sympathizers who considered the Home Guards to be little better than bandits.

Jennings was afraid that if he were caught, he would be court marshaled and shot, so he kept on the run. His intimate knowledge of the area plus an agreeable supply of relatives allowed Jennings to elude the best efforts of the Home Guards, but at a severe cost. His first wife died of exposure and fatigue after carrying food and clothing to him one cold and snowy winter night.

Jennings became a desperate man. He was saved when President Lincoln issued a blanket pardon to all deserters who would rejoin their regiments. Jennings did so at once, but his reception by his comrades-in-arms was somewhat less than cordial. They generally ignored him and would speak to him only in line of duty. When the regiment camped, he had to pitch his tent away from the others. At the end of the war, when the regiment returned to be mustered out, his fellow soldiers threw him overboard from the steamboat that was taking them home, and Jennings had to walk back to his home on Doolin Run. And while he was warmly welcomed home by his family, his neighbors still treated him as an outlaw.

It's here that versions of the story begin to differ. One version says that the Jennings sons became so upset by the treatment their father received from his neighbors that they began to rob and steal from his persecutors. As time went by, the gang attracted a diverse band of ex-convicts, fugitives and local juvenile delinquents and established a reign of terror in Wetzel County.

In his book *The History of Wetzel County West Virginia,* John C. McEldowny Jr. paints a slightly different if more detailed picture of the Jennings Gang. McEldowny describes Jennings as "a man of energy and courage who would sacrifice anything necessary for a friend but would shoot down those whom he considered an enemy as he would a dog."

According to McEldowny, three of Jennings' sons were in the gang: Frank, Thomas and Jackson. Frank Jennings was considered the leader. In 1864 he was sentenced to five years at Moundsville Prison for one of his crimes. He escaped and with the aid of sympathizers eluded recapture.

Thomas Jennings, the oldest of the brothers, deserted the Union Army around the same time as his father but he didn't accept Lincoln's amnesty. He shot and wounded George Forbes in Wheeling and later was thrown in jail for larceny. Upon his release he rejoined the gang but then was arrested and jailed for housebreaking. He died of an unspecified illness in the Moundsville State Prison hospital.

Jackson, better known as Jack Jennings, was generally considered to be the most unscrupulous member of the family. He and his father didn't get along, and on several occasions Jack allegedly threatened his father's life. John Jennings frequently complained that he had no control over Jack and that he was suffering the ill will of his neighbors because of the things Jack did.

The rest of the gang was composed of relations or people the Jennings boys met while they were serving time. The gang included women as well as men, plus several fringe members who served as spies or harbored members of the gang when they were on the run.

The gang undertook a series of armed robberies, burglaries and assaults on the good citizens of Wetzel and Tyler Counties. People locked their doors and windows at night out of fear of the gang. Despite the fact that almost every member of the gang was sent to jail at one time or another, their crime wave continued.

The people of Wetzel County became increasingly disgusted by the seeming inability of local authorities to control the gang, so they took the law into their own hands. In 1873 they formed a secret vigilante group they called the Red Men. To keep their identities secret, the Red Men would disguise themselves with red, pillowcase-like hoods. Other sources claimed they painted their faces red. Whichever way they disguised themselves, the group started visiting the homes of persons who befriended the gang. They would order the families to leave the county before burning down their houses. Quite naturally, this considerably diminished local support for the gang.

On the night of June 12, 1873, the Red Men decided to strike at the heart of the Jennings Gang. They went after John Jennings himself. Jennings was awakened by a shot, looked out of his window and saw two-dozen Red Men who ordered him to surrender. Jennings refused. Once again they ordered Jennings to come along with them. By this time Jennings had foolishly come out of his house. When he refused again the Red Men attempted to put a rope around his neck.

His wife (Jennings had remarried), thinking he was going to be lynched, handed him an ax so he could defend himself. The Red Men gunned John Jennings down and also wounded his wife. Upon hearing the news, Frank and Jack Jennings fled to the south and were never heard from again. The rest of the gang split up and went their separate ways.

But according to the local folks, that wasn't the end of it. There have been reports that the spirits of the Jennings gang roam the hills. Foxhunters claimed they could see the silhouettes of the gang members as they moved along the ridges.

The area along Doolin Run is still wild and beautiful country. There certainly is plenty of room to hide and plenty of room for ghosts. Do the spirits of the Jennings Gang still lurk in these woodlands, sizing up the living as possible robbery victims? Or did Jennings' relatives start the ghost stories to cover the return visits of Frank and Jack, who were not exactly Wetzel's favorite sons? Or on moonlit autumn nights, is the shade of John Jennings still pursued by spectral units of the Home Guards who can't let their enmity die?

How to Get There: From Route 2, on the south side of New Martinsville, turn east onto North Street (CR-3). (Yes, that's right, North Street is on the south side of town and it runs in an east-west direction!) CR-3 follows Doolin Run all the way to its headspring, near the junction with CR-5, on a plateau.

The Ghost Who Failed to Appear

West Virginia has the weird distinction of having not one, but *two* ghosts who "went to court." The Shue case (see Zona Shue, The Ghost That Testified) is world famous, but the other ghost who sought justice for his murder is all but unknown today.

Two authoritative accounts tell the story of John Gamble's ghost. The first was by D. W. Gamble, who had first-hand knowledge of the people and events even though he was only ten years old at the time of the incident. His account appears in John C. McEldowney, Jr.'s *History of Wetzel County*. The other account, written by Brent Gamble and published in a 1983 county history, tells the story as it still survives within the Gamble family. Significantly, the accounts complement one another without any important contradictions.

John Gamble, a house carpenter, was born in Beaver County, Pennsylvania, in 1814. In 1850, he settled on 50.5 acres of land that he purchased along the Ohio River, just above Paden City across from Sardis, Ohio. Gamble was an enterprising man who became a river trader, often buying up staves, wagon spokes, and tanbark and taking them down river for sale in Cincinnati. That year he sold a wagon to the Whiteman brothers, who also lived along the river. He accepted an IOU for $20 in payment from them. Gamble also bought and sold cattle, and on one occasion he bought a calf from Leb Mercer, paying him all but two dollars of the price. This seemingly inconsequential sale was the most important business transaction of his life.

The year 1850 was a good one for apples, so Gamble began making and selling cider. On November 12 he took his skiff to New Martinsville to buy some barrels because he was running short. On his way home, he stopped at the Whiteman brothers' farm to try to redeem their IOU. They still could not pay, so Gamble pocketed the note and prepared to leave, because it was getting dark. Leb Mercer was also visiting the Whitemans, and he asked for the two dollars he was owed. Gamble pulled a five-dollar bill out of his pocket, but Mercer had no change. Mercer asked whether that was all the money he had, and Gamble foolishly told him he had nearly $200, but no small bills. He asked Mercer to visit him in a few days, and he would pay him. Gamble then got in his skiff and pushed off, while Mercer was seen "moving toward him." At this point, darkness envelops the story, both literally and figuratively. Gamble was never seen again—not *alive*, that is!

In autumn of 1851, New Martinsville resident John Hindman attended a corn husking on Point Pleasant Ridge. Afterwards, he and some friends agreed to take different routes home to find out which route was best. Hindman went down Gamble's Run to a path along the Ohio River shore. There "he saw the form of a man," who said, "I am John Gamble. Leb Mercer killed me. Take him up and have justice done." Then the ghost suddenly disappeared. Terrified, Hindman walked quickly to town. The next day, he told his story widely. Few people believed him at first, but when he described Gamble's clothes, the way Gamble walked, and other personal characteristics, the number of believers swelled because *Hindman had never seen the living Gamble.*

A Wetzel County grand jury investigated the allegations in 1852. Mercer's mother testified that Leb was soaking wet and covered with mud when he returned home at 2 a.m. on the night of Gamble's disappearance. Leb claimed he had gotten that way from chocking a wagon up a muddy hill. It was also discovered that he had the IOU that the Whiteman brothers had given to Gamble. Consequently, Mercer was arrested for first-degree murder. Many people believed him guilty by this time, and his lawyer had a hard time keeping him from confessing.

According to Brent Gamble's account, Mercer was brought to trial in 1854. Since John Gamble's ghost was the only eyewitness to the crime, the defense demanded that the ghost appear and testify. When the ghost failed to appear, the judge held the ghost in contempt of court and directed the acquittal of Leb Mercer.

By contrast, D. W. Gamble's account is vague concerning the disposition of the case, saying only that Mercer "was released on the grounds that ghost evidence would not go in court." We tried to verify that the trial actually took place, but learned that a fire had long ago destroyed the original Wetzel County Courthouse and its records.

Mercer afterwards moved to St. Mary's, West Virginia, where, according to the account in McEldowney, "it is said he acts strangely, often muttering to himself." So go to Paden City and see for yourself. You might run into John Gamble's ghost trying to answer a summons for contempt at a courthouse that no longer exists.

How to Get There: *Take Route 2 south from New Martinsville, or north from Paden City. The murder and ghostly reappearance of John Gamble occurred on the Ohio River shore somewhere along this section of Route 2. The shore, though inaccessible private land, is often visible from the highway.*

TYLER COUNTY

The Wells Inn Spook

We discovered the Wells Inn spook almost by accident. It was two o'clock on a hot Sunday afternoon and we were driving up the Ohio River from St. Marys. We knew about the Wells Inn, in Sistersville, from our preliminary library research when we turned up an article in a now defunct magazine called *Mountain Trace.* The article mentioned in passing that there were reports of a ghost in the Wells Inn but that the skeptical owners claimed the haunt was just noisy pipes. And in many supposed hauntings, noisy pipes, not denizens of the nether world, are the cause of the phenomena.

The front entrance of the Wells Inn.

Since it was long past lunchtime and we had driven past the inn on our way down to St. Marys, we decided to give it a try. Who knows? Perhaps a talkative waitress or desk clerk would give us the real scoop. The worst we would get is that all-too-familiar cold look and abrupt denial that there was anything wrong with the inn, and you better not write that anything is or watch out. Many owners, particularly of hotels and motels, refuse to recognize that they share their establishments with the supernatural. While others think it is good business to have a spook about the place.

This time we were lucky. It seems that the skeptical owners were long gone and the new owners, Walker and Jody Boyd, did not deny the presence of a ghost but accepted it wholeheartedly. People working at the inn seemed eager to tell us what was going on, and our waitress told us about Nell Smith, who became our chief informant.

As we sat in the comfortable lobby, Nell pointed out the picture of Ephraim Wells, the man who built the original inn. As Nell talked, Ephraim, who was placed where he could see the comings and goings at the front desk and in the lobby, seemed to look benignly down on us.

Sistersville began to boom after oil was discovered there around the turn of the century. Like most boomtowns, it lacked the type of establishment that would cater to the quality, the higher class, and more gentile travelers. Ephraim Wells, the grandson of Sistersville's founder Charles Wells, filled the need by opening the Wells Hotel on January 15, 1895.

After many years of profitable and successful business, the hotel fell on hard times. It had a series of owners, and opened and closed several times. The hard winter of 1993-94 greatly damaged the hotel and almost caused it to be torn down. But the Boyds came along and saved it, pumping new life into the old place by adding such modern amenities as an indoor swimming pool and exercise area.

But what of the ghost? Those working at the inn feel that the elusive spirit is none other than Ephraim Wells, who haunts the inn he created. Ephraim is another one of those ghosts who are heard but usually not seen. Things are moved around rooms when no one is there. There are strange noises in the night, particularly when there is no one staying at the inn. Then there's the elevator that likes to come down from the third floor all by itself. Doors also like to slam when there's no one around.

Perhaps the most unusual incident happened to a housekeeper on the third floor. There's a pleasant corner room, #324, down at the end of the hall.

Room 324, the door that refused to open at the Wells Inn.

One day the housekeeper tried to open the door to the room, and it literally sucked itself shut. Being somewhat pluckier than most, she tried twice more with the same results. On the fourth try, the door opened normally.

When we examined the door we could find nothing wrong with it. It opened and closed quite smoothly, and this was on a hot and humid summer day. Was Ephraim having a little joke with the help? Or did some unknown spectral tenant want a little privacy? There's no way to tell. Spooks do the darnedest things and no one really knows why.

People working at the inn say that things have calmed down quite a bit since the new owners took over. Perhaps Ephraim is signaling the Boyds that he approves of what they've done to save his beloved inn. Maybe he's happy that people have acknowledged him. In some instances, the complete denial of a ghost's existence will make it try harder to be noticed, and not always with the most pleasant results.

And now for a final bit of irony. Nell Smith told us that Walker Boyd bears a startling resemblance to Ephraim Wells. We didn't meet Mr. Boyd so we can't personally verify this. If you stay at the inn, you may meet Mr. Boyd or maybe you'll meet Ephraim himself.

How to Get There: *From Route 2 in Sistersville, turn onto Charles Street. The Wells Inn stands at 316 Charles Street.*

MID-OHIO VALLEY

CHAPTER SEVEN

Pleasants County

The Virgin Mary in the Ohio Valley

How many towns in the United States can claim that they were founded upon the direction of the Blessed Virgin Mary? Not many, we'll venture, but the riverside town of St. Marys does make that claim.

According to local legend, it all started with Alexander H. Creel, a businessman who came from somewhere in eastern Virginia to seek his fortune in the Ohio River Valley. One night in 1834, he was taking a steamboat up the river to Wheeling to conduct a bit of business. While he slumbered, Creel said that the Blessed Virgin Mary appeared to him in a vision. She told him to go out to the rail and to look on the Virginia side of the river. "There," she said, "You will behold the site of what someday will be a happy and prosperous city."

Creel awakened immediately and kicked open the outer door of his stateroom. Looking out, he saw the site of the current city of St. Marys. Creel bought the land in 1834, sold it, repurchased it in 1849 and laid out the town of St. Marys. According to some local historians, it was Creel's father, not Creel, who first purchased the land, but it was Creel who actually laid out the town.

The inhabitants of St. Marys don't seem to make much fuss about the possible heavenly origins of their town. The day we visited we found the town slumbering in a hot and humid Sunday afternoon in August. As we drove around the quiet streets, we could find few references to St. Mary herself. Even the local Roman Catholic Church was named St. Johns. The weekly paper, however, is called the St. Marys *Oracle*. We understand that the fishing is quite good, and every July the town holds a bass-fishing tournament.

Did Alexander Creel really have a visitation from the Blessed Virgin Mary? Who can say, for these things are largely a matter of personal faith, and there's nothing in the literature that indicates that Creel was a Catholic, or even particularly religious. Most people who claim to see the Blessed Virgin Mary normally don't get commercial messages from her, and she usually comes more than once. Perhaps this was just an unusual advertising ploy on Creel's part, or maybe he named the town St. Marys for reasons known only to him and invented this tale of a visitation to account for its unusual name.

For whatever reason, it was a strange decision because the 1840s and 1850s was a time of intense anti-Catholic agitation on the part of several nativist groups, who eventually formed the Know Nothing Party and ran Millard Fillmore for President in 1856. The Know Nothings were a secret lodge whose members, when quizzed about lodge activities, were instructed to answer "I know nothing." Perhaps Creel was striking out at these groups, or maybe he was just one of the many eccentrics that populate the fringes of American history. Whether or not the town's name was divinely inspired or had more earthly origins is a mystery that Creel took to his grave.

How to Get There: *St. Marys lies on Route 2, about midway between New Martinsville and Parkersburg.*

RITCHIE COUNTY

Silver Run's Woman in White

The road to Cairo twists and turns in the hollows and in the autumn light has an aura of the supernatural about it. As you follow Route 31, you come to places where the sun seldom shines, perfect spots for spooks or haunts. Cairo is not what it used to be. The railroad that gave it life is now a bicycle trail. You can rent bikes at what used to be the depot. But we couldn't linger for we were on the road, such as it is, to Silver Run, to look for the site of one of the more interesting haunts we've come across.

In the summer of 1910, a young William B. Price heard this tale from an old engineer on the Baltimore & Ohio Railroad. It would be more than 50 years before he recorded the story in his book, *Tales and Lore of the Mountaineers*, but others must have passed the tale on down, because it is a long-standing tradition in Parkersburg.

The engineer told Price of a frightening series of experiences he had some 40 years before. One foggy night on the run to Parkersburg, he saw a "woman in a white evening gown standing on the track" just before the Silver Run tunnel. He brought the train to a screeching halt, and with the fireman, jumped down and ran to the woman. Before they reached her, however, she drifted off the track and "faded from sight into the fog...." The engineer and the fireman searched the area but found no trace of her.

Silver Run Tunnel is now a bike path.

As we stood looking at the entrance of the tunnel, we could easily imagine their unease. Before us was the tall, narrow tunnel, arched with brick in 1857 and bearing the designation #19 over its entrance. On each side, the high, sheer rock walls of the railroad cut permitted no escape. Where could the woman in white have gone?

Some of you may doubt that the engineer could have stopped the train in time, but it is quite likely that the train had barely begun to get up steam for the tunnel is only about a third of a mile from the Silver Run Station. A notable stop in its day, the station is long gone. Today, the forlorn community has barely a house left to mark its existence.

Our engineer quietly questioned his colleagues, but the engineers on other runs along the line had seen nothing. This reassurance was short-lived, however. On his next run, our engineer saw the woman in white again and made the same frantic stop and futile search. This time he had the presence of mind to note additional details about her appearance before she disappeared. She had raven black hair and wore a sparkling bejeweled pin on the neck of her dress.

A month later, he saw the apparition yet again. By this time, railroad officials had gotten wind of his story and decided to give his run to an engineer named O'Flannery, who they hoped would be less prone to "seeing things." The strategy failed, for O'Flannery too saw the ghost. O'Flannery seems to have been made of sterner stuff, however, for he vowed to run her down if she stood in his way again.

He soon got the opportunity. When the woman in white appeared on the track he plowed into her mercilessly. When O'Flannery pulled into the station at Parkersburg, he was surprised to see a large, excited crowd waiting for him. They had gathered because railroad workers all along the line had reported seeing a woman sitting on the train's cowcatcher. But the apparition vanished when the train reached Parkersburg.

Who was the woman? The railroad company investigated and discovered a case of a woman who had disappeared on a train on that line 25 years before. On the other hand, our anonymous engineer said that he later learned that the skeleton of a woman was once found buried in the cellar of a house near Silver Run. A variation of this story tells of a woman in a bridal gown who was found bricked up in the chimney of a old house by Silver Run.

Like so many things in West Virginia, the trains are gone and so is most of Silver Run. Today you can ride along the bike path that follows the abandoned railroad grade. If you see a woman in white, standing in the middle of the trail, get off your bike and walk around her. For if you try to run down Silver Run's woman in white you may get a bike ride you'll never forget.

How to Get There:

Silver Run Tunnel: From US-50, take Route 31 to Cairo. Turn right at the green bridge in town, onto CR-31-4 (no sign). (If you reach the Cairo railroad crossing, now a bike path, you've missed the turn.) Pass School Street, cross the old railroad grade, and curve to the right on Carroll Street. The road becomes gravel, well kept, but narrow. Park at the next crossing of the railroad grade, but do not block the gates. The distance is 3.2 miles from the bridge. Walk to the left on the old railroad grade, now a graveled bike path. The path curves through a substantial rock cut and reaches the tunnel in about a third of a mile.

Parkersburg Railroad Station: To reach the site of the Parkersburg railroad station, torn down a few years ago, turn left onto Green Street from westbound US-50 (or right, if eastbound). The station stood where Green Street crosses the railroad tracks.

Wood County

Haunted Parkersburg

Most of the stories that we've researched take place in the West Virginia backcountry, down twisting mountain roads, in dark hollows or on old battlefields. Sometimes it seems that the better a story is, the harder it is to get to. This stands to reason. Since West Virginia is largely rural, most of its ghosts are in the country.

Parkersburg is an exception to this rule. Sitting next to a beautiful spot on the banks of the Ohio and Little Kanawha Rivers, the city has a certain air of decadence and good times long past about it. And probably with good reason, for Parkersburg was once called the wickedest city on the Ohio River. The downtown has great gaps in it where urban renewal slashed and burned its way through the center. So block for block, downtown Parkersburg has more parking lots than most cities its size. This gives the city a fragmented, almost ephemeral nature, particularly on moonlit autumn nights, and we think this adds to its attractiveness.

The hills in the northern part of the city are full of beautiful Victorian homes and speak of the days when the name Parkersburg meant wealth. Many of its hauntings stem from those days. The Civil War has also added its numbers to the ranks of Parkersburg spooks.

The Blennerhassett Hotel

The Blennerhassett Hotel seems to have more ghosts than the fictional Overlook Hotel in Steven King's novel *The Shining.* The spooks at the Blennerhassett, however, are of a much gentler sort and don't seem to have evil on their minds. They seem to be curious about what's going on and like to liven things up with an occasional prank.

Colonel William Chancellor, a banker involved in the oil business, built the hotel in 1899. At one time, it was considered to be the grandest hotel in the

William Chancellor.

state. But then, like so many older establishments, the hotel fell on hard times. It was converted into a bank and then a restaurant. Then, after dodging the wrecking ball, it became a hotel again in 1986.

Since 1986, the ghost of Mr. Chancellor likes to come back and see how things are going. This sometimes happens in buildings that undergo extensive renovation. Guests have reported seeing a gentleman of serious demeanor, dressed in 19th-century clothes, in the halls and even in the rooms. Guests are sometimes awakened in the middle of the night and startled to find Mr. Chancellor standing next to their beds, staring at them. Mr. Chancellor then fades away, leaving them to mull over their grasp on reality.

They say that when Mr. Chancellor appears at the front desk, he wears a brown suit—1890s business attire, no doubt. It's also reported that the smell of cigar smoke accompanies Mr. Chancellor's visits. How do those who see him know that this cigar-puffing, disappearing phantom is really Mr. Chancellor and not some other misguided spirit? Easy. They all say that the ghost looks just like the picture of Mr. Chancellor that hangs over the mantel in the hotel library.

Mr. Chancellor isn't the only one who haunts the Blennerhassett. Some female ghosts, unlike Mr. Chancellor, like to be heard but not seen. Disembodied female voices are heard at odd places in the hotel. Once in the Wheeling Room, a hotel employee heard a woman's laughter come over the sound system. Women's voices also pop up on the intercom from time to time, when no human is using it.

Strange music, too, sometimes comes from the Wheeling Room in the wee hours of the morning, when the room is empty. One witness reported that the music sounded like "live" dance music from another era. The Charleston Room has spectral activities as well. The silverware gets rearranged by invisible hands, and the chandelier occasionally sways and shakes for no known reason. People also say that from time to time, you can hear women laughing, sobbing, and wailing.

The hotel library is a pleasant enough place where civic meetings are often held. But employees report that strange things happen there too. Books mysteriously move off their shelves, and the room often fills with the smell of cigar smoke, even though no one there is smoking.

Then there's the four a.m. knocker. On some nights when business is slow, the night desk clerk will go into the front office and work there. Then someone, or something, raps sharply on the office door, always precisely at four a.m. When the startled clerk goes to the door, no one is there. Maybe Mr. Chancellor wants to make sure that everyone is awake and on their toes.

The main desk of the Blennerhassett. The door to the right is where the 4 A.M. knocker plays his little tricks.

Finally, there are the haunted mirrors over the lounge bar and in the hall. Some nights, just around closing time, the reflection of a man in a white tuxedo floats by in the mirror over the bar. This would not be unusual except that the reflection is not caused by any physical entity wearing a white tuxedo in the bar. Since these mirrors were imported from an old apartment house that was torn down in New York City, it's possible that this is an imported big city ghost wondering just what the heck he's doing in a lounge bar in West Virginia.

The Blennerhassett Museum

The Blennerhassett Museum is one of the nicer museums we visited in West Virginia. It is a relatively new building containing materials from Blennerhassett Island plus local fossils and Indian artifacts and various memorabilia from the history of Parkersburg. The third floor contains a fine collection of antique furniture along with two ghosts. The first is a little old man in a straw hat. The second, a rather large woman who is fond of the color scarlet. While it seems unusual that such a modern building would have spooks, it may be that these wandering spirits are attached to one of the artifacts in the museum.

The Smoot Theater

Ghosts seem to be drawn to theaters like moths to flames. Perhaps the ephemeral nature of plays and movies attracts them and makes them feel more comfortable. Perhaps it's because actors in a play are much like ghosts, doomed to repeat the same lines and go through the same actions night after night. For live actors, the drama stops at the end of the performance and totally ceases when the play closes. For ghosts, the cosmic drama continues until it gradually fades away.

The Smoot Theater in Parkersburg is no exception to the rule. It was built in 1926, during the vaudeville era, by the Smoot Amusement Company. In 1986 there were plans to tear the old place down, but concerned citizens saved it from this grisly fate. The theater still stands and performances are put on periodically.

At the Smoot, some fragments of its storied history may still be lingering about. Although the current theater management admits nothing, there are tales of strange shadows and sounds behind the curtains late at night. There are also many unexplained technical and electrical problems during productions. Faulty wiring or spectral meddling? And then there's the place in the theater that always seems cold and never warms up. Cold spots are quite common in haunted buildings. So if you go to a play at the Smoot, you may be seeing a double feature, one earthly performance and the other—not of this world.

The Trans-Allegheny Book Store

The Trans-Allegheny Book Store started life as the Parkersburg Carnegie Public Library and remained that until 1976. Now it is one of the finest bookstores in West Virginia, and compares favorably to many in the mid-west. There are three stories chock full of new and used books. The upper stories can be reached by climbing a spiral iron staircase which give you the feeling of being back in the 19th century. The building was constructed with money from a grant donated by Andrew Carnegie, famed industrialist and financier. The stained glass window in the front contains the Carnegie coat of arms.

The staircase at Trans-Allegheny Books where the ghost of a little girl is said to appear.

The Trans-Allegheny is home to two different spirits. The first is a little girl around eight years old. She likes to appear sitting on the main wooden staircase and vanishes when she's approached. The second is a middle-aged man seen in the world history section. He seems to be looking for a book. No one knows why these two have chosen to haunt the bookstore. (When we took a picture of the world history room, our camera malfunctioned and we got light on the print. Maybe the gentleman doesn't like to have his picture taken either.) Have these two disparate souls journeyed across time and space to attempt to return overdue books? We'll never know.

916 Juliana Street

The house at 916 Juliana Street belongs to a long-since-vanished era of opulence, when Parkersburg was home to wealthy oil barons. According to a psychic, two women allegedly haunt the house, one from the Victorian era and the other from more recent times. The house has several cold spots that never are warm, even on the hottest August day. Visitors report a sense of unease in the kitchen that has nothing to do with the culinary events that have taken place here. There are also reports of a strange woman who looks out the upstairs window in the front of the house when nobody is home and vanishes when people go in to check.

Now before you dismiss 916 as a drafty old house, consider this. In the summer of 1997, the folks who run the Haunted Parkersburg tour every October were taking pictures of the house for their tour. They knew the owner quite well and were sure that she was away and the house was empty. They shot two rolls of film. A picture from the first roll showed the upstairs window with the blinds open with something white in the picture. It looked like the shoulder of a woman, standing slightly back from the window. The same picture from the second roll showed that the window blind was pulled. Maybe even ghosts like to have a little privacy.

Little Bessie Bartlett

This is the story of the ghost of a little 10-year-old girl named Bessie who died of scarlet fever around the turn of the century. Bessie's father was a prosperous dentist who lived in a house on Ann Street. Since scarlet fever is an extremely contagious disease, the standard practice of the day was to quarantine the victims. This placed Dr. Bartlett in a dilemma. If he kept Bessie with the family he would be put into quarantine and his prosperous practice would be ruined. Further, he loved his daughter so much that he couldn't bear to be parted from her. Thus the hospital was out. So he hid her in the basement, with the hope that the coolness down there would help to break her fever. His hopes were in vain, for little Bessie died.

For years, nothing was reported to have happened in the house. Bessie and Dr. Bartlett were forgotten, and little remained to show that they ever lived in the house, except for their last name on the carriage stoop in the front yard next to the street.

In the 1980s, a family was looking for a house to buy and ended up at the old Bartlett place. They felt strangely attracted to the house. When they were in the basement, they took a photo of the spot where poor little Bessie breathed her last so many years ago. They had quite a shock when they had the picture developed. In it was a young girl, about 10 or 11 years old, dressed in turn of the century clothing. The girl was unknown to anyone in the family. Did Bessie Bartlett reach out from somewhere in time to touch this family, so she wouldn't feel quite so alone?

Quincy Hill Park and 10th Street

Full of trees and with a beautiful view of the Ohio River and Blennerhassett Island, Quincy Hill Park looks like a pleasant enough place. As we stood there on a soft October night, it was hard to realize that this beautiful park was the scene of endless suffering and death.

During the Civil War, Parkersburg was a rear area where supplies and reinforcements were gathered to be sent into battle, and where the sick and the wounded were sent back to heal or to die. Disease presented a greater problem than wounds, and illnesses such as typhoid fever, typhus, measles and smallpox killed more Civil War soldiers then all the bullets, bayonets and artillery shells combined.

Five hospitals sprang up in Parkersburg, and soon the city was filled with sick and dying men. One hospital was established on Quincy Hill, then called Prospect Hill, and soon the moans and desperate cries of the sick and dying could be heard all hours of the day and night. A smallpox epidemic struck the camp which contained some 5,000 souls and overwhelmed the medical help that was available. Since there is no cure for smallpox even today, only vaccinations to prevent the disease, many died on the hill. Many crawled down from the hill to find aid where there was none.

Well, this is all part of the gloomy past, or is it? On September 26, 1996, two young girls decided to watch the total eclipse of the moon from the vantage point of the park. While they were admiring the moon, they heard a rustling movement down the side of the hill, the sound sick Civil War soldiers made as they crawled to their doom.

The spirits of dying Civil War soldiers aren't the only ones that haunt the park. If you go to Quincy Hill, you'll notice that there's a long concrete stairway leading down to Avery Street. There's a landing with a streetlight about half way down. Several early morning joggers have been startled to see a Shawnee Indian standing approximately where the street lamp is. No one seems to know who he was or why he's there. Psychic residue from the Civil War or one of the earlier conflicts that raged up and down the Ohio Valley?

The stairway at Quincy Park, where the ghost of a Shawnee Indian has been seen lurking.

The Yankee Ghost and the House Below the Hill

This next story is a truly astonishing one and makes you wonder about buying an old house. During the 1970s, a single woman bought a house located between 13th and Avery and Quincy Hill. Soon some very odd things started to occur. Doors slammed by themselves. There were raps on the wall, yelling and the sound of footsteps running in the basement. The woman, who had plenty of West Virginia grit and spirit, assumed that the noises were partly her imagination and partly the old house settling.

But then things began to happen that couldn't be accounted for by ground water noises or wind in the chimney. First there was the chair in the dining room that refused to stay put. No matter where in the room she placed the chair it was always end up next to the front window.

Then things began to escalate. One night she was roused from her sleep to find that every candle she had in the house had been placed on the bedroom dresser and lit. Needless to say she was considerably unnerved by this unusual act. She decided to check things out. With her heart in her throat she crept down the stairs to see if this bizarre burglar was still in the house. When she got to the dining room, she was shocked to see a red-haired, bearded Union soldier seated in the chair that liked to wander around. The man stood up as if to greet her and then vanished.

By this time most people would have cleared out of that house as quickly as they could, but not our heroine. Deciding that no spook, Yankee or otherwise, was going to force her out of her home, she sent for reinforcements in the person of her boyfriend.

Things settled down for a while, and it seemed that maybe the Yankee soldier had finally found peace. But then one night, when the boyfriend was alone in the house, he heard noises coming from the basement. When he opened the door to check, he saw the bearded soldier running towards him, pistol drawn and ready for action.

The boyfriend fled, never to return. The lady soon gave up, sold the house and moved away. There are no subsequent reports that the current residents are bothered by this gun-toting blue-clad specter. Does the Avery Street ghost pine for his lost love? Does he stand by the window, staring out at a world he can never be part of? Or has he finally found peace?

The Phantom Nurse of Camden Clark

Sometimes people who are devoted to their duties in life don't know when to stop after death. Camden-Clark Hospital, which was built on the site of a Civil War hospital, has one such ghostly inhabitant, a nurse named Mrs. Blumbit. Dressed in her old-time nurse's garb, Mrs. Blumbit is seen on the second and fifth floors, checking beds and making the rounds. Some of her old students have seen her and recognize her. Interestingly enough, she didn't start her nocturnal rambles until after the hospital was remodeled.

The east wing of the hospital also has a phantom, an invisible patient. Witnesses say that he or she likes to lie down on made-up hospital beds. They say you can see the impression of a human form on the covers. It makes a weird sort of sense that a hospital with a phantom patient has a ghostly nurse to look after it. Or maybe Mrs. Blumbit just gets tired once in awhile.

How to Get There: From US-50 in Parkersburg, turn onto Green Street (left if going west, right if going east). The Trans-Allegheny Book Store stands at 725 Green Street. Turn right on 5th Street and continue past Market Street. The Smoot Theater stands in the middle of the block on the right. Circle the block by turning right on Juliana, right on 6th, and right on Market. Continue on Market to the Blennerhassett Hotel, which stands on the left, on the southeast corner of Market and 4th. Continue two blocks, turn right on 2nd Street, and go one block to Juliana. The Blennerhassett Museum stands on the northwest corner of 2nd Street and Juliana. Turn right on Juliana. As Juliana crosses US-50, the Camden-Clark Memorial Hospital can be seen; it is the large building one block to the left. Turn left on 13th Street and left on Ann Street, where the Bartlett house stands. Take Ann Street back to US-50, and turn left (east) on US-50. Turn left on Avery Street, pass the house at 13th and Avery and turn right on 13th Street. In one block, turn right on Quincy Street and follow it all the way to Quincy Hill Park.

The Lady in White - Haunted Blennerhassett

If you go down to the Parkersburg waterfront on an October evening around sunset, face the river and look to your left, you'll see, rising up out of the glowing mist, beautiful, enchanted Blennerhassett Island. At the beginning of the 19th century, Blennerhassett Island was the center of romance, tragedy and conspiracy. Its story would make a good Shakespearean tragedy. And like many Shakespearean tragedies, Blennerhassett Island has a ghost or two, waiting in the wings.

The reconstructed mansion on Blennerhassett Island.

The island takes its name from Harman Blennerhassett, an Irish aristocrat who purchased it in 1797. With his wife Margaret he built one of the most beautiful mansions in America and his estate became the center of cultural and economic life for that portion of the Ohio Valley. Unfortunately, Blennerhassett ran afoul of Aaron Burr, and in a very short time he was put under arrest and the mansion was reduced to ashes.

About four miles long, Blennerhassett Island has eight miles of shoreline and contains approximately 500 acres. Archaeological evidence shows that paleo-Indians inhabited the island over 9,000 years ago. The island was first mentioned in trader George Crogan's journal, and the first recorded resident was the Delaware Indian Chief Nemacolin, who built a cabin there, and who, by some accounts, may still be there.

But the island slumbered in primordial beauty until Harman and Margaret Blennerhassett decided to make it their home. Harman Blennerhassett was one of those people who are doomed by personality, temperament or fate to lead lives filled with tragedy and disaster. He was a practicing attorney who inherited a large estate in his native Ireland, so had he chosen, he could have led the quiet life of a country squire. But something in Blennerhassett's restless spirit would not allow this to happen. He liked radical politics and joined

The British Society of United Irishmen, a clandestine organization dedicated to freeing Ireland from British rule. Blennerhassett became so taken up by the cause of Irish freedom that he became an officer in the society.

Not content with being a political rebel, Blennerhassett became a social rebel as well by marrying his niece Margaret. While the church forbade this union, it was not forbidden by civil law, although many considered the marriage incestuous. Because of this —plus the rising of the political tempest in Ireland—Blennerhassett thought it would be prudent to get out of the country, so he sold his estates and moved to America.

Once they arrived in the United States, the Blennerhassetts decided to settle down on the frontier so they moved to Pittsburgh. In 1797 they purchased Blennerhassett Island and during the next two years proceeded to build a mansion that would rival Jefferson's Monticello or Washington's Mount Vernon. The house, which was built in the Italian Palladian style, cost some $40,000, a veritable fortune in those days. It was built of hardwood rather than bricks because Harman Blennerhassett feared earthquakes. (If Harman had feared fire as much as he feared earthquakes, perhaps more of the original house might be left today.) The grounds included extensive gardens as well as an English maze and fruit orchard.

One of the unusual features of the house was Harman Blennerhassett's study and library, which was separate from the main house. The library was one of the largest private libraries west of the Alleghenies. From here, Blennerhassett ran his widespread business interests, which included shipbuilding, cattle and fur trading and a chain of general stores.

Blennerhassett also had a keen interest in the sciences, so his study included a scientific laboratory. He explored the paleo-Indian remains and would often give guests an artifact discovered on the property as a gift. He was also a gifted musician and skilled physician, whom the local people would often consult when they became ill.

Apart from being quite beautiful, Harman's wife Margaret was also an intellectual who wrote poetry (she was the first published poet from the state of Virginia) and liked to discuss politics and philosophy. She shared Harman's interest in science and was responsible for having the local children vaccinated for smallpox. She was also an accomplished horsewoman, liked parties and loved to dance.

The couple had four children: John Claudius Petit, an eight-year-old French boy whom they adopted; Dominic; Margaret or Snowdrop, who died at the age of two and is buried somewhere in the estate garden; and Harman Jr.

Unfortunately Harman's skill as a businessman didn't match his talents as a physician or musician. By 1805, the Blennerhassetts were headed for bankruptcy. The couple's high-living life style made sure that income would never catch up with outgo, and contemporary sources report that Harman was gullible and the constant victim of swindlers and confidence men. Thus in 1805, Harman was considering selling the estate and moving south to start a cotton plantation.

Harman, the revolutionary, was also making a reappearance. Using the pen name Querist, he began publishing articles in the *Ohio Gazette and Territorial and Virginia Herald* calling for the peaceful separation of the northwest from the Union. Blennerhassett might rightly be called one of Virginia's pioneer secessionists.

Into these troubled waters sailed the charismatic Aaron Burr, who entangled the idealistic couple in his schemes. Burr had been a rising star in Jefferson's Democratic-Republican Party. He became a senator from New York and, after the disputed election of 1800, Vice President. He made many enemies including his Federalist New York archrival, Alexander Hamilton and President Thomas Jefferson. He later killed Hamilton in an infamous duel fought in 1804.

Burr first visited Blennerhassett Island in 1805, while seeking support for his most infamous escapade, an expedition that some say was intended to separate the western states from the Union. Burr maintained that he intended to launch a filibustering expedition against Spanish Texas to add it to the Union. Burr's exact intentions will always remain a mystery because all of his notes and papers were later lost at sea. (Harman Blennerhassett's predilection for disunion and secession might add weight to the first accusation.)

Whatever Burr's real intentions, he found willing recruits in Margaret and Harman Blennerhassett. They became one of Burr's largest financial backers. Blennerhassett underwrote the construction of some 15 riverboats, purchased and stored supplies on the island, and tried to use his local influence to recruit locals to join the expedition.

Things came to a head when the notorious General James Wilkinson, one of the chief plotters, turned Burr in. On November 27, 1806, an angry Thomas Jefferson called for the arrest of Burr and his followers for planning an illegal attack on Spanish possessions. On December 11, Harman fled south, just ahead of the local militia who were red hot to arrest the "traitors." He joined up with Burr at the mouth of the Cumberland River in Kentucky on December 27. Margaret and the children followed on December 17. This was the last that any of the family saw of their beloved island. Harman was later arrested along with Burr and they were brought to trial.

In July 1807, a court sitting in Richmond, Virginia found Burr and Blennerhassett not guilty of treason. Eager to start again and recoup their fortunes, the Blennerhassetts purchased a cotton plantation at Port Gibson, Mississippi, but like so many other things, it failed. Here they had another daughter named Margaret who also died. From there they bounced around from Montreal to England where they lived with relatives. Harman died in 1831 from a series of strokes. Margaret then moved to New York City and died there of a heart attack in 1842. All of the surviving children led dissolute lives and died or disappeared at an early age.

The mansion, which was allegedly looted by the militia, was accidentally set on fire on March 3, 1811 and totally destroyed. Up until her death, Margaret Blennerhassett petitioned the Federal government for payment for damages to Blennerhassett but was unsuccessful. When she died, the tragedy came to an end.

After the fire, Blennerhassett Island faded into quiet obscurity. It became a farm, and in 1833 George Neal Jr. built a fine brick home on the island. In 1847 the poet Walt Whitman visited the Neal home, which is in ramshackle condition today, and later wrote a poem about it. The island later became a local park and popular picnic ground with the local inhabitants. In 1970 it was put on the National Registry of Historic Places. After conducting an archeological dig, the state of West Virginia decided to restore the plantation to its original splendor, so the mansion was reconstructed on its original site. Unfortunately, very little of the original furniture could be recovered.

But what of the ghosts? Well, it seems that the ghost of Margaret Blennerhassett may have taken to strolling the grounds of her beloved home once again. There have been several sightings of a woman dressed in a white gown with an Empire-style waist particularly in October. Take October 17, 1997 for example: a woman who was cruising down the river on a sternwheeler happened to look toward the island shore and saw a woman dressed in a long white gown walking along the shore line. After a few minutes the lady in white disappeared into the trees. The curious woman then asked if there was a nunnery around Parkersburg and related what she saw. The guides replied that the only nunnery in Parkersburg had been closed a few years before.

In 1992, a writer for a Pittsburgh magazine was canoeing down the Ohio. He decided to camp out on Blennerhassett Island on the grounds below the Neal house. Early in the morning on October 1, he woke up to the strong smell of perfume. He got out of his tent and was surprised to see a young woman stride out of the morning mists. He offered her a cup of coffee but she said nothing and retreated into the mists.

Thinking that this nocturnal encounter was a bit strange, the writer decided to get some more sleep. A little while later he was awakened by the sound of someone rummaging through his knapsack that he left outside. Being a bit spooked by the earlier visitation, he decided to ignore the noises and went back to sleep. When he awoke the next day, he discovered all of his books and papers stacked neatly on top of his knapsack. An elaborate practical joke played on an impressionable writer or was Margaret catching up on her reading. The writer's description of the woman tallies with other descriptions of Margaret's ghost.

During the summer of 1996, Margaret finally came home to her beloved island. Her body was disinterred from the New York cemetery where it was buried. She was given a full funeral and a Christian burial on the grounds of the plantation. Strangeness started right at the funeral when a lady who attended thought she saw Margaret standing where they used to tie up her horses. And things haven't settled down since. Lights in the mansion sometimes flash at the mention of Harman's name. Sometime ghostly noises come from the attic when *East of the River,* a play based on the Blennerhassetts, is performed. One time someone in a tour group made a derogatory comment about Harman, and the electronic alarm system went off for no reason. On another occasion everyone in a tour group on the second floor distinctly heard the front door slam, but when they went downstairs the door was open. Finally, on July 4,1997, a woman who looked an awful lot like Margaret was seen atop the mansion's stairs by a guide who thought all the stories were bosh.

Margaret's ghost isn't the only one seen on the island. Some people have seen a Native American man standing near the Neal

House looking towards Parkersburg. No one ever sees his face—not that they would recognize him if they did see his face. Without turning around, he slowly fades away. Perhaps Chief Nemacolin has returned to see what happened to his cabin.

Does Margaret Blennerhassett's ghost walk her old home during October? Is she searching for the grave of her beloved little daughter, Snowdrop? Or is she giving mute criticism to the reconstruction job done by the state of West Virginia. Did disturbing her bones just stir things up? Or do they have the right person buried on the island? Cemetery records from that time could be somewhat vague. Or maybe she's looking for Aaron Burr to give him a piece of her mind.

So come to Blennerhassett Island and enjoy all the attractions the state has put there. And if you happen to spot Margaret, give her a wave and a smile.

How to Get There: Blennerhassett Island lies a short distance down river from Parkersburg. From the first weekend in May through the last weekend in October, a 19th-century sternwheeler carries tourists to and from the island (20 minutes each way). Boat and tour tickets can be purchased at Blennerhassett Museum, on the corner of Juliana and Second streets. From US-50 in Parkersburg, turn onto Market Street (left if going west, right if going east). Then turn right on 2nd Street and go one block to Juliana. The boat departs from Point Park, which lies at the foot of 2nd Street.

The Parkersburg Aerial Apparition

Many strange things are seen in the skies of the Ohio River Valley from time to time, but nothing quite so strange as this. It was a cloudless July evening in 1878. A local farmer was working in one of his fields with several other men. About seven o'clock he looked up from his labors and saw a white, opaque cloud, in the shape of a horse about a half-mile to the west. The cloud had a clearly defined horse's head, neck, legs and tail. It appeared to be swimming through the sky, while moving its head from side to side. Further, the horse seemed to be heading up at a 45-degree angle.

The farmer shook his head and rubbed his eyes in disbelief, but after all that the horse was still swimming across the sky. He called to the nearby field hands and asked them to tell him what they saw. They unanimously stated that they saw a white horse swimming in the sky. The apparition frightened the farm hands so much that they hurriedly left the field. Our intrepid observer, made of sterner stuff, sat down on a stump and watched the phantasm until it disappeared into space.

So just what was this West Virginia version of Pegasus? A mirage, an hallucination or optical illusion? A weird cloud formation turned into a horse by a superstitious farmer and his equally superstitious hired hands? Or was the story concocted by some shrewd farmer as a joke on the city slickers or even a reporter or editor looking for items to boost circulation? This was the age of liars' clubs and tall tales, and what a laugh everyone would have when the story was picked up by the *New York Times*.

Or was the cloud a real, paranormal phenomenon? Was it some sort of portent or warning? The white horse is thought of as a death sign in West Virginia folklore, and this may explain the hurried exit of the farm hands. And there are other stories of phantom white horses that don't simply "swim" over in a clear sky and disappear towards Mars. In Revelations chapter 6 verses 2 and 8, we read, "And behold a pale horse: and he that sat upon him, his name was Death." Of course, earlier in Revelations, Christ is identified as riding a white horse, so maybe this is a good sign. And what color is a pale horse anyway?

What did the farmer really see? Who can say for sure? It doesn't sound like one of the fabrications of the hoaxer's and liars' clubs. The source seems to be level headed and didn't add a lot of window-dressing to zap up the story, in the way a hoaxer might have. Thus we can't really make a judgment as to the truth of this tale but only can report it.

How to Get There: *This haunt is fairly easy to find. Just drive to any place around Parkersburg with a clear view of the sky and look up. Who's to say what you'll see swimming out of the west.*

JACKSON COUNTY

The Ghost in the Ravenswood Theater

Ravenswood is a pretty town located on the big bend of the Ohio River, just a little ways down from Parkersburg. George Washington liked the Ravenswood area so much that he commented favorably on it in his journal. Indeed, there is a Washington Lands Museum located in the upper two floors of a converted lock building along the waterfront. There's also a log house built in the style of the 1840s. And there's a ghost, but not in the historic area where you might expect to find it. The spirit that haunts Ravenswood is a lot more modern in origin.

Earlier in this century, before the advent of giant shopping malls and multiplex theaters, every town of any size had a movie theater that probably started life as a vaudeville theater before the movies became common. Ravenswood was no exception. This story comes from a boy who worked part time in the theater, running the projector and sweeping out the place after the last show.

One night the boy was getting ready to secure the theater and lock up for the night when someone or something passed behind the screen, carrying what looked like a lantern. The thoroughly frightened boy, who thought he was alone in the theater, ran to the ticket booth where he called the police and then the theater owner. The police searched the theater from top to bottom but found no one. The rear door, which could be locked only with a key from the inside, was indeed locked, and the boy knew that he had the key.

When the boy told his story to the lady who owned the theater, she calmed him down and told him not to worry. She said that she wasn't worried about some burglar or other such person being locked in the theater for other employees had the same experience over the past 30 years and that whoever it was that walked the night probably wasn't of this world.

She then told him the following story. At some time in the past, there was a lodge hall on the second floor of the building beside the theater. The lodge shrouded its activities, particularly its rites of initiation, in deepest mystery. No one knows, or will say if they do know, exactly what took place during an initiation, but it was well known that many prospective members couldn't stay the course and fled. A modern informant told us the lodge was probably the Ku Klux Klan. We have, however, found no evidence to corroborate this allegation so the lodge must remain a mystery.

It all came to a tragic end one night, when a fire broke out and the building was gutted. Everyone escaped, but for one man who was in the attic where the fire started. His body was never found. The owner said that she thought that the light-bearing phantom was the ghost of the poor man lost in the fire and that she had seen it many times. She further explained that the two buildings were connected before the fire and that some passages between them still existed.

The perplexed youth went home and told the tale to his father, who confirmed the story and added one important detail. It seems the man who died in the fire was the owner's husband.

It was never determined if the fire was part of the initiation, but no legal proceedings were raised against the lodge. It is significant to note, however, that the fateful fire spelled the end of the lodge, for it never met again.

Like so many other local movie houses, the Ravenswood Theater closed in the 1960s. In its present incarnation it is a women's clothing store called Almeda's. From the outside the building shows its origins as a theater, but inside it looks like a typical clothing store. The present manager told us that nothing untoward has happened in the store and that no ghost has been seen. Perhaps it was the extensive alterations. Perhaps since his wife no longer runs the theater, the ghost has no need to walk there anymore. Or maybe, like many men, he just doesn't like to hang around women's clothing stores. Whatever the reason, the Ravenswood ghost seems to have found peace, and walks no more, for the moment.

(There's an interesting personal note to go with our hunt for the theater. About a week before we started our field research, someone rear-ended my car. I went to a local car rental place to get a replacement while my machine was in the body shop. As is usual, the girl behind the counter asked if I were going outside the Washington area. I replied that I might take a day trip to West Virginia to do some field research for a book on West Virginia ghosts. She smiled and said she was from Ravenswood and asked if I were going to go there. I told her the story we'd found about the Ravenswood Theater and asked if she'd ever heard of it. She didn't know the ghost story but she did know where the theater was. It had been converted into a clothing store called Almeda's.

Almeda's Clothing Store - The site of the haunted theater in Ravenswood.

Serendipity struck again and this chance encounter saved us hours of tramping around Ravenswood. This was not the last time we'd feel that a hidden hand was guiding us in our quest, but I wish it would find less expensive ways to pass on its suggestions. WJG)

How to Get There: Ravenswood is located on Route 68 in the Ohio Valley. Route 68 becomes Washington Street. Drive down Washington Street to Mulberry Street and you will recognize an old theater masquerading as a dress shop. It's located next to Almeda's Music and Photo, which is in a very old building, quite possibly where the lodge hall was located.

METRO VALLEY

CHAPTER
EIGHT

Mason County

Chief Cornstalk's Curse

As we drove into Point Pleasant on a sunny October day, its name seemed to suit it most admirably. We were on our way to the Point Pleasant Battlefield State Park, looking for the grave of Cornstalk, Chief of the Scioto Shawnee, who was murdered in 1777 by Virginia militiamen at Fort Randolph.

The day was bright and sharp. The west wind played games with whitecaps on the Ohio River. As we stood in the park, watching barges cruise up and down the Ohio, it was hard to believe that Point Pleasant has a darker side, for some say that before he died, Chief Cornstalk laid a curse on this place, a curse that has reached out from beyond the grave and even affects the lives of the people who live there today.

Times were tough on the Virginia frontier, particularly during the American Revolution. First, the land that is now West Virginia was a battleground between French and British interests. Then, during the Revolution most of the Indians supported the British, and the resulting battle for West Virginia was probably one of the most brutal in American history.

There were very few set-piece battles in this war. It was a war of ambush and massacre, of unspeakable atrocities and great heroism on both sides. On one side were the Shawnee, the Mingo and the Delaware with their British advisors. On the other were rugged frontiersmen, who defied British edicts not to settle west of the Alleghenies. In the war between the Virginia militia (called the Long Knives by their Indian enemies) and the Shawnee and Mingo warriors, no quarter was asked or given.

Out of this violent, vitriolic brew rose Cornstalk, a famed diplomat and statesman, capable warrior, general, and leader of the Scioto Shawnee. Cornstalk learned to fight in Pontiac's War in 1763. During that time, Cornstalk led a Shawnee war party that destroyed pioneer settlements at Muddy Creek and Big Levels. The Shawnee gained entry to the settlements by feigning friendship then turned on their hosts during a welcome feast. Almost everyone in the settlements was killed or captured.

After peace was restored, the British still pursued their policy of trying to keep colonial settlement east of the Alleghenies. In 1774, Lord North, the British Prime Minister, ceded the Northwest Territories to the Indians and proposed to supply them with arms and ammunition. This did not sit well with the frontiersmen who felt that their government was betraying them. Then in the spring of 1774, a group of drunken traders massacred the family of Logan, leader of the Mingos, at a place called Yellow Creek. Logan, who up to that time had been pro-Virginian, swore vengeance, and the Mingo and Shawnee began attacking settlements.

Lord Dunmore, the governor of colonial Virginia began to organize two expeditions to defend the frontier. The first, 1,100 Virginia Militia under Colonel Anthony Lewis, set off from Greenbrier towards Point Pleasant on September 11, 1774. Dunmore raised another army at Fort Pitt (modern Pittsburgh), which was to rendezvous with Lewis at Point Pleasant. Instead, Dunmore decided to take his army into Ohio and negotiate with the Shawnee. Lewis arrived at Point Pleasant and settled down to wait for the arrival of Lord Dunmore.

Early in the morning on October 10, Cornstalk struck. The Virginians, who had constructed a defensive line across the point of land between the Ohio and Kanawha Rivers, were alerted by some hunters that the Shawnee were coming. A bloody daylong fight ensued. It was said that Cornstalk's commanding voice could be heard all over the battlefield and that he personally tomahawked any Indian trying to flee the field. In the end the Shawnee left the field to the Virginians and fled across the Ohio. The Virginians had lost 75 killed and 140 wounded.

Historians disagree on the results of the battle. One side says that the Shawnee won because they killed more Virginians than the Virginians killed Shawnee. Others refute this claim contending that the Shawnee casualties were difficult to estimate because they removed their dead from the battlefield. Further, they maintain that it was the Shawnee, not the Virginians, who left the field.

After the battle at Point Pleasant, Cornstalk negotiated a peace treaty with Lord Dunmore in which the Shawnee agreed to stay on the north and west banks of the Ohio River. Dunmore ordered Lewis to join him in Ohio but Lewis refused. He felt that Dunmore had betrayed him, hoping the Virginian Militia would lose and thus add to the British control of the Virginia colony. This ill feeling was made worse because Lewis' brother was among the casualties in the battle. Lewis became the first American officer to directly defy British authority. This is why many scholars consider Point Pleasant, rather than Lexington and Concord, to be the first battle of the War of Independence.

As the cause for independence gained strength, the British once again adopted the time-honored tactic of stirring up the Indians on the frontier. Things had remained relatively peaceful after Point Pleasant until 1777, when the British began exerting heavy pressure on the Shawnee to take up the hatchet against the Americans. Cornstalk, however, wanted to remain out of the fight. In late September 1777, he, along with Red Hawk, a Scioto Shawnee warrior and sub-chief, went to Fort Randolph, located at Point Pleasant (and now the site of a facility for the elderly), to warn the Americans of their grave danger. He told Captain Arbuckle, the American commander, that although he favored peace, most of the Shawnee would go with the British.

Arbuckle decided to hold the two Shawnee hostage towards the good behavior of the rest of the tribe. Cornstalk's son, Ellinipscio came to the fort to check on his father. That same day, a militia ensign named Gilmore was murdered and scalped by unknown Indians while hunting deer. Gilmore's militia comrades became enraged and, despite the protestation of their officers, they vowed to kill every Indian in Fort Randolph. They found Cornstalk and put seven musket balls in him. Then they killed his son and Red Hawk, who tried to escape by climbing up the chimney.

The Virginia government was outraged by the murder and had the perpetrators arrested and brought to trial for "crimes against humanity." A sympathetic local jury found them not guilty. The Shawnee were not so sympathetic and started a blood bath on the frontier that would end only with the battle of Fallen Timbers in 1794.

In the years following Cornstalk's death, Point Pleasant didn't prosper, despite all of its natural advantages. It became a popular superstition that Point Pleasant's misery was the result of a curse that Cornstalk placed on the town with his dying breath. The curse, according to the believers, went as follows:

I was the friend of the bordermen. Many a time I have saved him and his people from harm. I came to your house as a friend and you murdered me. For this may the curse of the Great Spirit rest upon this spot. May its people be paralyzed by the stain of my blood.

This would be quite a speech for anyone with seven musket balls in him. Further, contemporary accounts of Cornstalk's death do not mention that he said anything, much less a curse.

As near as we have been able to determine, the story of the curse probably began in the early 19th century as a local superstition brought on by guilt. The earliest known source is an account by an anonymous traveler that appeared in *The Spirit of the Old Dominion*, a periodical published in Richmond sometime before 1825. Speaking of a giant oak tree that stood at the spot where Cornstalk was buried, it says, "The lightenings [sic] have shattered it and the whirlwinds have twisted its bows...It would appear that the indignant spirit of the old warrior was still imbued with the power of affecting vengeance and exercised retribution by spreading desolating influences over the place of his massacre."

The traveler went on to say, "...the situation of the village of Point Pleasant is of a commanding nature...yet it presents the most wretched appearance possible." Was the town truly cursed or did the residents of the town use the idea of a curse to disguise their own failings?

Before we dismiss the idea of a curse out of hand, we must consider the fact that Point Pleasant's history reads like a litany of catastrophes. In his book, *The Ghosts of Virginia, Vol. III*, L. B. Taylor compiled the following list of disasters that struck the unfortunate town.

• During the 1880s, a city block was destroyed by a fire.

• In 1913, 1927, 1936 and 1937, floods inundated the area.

• In 1944 a tornado ripped through the area and killed 140 people.

• On Friday December 15, 1967 at 4:58 p.m., the Silver Bridge collapsed in the Ohio River killing 46. Some of the bodies were never found.

• In 1968 a Piedmont Airliner went down in the area killing all 45 aboard.

• Buffalo Creek, a tributary of the Kanawha River, overflowed in 1972 taking 155 lives.

• In 1978 a freight train derailed dumping toxic chemicals into the ground. The chemicals contaminated Point Pleasant's water supply.

The results of a curse, or very bad luck combined with the usual hazards of living where two rivers meet? And it's not as though the people of Point Pleasant don't respect the memory of Cornstalk. In 1840 they moved Cornstalk's bones to the grounds of the Mason County Courthouse. In 1899 they put up a monument. When a new courthouse was constructed his body was moved to the town park (which later became the Point Pleasant Battlefield State Park), where the Daughters of the American Revolution erected a 12-foot monument in his honor.

Cornstalk's aren't the only bones that have been moved. Many of the dead Virginians were buried in a magazine pit near the point, but their remains have never been found. Because of huge changes caused by floods and erosion, the remains may have been washed away.

The Shawnee casualties were either removed from the battlefield by their retreating comrades or thrown into the river. Further the bodies of Red Hawk and Ellinipscio were also thrown into the river without a

Chief Cornstalk's final resting place.

proper burial. And we all know (by now we hope) that a massive disturbance of bones done in a disrespectful way, can sometimes have interesting consequences, even many years after the fact.

And then there's the problem of the 86-foot-high obelisk, erected to commemorate the battle and honor the dead. On July 22, 1909 lightning struck the crane that was to be used to lift the monument into place. This delayed the opening ceremony for about a month. Then on July 4, 1921 lightning struck the capstone, knocking it loose along with some heavy granite blocks. Is Cornstalk still commenting from beyond the grave? Remember the old oak tree reported on earlier.

Whether it's Cornstalk, Red Hawk or something completely different, strange things have happened at Point Pleasant. If you want to read more about high weirdness at Point Pleasant, read the next chapters: The Point Pleasant Ghost Blimp and Mothman: Space Alien or Old-Fashioned Haunt?

How to Get There: *Point Pleasant lies one mile north of the junction of US-35 and Route 2. From Route 2, in the city, take First, Second, or Third Street one block west. Turn left on Main Street and follow it to Point Pleasant Battlefield Monument State Park.*

The Point Pleasant Ghost Blimp

Point Pleasant is a area of West Virginia that is well known for bizarre aerial phenomena. It's the home of Mothman, Cornstalk's curse, and many UFO sightings. But perhaps the strangest incident of all occurred on October 10, 1931.

The 1930s were the heyday of lighter-than-air travel, and the air was filled with blimps and dirigibles both military and civilian. On October 10, the Akron, America's newest dirigible and the pride of the U. S. Navy, was scheduled to fly over Fairfield Stadium in Huntington, West Virginia, as part of the half-time show for the Washington and Jefferson versus Marshall football game. But the fans of the Thundering Herd would be disappointed, for the Navy denied the request, and the Akron spent the day flying over the Ohio cities of Toledo and Sandusky and out over Lake Erie.

However, according to many residents of Gallipolis, Ohio and Point Pleasant, an airship did fly over the Ohio Valley that day and, in front of hundreds of witnesses, crashed in flames in the hills behind Gallipolis Ferry, West Virginia. The mystery ship was first seen by Herald MacKenzie and his friends at the Foster Dairy as it flew over Gallipolis and headed towards Point Pleasant. The aerial craft was also seen by residents of Point Pleasant, highway workers just south of the city and by employees working on a sand dredge near Raccoon Island in the Ohio River.

Mr. Robert Henke observed the vessel through field glasses and estimated that it was between 100 and 150 feet long and flew at an altitude of around 300 feet. The size would put the ship in the blimp rather than zeppelin class because dirigibles were usually much larger. The Hindenberg, for example was 803 feet long.

At around 2:50 p.m., a shocking thing happened. Witnesses reported that the ship seemed to buckle in half and fall. Other witnesses reported that the stricken craft fell in flames and that as many as four individuals parachuted out. Despite an aerial search and a ground search by West Virginia state troopers and the Mason County sheriff's department, no trace of the blimp or its occupants was ever found.

Lt. D. Eckford Hodgson, who took part in the aerial search, later talked in depth to 25 or 30 individuals who claimed to have seen the airship and reached the following conclusions from compiling their testimony. The witnesses observed the ship for an hour. They said it turned end-for-end and had a rolling motion and stayed in approximately the same spot. Then suddenly, both ends of the craft bent upward and smoke and debris fell into the woods. The witnesses then said that they saw three objects leave the stricken craft and descend in parachutes. Hodgson reported that none of the witnesses remembered seeing an identification number or a cabin.

So what was this blimp that wasn't? All American airships were accounted for so it wasn't one of them. Hodgson's description makes the blimp sound like a kite balloon, a tethered balloon that most armies of the day used for observing enemy forces. But there was no record that a kite balloon broke loose from any nearby army base. Further, there were no foreign airships within 2,000 miles of Point Pleasant on that day. A more prosaic explanation was provided by Robert Henke, who claimed that people told him that they had seen millions of black birds flying in a dirigible like formation high above the clouds. The flock suddenly separated, landing in a heavily wooded area, which would make it seem to crash.

This might explain why there were no markings on the blimp and why observers don't remember seeing a cabin. But it doesn't explain why Henke, who allegedly observed the machine through field glasses, was unable to determine that it was composed of birds. So this seems like an unlikely explanation, although any weird things birds might do around Point Pleasant would not surprise either of us.

Hodgson stated that two weeks after the initial incident he saw the nose of a dirigible headed for the Gallipolis airport. The craft turned broadside to him and then vanished. Hodgson jumped into his plane and flew down the river, but all he saw was the dredge at Raccoon Island sending up great clouds of smoke.

Several individuals have pointed to the Point Pleasant ghost blimp as a possible early UFO report. This doesn't seem like a typical UFO sighting, and there is still a lack of physical evidence that anything crashed into the hills behind Gallipolis Ferry. This was either one of the craziest mass hallucinations on record or it belongs in the realm of the supernatural.

Consider this. The dirigible USS Shenandoah went down in a storm in Ohio on September 2, 1925 after breaking up into three pieces. Was this some sort of reenactment of the Shenandoah's death struggle, rolling, tossing and swirling in a squall line? A survivor of the disaster said that the Shenandoah was spinning like a merry-go-round before she broke up.

The Akron, which was supposed to fly over the Ohio River Valley that day, was considered a jinxed ship by those who flew in her. Sometime during the early hours of April 5, 1933, the Akron plunged into the stormy Atlantic taking most of her crew with her. This was the deadliest dirigible accident in U. S. Navy history. Could this have been a premonition of the Akron's ultimate destiny?

The Upper Ohio Valley seems to attract strange aerial objects much as a magnet attracts iron filings. According to a report in the New York *Herald,* a luminous object flashing red, white and green lights flew over Sistersville on April 18, 1897. An eyewitness reported, "An examination through strong glasses left the impression of a huge cone shaped arrangement, 80 feet long with fins on the side."

This event occurred during a wave of mystery airship sightings that occurred during 1896 and 1897, all throughout the Midwest. The thing that made this unusual is that the few airships that existed during that time were primitive craft that would be flown at night only by someone intent on suicide.

Again on December 31, 1909 three white lights appeared in the early morning sky over Huntington, West Virginia. A local farmer named Joseph Green claimed the lights were meteors that crashed on his farm, although a subsequent search revealed nothing. Others who saw the lights believed that an airship had flown over the city.

Sightings of out-of-place aircraft continue to this day. We picked up a similar interesting tale while doing fieldwork in the museum in Middlebourne, West Virginia (an excellent museum that we would recommend to anyone) from Louise Sinclaire, one of the volunteers working at the museum. One day in 1986 she and her husband were driving down West Virginia Route 18 when they both noticed a two-engine prop plane wobbling out of control. Mrs. Sinclaire said the plane looked like a World War II-vintage bomber but she couldn't identify it any further.

The plane seemed to crash at the bottom of a hill near Middle Island Run. What was really strange is that it made no noise when it crashed, and afterwards no one could find the wreck. While preparing to write this section, we examined a topographic map of the area and another interesting little coincidence sprang out at us. It seems that a Point Pleasant Creek runs right next to Route 18 in that area. Hmmmm?

So was this mysterious Point Pleasant airship a harbinger of the Akron's or perhaps the Hindenberg's doom? Did somebody's captive balloon get away? Was it a monster flock of blackbirds that decided to play silly buggers that day? Did an airship from somewhere else turn around a corner in infinity and wind up over Point Pleasant? Is it one of a parade of weird aerial contraptions that have skulked around the skies since the turn of the century or is the Ohio Valley haunted by a Flying Dutchman of the air, doomed forever to cruise above the river and crash into the hills. Watch the skies!

How to Get There: Point Pleasant lies one mile north of the junction of US-35 and Route 2.

Mothman: Space Alien or Old-Fashioned Haunt?

No book about West Virginia ghosts would be complete without at least a mention of Mothman, one of the state's most famous monsters. Mothman fluttered into public notice in November 1966, when reports of a giant winged man or large bird seen around the Point Pleasant area began to hit the national press. One of the more popular television series of the day was *Batman*. So some enterprising newspaper reporter christened the creature Mothman, despite the fact that it resembled neither moth nor man.

There has been a great deal of debate about who or what Mothman really is. Some people have tried to tie Mothman's appearance to UFOs and flying saucers. (West Virginia has had more than its share of aerial glowing bodies for the last 100 or so years.)

Others have said that Point Pleasant is the location of a "window" to another dimension through which extra-dimensional creatures enter our world from time to time. John Keel, the best-known chronicler of Mothman, is the chief exponent of this theory and his books on the subject, particularly *The Mothman Prophecies,* are one of our main sources of information about the phenomenon. But our research has led us to consider a third explanation, which lies buried at the roots of Scottish, Irish and American Indian mythology and folklore, not in esoteric aliens from outer space nor in strange creatures from hidden dimensions.

So what does Mothman look like? There seem to be two different varieties. The first is a birdlike or bat-like flying man generally seen close up and at night while the second variety are more like giant birds. We'll call these Big Old Birds (BOBs) to keep them separate from Mothman. Therefore it's possible that there may be two different kinds of Mothman.

John Keel put together a composite description of Mothman that he gleaned from a variety of reports. Mothman is big, between five and seven feet tall with broader shoulders than a man. He's gray or brown, and none of the witnesses could determine whether Mothman wears clothes or is covered with fur.

His most noticeable feature is ten-foot-long bat-like wings that he folds back when he isn't flying and that never flap when he does. Mothman doesn't walk but he shuffles or waddles. No witness remembers seeing any arms. Mothman's second most noticeable feature is his luminous red glowing eyes that measure between two and three inches wide and are set at the top of the shoulders. When seen from the back, Mothman appears to have no head, and none of the witnesses have described his face. (Maybe this is a good thing.)

For all of his physical impressiveness, the only sounds Mothman can make are loud squeaks, like a large mouse. One witness said he sounds like a squealing fan belt. When he flies, Mothman can move out, and he seems to have a predilection for chasing cars. He has allegedly kept pace with cars going between 70 and 100 miles an hour, and all of this without flapping his wings.

The BOBs are much more birdlike than manlike. They are usually brown or brown and gray. Some are big enough to be taken for small airplanes when they are first sighted. BOBs don't have red glowing eyes nor do they seem to like to chase things. They do like to skulk around woods a lot not unlike some known species of birds.

Mothman was first seen on November 1, 1966 when National Guardsmen at the armory on Camp Connerly Road near Point Pleasant saw a large, brown, man-shaped figure on the limb of a nearby tree. On November 12, five men who were digging a grave in Clendenin saw "a brown human being" that fluttered from the trees, maneuvered over their heads and glided back into the trees. They all agreed that it looked like a man with wings. This is not something you would care to see while digging a grave.

On November 12, 1966, the night-lurking, eye-glowing, car-chasing Mothman made his debut to Roger Scarberry, Steven Mallette and their wives. The two couples were driving through the TNT area, so called because it served as an ammunition dump during World War II. Located about seven miles from Point Pleasant, the area is full of abandoned, igloo-shaped, concrete, ammunition storage bunkers and crisscrossed by roads. Overgrown with brush and second growth trees, it is used by the locals for hunting.

As the two couples came up to the abandoned power plant, Mothman rose up silently beside the road, red eyes glowing, wings folded against his back. Scarberry floored it and tried to get out of the area as fast as he could. To the couple's dismay, the creature went airborne and chased the car. It managed to keep up with the car without flapping its wings. One of the women said that it squeaked like a mouse.

This set off a wave of sightings in West Virginia, Kentucky and Ohio. Apart from Point Pleasant and Clendenin, strange birdlike creatures were seen in Campbell's Creek, St. Albans, Mason and Chief Cornstalk Park, in West Virginia; Cheshire, Gallipolis and Letart Falls, Ohio; and Maysville, Kentucky. The sightings lasted from November 1966 to May 1967.

To document all of the sightings would take far too much space. So we've decided to include some of the more unusual ones of both the Mothman and BOB variety. If you wish more detail, consult any of John Keel's works on the subject.

On November 27, 1966 Connie Carpenter was chased by Mothman and ended up suffering from conjunctivitis, an inflammation of the conjunctive tissue of the eyes. This side effect is also reported by many UFO witnesses.

On November 26, 1966, four gigantic birds were seen in the woods near Lowell, Ohio. Witnesses said that the birds were as big as a man and had dark brown backs with dark flecks and gray breasts.

The birds also had straight bills and a reddish cast to their heads. On December 5, 1966, five pilots at the Gallipolis Airport saw what they thought was a small plane coming in for a landing. Imagine their shock and amazement—pilots being a rather practical and hardheaded lot—when the "plane" turned out to be a prehistoric-looking bird with a long neck. It buzzed the runway at an altitude of 300 feet, going at least 70 miles-per-hour.

Tiny's Restaurant was one of the local gathering places in Point Pleasant where the townsfolk went to gossip and discuss the happenings of the day. On January 11, 1967 Mable McDaniel saw a large bird circling the restaurant. When she first saw the creature, she thought she was seeing an airplane but then noticed the beast had two legs. It circled the restaurant for a while and then flew away. It flew without flapping its wings.

The Mothman wave of 1966-67 was not the first time in history that such a creature had been seen by West Virginians in the same area. In his book *The Haunted Valley*, history professor James Gay Jones reports that on several occasions early in this century, people have reported seeing a large bird with the head of a man and a 12-foot wing span. This usually happened immediately before or just after tragic events in the Point Pleasant area. This creature was allegedly seen by rural families in Mason, Jackson, Roan, Clay and Kanawha Counties.

Around the time that World War I started, people in the town of Looneyville looked up one day and saw the birdman flying over their town. The creature cruised up Johnson's Creek, down Galie's Creek, down the Elk River to the Kanawha River. The bird was of "monstrous size and [had] dark reddish feathers, which glistened in the sunlight." People in the area were so frightened that they kept their children indoors so that they wouldn't be snatched up and carried off by the huge bird.

According to Jones, local people believe that the birdman is the spirit of Red Hawk, the Shawnee who was murdered at Point Pleasant along with Chief Cornstalk and his son (see Cornstalk's Curse). Some say Red Hawk appears to warn people of an impending disaster, while others say that Red Hawk is merely witnessing the destruction after the catastrophe. The Silver Bridge collapsed in December 1967, killing 46 people so perhaps Mothman is an updated version of the birdman, and a harbinger of doom.

Along these lines, while connections with UFOs and/or extra-dimensional creatures are interesting speculations, we believe Mothman owes more to Celtic or American Indian mythology than to inhuman aliens from Zeta Reticuli. Perhaps a brief look into both these traditions might shed some more light on the Mothman puzzle.

According to American Indian traditions, birds are associated with death. The Powhattan Indians of Virginia believed that birds received the souls of their chiefs at death. The Algonquins thought that the owl was an attendant of the Lord of Death, while other tribes thought birds were helpers who could render magical aid.

Then there's the story of the thunderbird, common throughout many of the North American Indian tribes. Thunder was caused by the giant thunderbird flapping its wings. In the Mississippi Valley there's the legend of the Piasa Bird (whose name means "birds which devour men"). At one time a large painting of a Piasa bird adorned the cliff at Alton, Illinois. No one knows why this picture was painted. Was it a warning symbol or some sort of pre-Colombian psychological warfare to scare away trespassers? The painting is long gone now, but fortunately copies were made. By the way, the Piasa Bird was pictured with red glowing eyes.

When we look at Celtic myths and legends, the picture gets even more interesting. West Virginia was settled by Scotch-Irish families who brought many of their stories and traditions with them. And some of these tales have more in common with Mothman than you might think.

Ireland is the land of the fairies, the "good people." There's one fairy animal spirit called the pooka that has some similarities to Mothman. (Those of you who have ever seen the movie *Harvey* starring James Stewart know that his giant, invisible rabbit friend named Harvey, was a pooka.) Pookas always took animal form, usually that of a horse, but also appeared as a bull, jackass, goat or eagle. Whatever form they took, they had red glowing eyes and could communicate with people. They generally were considered evil spirits because they took delight in causing travelers to come to harm.

In his book *Irish Folk Stories and Fairy Tales*, William Butler Yates tells the tale of a pooka that took the form of a horse. Every November 1, the pooka would grow tame and civil, and if you asked him politely he would tell you your future for the next year. The whole month of November, but particularly November 1, was sacred to pookas, and if you will recall, Mothman started romping around the Point Pleasant countryside in November 1966. He also liked to harass travelers, in fine old pooka tradition.

In Celtic lore, the banshee is a female spirit who announces an impending death in the house by wailing outside the gate. The Welsh banshee is a little different, for it is a woman with leather bat-like wings that flutters around Welsh houses, wailing and moaning to foretell a death.

The Scots also have a winged fury that's a harbinger of doom. Called the skree, it takes the form of a big black bird and appears to the highland people as an omen of death. During the battle of Culloden, which ended the Jacobite Rebellion of 1745, a skree with red glowing eyes and leather wings hovered over the battlefield as the Scots were being slaughtered by the Duke of Cumberland's troops. Thus the legend sprang up that the skree would appear whenever the Northern Scots were on the brink of disaster or pestilence.

The skree appeared again on May 22, 1915 to 500 officers and men of the Royal Scots, who were preparing to board a train at Larbert. The men refused to board and had to be forced by officers with drawn guns. Later that day, the train crashed and caught fire, killing 227 passengers and injuring 246. You should also remember that the giant bird reported by Professor Jones, which frightened so many residents of Central West Virginia, appeared around the time we were getting involved in that bloody mess known as World War I. How many young West Virginians met their doom in the muddy trenches of France? Then there was the Silver Bridge disaster in December 1967. How many people of Northern Scots descent died when the bridge collapsed into the Ohio that gloomy December evening? Was Mothman really a creature of the Celtic twilight, giving warning to those who, because of the passage of time, didn't understand?

The pooka had red glowing eyes and some would tell your fortune. The leather-winged Welsh banshee flew around the house bewailing the doom of someone in the house. The skree foretold disaster on a grand scale. To the Indians, birds were symbols of death and the Powhattan believed that birds carried away the souls of their dead chiefs. Red Hawk was a sub-chief of the Scioto Shawnee and murdered in Point Pleasant. And don't forget the glowing-eyed Piasa, the bird that devours men. Is Mothman the product of a cross between Celtic and Indian traditions, with a little mountaineer yarn-spinning tossed in just for the flavor? And does he still haunt the back roads around Point Pleasant, waiting to pop up and scare the dickens out of some poor mortals out for an evening drive?

How to Get There: The former "TNT" area, site of the most dramatic Mothman encounters, is now the McClintic Wildlife Management Area. From Point Pleasant, take Route 62 nearly seven miles north. Turn right on CR-11, which leads into the area.

The Other Lost Colony

Almost everyone has heard of the Lost Colony on North Carolina's Roanoke Island. Sir Walter Raleigh planted the settlement in 1587, but when a supply ship returned in 1590, it found the colony abandoned by its inhabitants, who left the cryptic message, "Croatoan," carved in a tree before vanishing forever.

By contrast, hardly anyone today knows of George Washington's "lost colony," although its disappearance was more complete and more mysterious than that of Raleigh's doomed band. Not only did Washington's settlers vanish, but it seems as if the site itself was swallowed by the earth. Today, you can visit Raleigh's Lost Colony, but just try to find Washington's lost colony!

In a 1754 proclamation, Virginia Governor Robert Dinwiddie promised 200,000 acres of land to Virginia officers in exchange for their service in the French and Indian War. The officers served, but in 1770 they were still waiting for the land. On behalf of his brother officers, George Washington went to the Ohio valley that year to locate and claim the promised land. He set out for Fort Pitt (Pittsburgh) on October 5, accompanied by his friend Dr. Craik, Craik's servant, and two of his own servants. In Fort Pitt, they picked up Washington's land agent, Captain William Crawford, and then descended the Ohio River to the mouth of the Kanawha. Writing in his diary, Washington observed, "The Land on both sides of this River just at the Mouth is very fine....." From here the band went 14 miles up the Kanawha. On November 2 in the vicinity of present-day Arbuckle, Washington's party killed five buffalo and three deer, prompting Washington to write, "This Country abounds in Buffalo and Wild game of all kinds as also in all kinds of wild fowl...." After sending scouts another four or five miles up river, the company began to retrace its steps. On the lower Kanawha, they marked trees to claim the land due the officers. Washington returned to Mount Vernon on December 1.

Impressed by the rich land and abundant game, and doubtless recognizing the commercial potential of the Kanawha River, Washington concluded that settlement of the area could prove profitable. He employed Crawford to survey some choice land on the south side of the Kanawha River in June 1771. The next year, Washington used this survey to obtain from the Virginia colony a patent for 10,990 acres along a 17-mile portion of the river, from about two miles above the river's mouth to the Putnam County line. Then Washington tried, but failed, to sell parcels of this land to settlers in July 1773. He found no buyers, because conflict between Indians and settlers engulfed the whole Ohio Valley frontier by that time.

This period of conflict culminated in the Battle of Point Pleasant in October 1774 (see Cornstalk's Curse). The colonial victory in that battle resulted in a temporary peace with the Shawnee and gave Washington hope for the development of his land. He appointed James Cleveland overseer of his western property in January 1775, and instructed him to make improvements at a site in the middle of the tract. The idea seems to have been to establish a preliminary settlement of workers who would improve the land sufficiently to attract pioneer families. The venture had little appeal even to freebooters, however, forcing Cleveland to buy indentured servants in Alexandria, Virginia, in order to man the expedition.

Cleveland established the settlement just above the mouth of Nine Mile Creek, which would place it in the vicinity of present-day Beech Hill. He wrote a number of letters to Washington reporting on the progress of the colony. Three of these letters survive, the first dated May 12, 1775. They tell of a host of troubles that beset the colony from the beginning. Dense scrub brush made the land hard to clear, and clothing and food were running short. The game that had so impressed Washington in 1770 had vanished from the area, and even the fishing proved poor. Several of the indentured servants-cum-settlers ran away, although most were recaptured and brought back.

Events took a turn for the worse as news of the American Revolution spread. The Indians in the Kanawha Valley took advantage of the situation and began to terrorize settlers in August 1775. There is no evidence, however, that they attacked Washington's colony. The last known historical record of the colony is a tax appraisal that Captain Crawford delivered to the Fincastle Court House, in Botetourt County, on April 2, 1776. The document, preserved among historical records in Christianburg, Virginia, was drawn up on August 4, 1775. It noted that Cleveland and his men had cleared 28 acres and had planted "large crops of corn, potatoes, and turnips" and 2,000 peach seeds. In addition, they had built three two-story log houses, a barn, and ten smaller cabins.

After that, there is silence. As historian Phil Conley notes, despite the "hundreds of documents, letters, and other records [that] tell the history of the region.... No written stories of the border have ever mentioned the group of 14 buildings, or the 28 acres of cleared land or any of the 2,000 peach trees that might have grown..."

What happened? It is tempting to suggest that the men fled or were massacred, that the Indians burned the buildings, and that the clearing rapidly became overgrown. But it is strange, with Point Pleasant nearby and the Kanawha a highway for travelers, that no one noted for posterity the massacre, the charred remains, or the prominent clearing. It is also tempting to attribute the disappearance to Cornstalk's Curse (see Cornstalk's Curse), except that the colony disappeared two years before Cornstalk's death. In any case, the colony's mysterious disappearance certainly contributes to the uncanny quality of the Point Pleasant region.

This road sign marks the approximate location of Washington's "Lost Colony."

Finding the colony's remains is a worthwhile challenge for historical archeologists. But to anyone who might take up the quest, we say, watch out for Mothman, who once put in appearances in the adjacent Chief Cornstalk Wildlife Management Area and along US-35 (see Mothman: Space Alien or an Old-Fashioned Haunt?).

How to Get There: *A state historical marker commemorates the colony in the vicinity of its suspected location. It stands a short distance west of Beech Hill, on the north side of US-35, the main highway between Charleston and Point Pleasant.*

LOGAN COUNTY

The Hatfields' Repentance

The Hatfield-McCoy feud has become a symbol of all mountain feuds, embodied in our language and copied or spoofed in countless films and cartoons. Indeed, it is perhaps the most famous of all feuds (if not second to the Montagues and Capulets of Romeo and Juliet fame). As the story has been retold, sometimes casualties were said to have mounted into the hundreds, but in fact fewer than 20 deaths can be definitely attributed to the feud.

The root of the feud can be traced to the Civil War. The Hatfields, living on the West Virginia side of Tug Fork River were Confederates, while the McCoys, on the Kentucky side, were for the Union. Devil Anse Hatfield commanded a partisan unit during the war. (Devil Anse got his colorful name because of his skill as a wrestler in his youth, not because of the feud.) These political differences meant that any dispute between the two families had the potential to turn violent. The feud started in 1873 in a dispute over the ownership of a hog. The McCoys lost the case in court, which kept the pot stirred. Then came a real Romeo-and-Juliet romance between Johnse Hatfield and Rose Anne McCoy. The patriarch of the McCoy clan refused to let his daughter marry Johnse Hatfield. Had he not been so prideful, then the feud might have never taken place.

But the incident that led to warfare was the drunken murder of Ellison Hatfield during election day festivities in 1882. In reprisal, the Hatfields kidnapped the three culprits—Tolbert, Phamer, and Randolph McCoy—and killed them when they got word that Ellison had died of his wounds that night. Then there followed ambushes, trials, a legal hanging, and innumerable posses chasing each other. The feud climaxed in 1888 with the Battle of Grapevine Creek, where two posses, each bearing warrants for members of the other, clashed in a deadly shoot-out. Other incidents occurred over the next eight years, but after Grapevine Creek, William Anderson "Devil Anse" Hatfield, the clan's leader, declared, "The war spirit in me has abated."

In view of such strong and long-lasting passions and their legacy of death, you might expect to find a host of feuding ghosts in Logan County. To our surprise, the only Hatfield ghosts we could find perpetually reenact a pious repentance. The scene of this ghostly ritual is the Hatfield family cemetery, near Sarah Ann, in Logan County. Awkwardly situated on a steep mountain slope, the cemetery overlooks Island Creek (formerly Main Island Creek), where Devil Anse relocated in 1888. Here on a cold rainy Sunday—January 9, 1921—Devil Anse was buried at the age of 82. Soon after, relatives and friends erected over the grave a life-size statue of him in white marble, sculpted in Carrara, Italy, at the astounding cost of $3,000. In time, all of his immediate family came to be buried under that ever-watchful stone sentry.

According to tradition, the spirits of Devil Anse and six of his sons rise from the grave on foggy nights and march down the mountain to Island Creek. There the ghost of William "Uncle" Dyke Garrett duly baptizes them. It would be easy to dismiss this story as a pious invention, but it does contain some good history.

Two of Anse's nine sons, Elias and Troy (Detroit), were shot to death in 1911 in a private dispute unrelated to the feud. The sorrow of that event, which he could not avenge, plunged Anse into a depression. His long-time friend Dyke Garrett, widely beloved as "The Mountain Preacher" and "The Good Shepherd of the Hills," saw that the opportunity was near to win Anse over to the Lord, but he bided his time. Soon Anse brought up the subject of religion, and shortly after Uncle Dyke baptized him, along with his sons Johnse and Cap, in Island Creek. Garrett afterward told someone, "I baptized the Devil today," and he often recalled the moment as one of his proudest.

Anse Hatfield's statue in the Hatfield Cemetery near Sara Ann.

It is notable that six sons join in the ghostly procession. Elias and Troy died before Anse was saved, and the youngest son, Tennis, never took part in the feud. Hence, there is logic in the story even if it is a pious invention.

We trudged up to the Hatfield cemetery through rivers of mud to pay our respects on a cold, rainy day much like the day Anse was buried. Seeing his white statue standing there stoically among the weedy tombstones certainly gave us a feeling of ghostly melancholy. But visitors—even a McCoy—need fear no ghosts here, for as Uncle Dyke used to say, "The ghosts of them that has been baptized, they won't harm nobody."

How to Get There: The Hatfield cemetery lies on the west side of Route 44, about one mile south of Sarah Ann, in Logan County. Park by the historical marker and follow the dirt path across Island Creek and steeply up the mountain for a couple hundred yards.

MINGO COUNTY

Old Thump

One day early in the century, a young boy named O. M. Perry was playing in the road by his house in Codger Town when he heard the sound of an approaching horse-drawn wagon. Scrambling to get out of the way, he ran into his yard and waited for the wagon to pass.

The sound got louder and louder, but no wagon appeared. Then the sound passed by—in the middle of the river rather than the road—and faded away. Perry saw nothing, no wagon, no horses, just the river.

The people in this small community—just a handful of houses on the Guyandotte River about a mile and a half above Justice—called this mysterious sound Old Thump. They speculated that it was the ghostly wagon of a pioneer family killed by Indians or drowned while trying to cross the river.

In 1956, Perry's son Michael also heard the sound. He was playing with some friends at neighbor Al Cline's house, which stood between the dirt road and the river. They heard a noise resembling a horse-drawn wagon in the nearby river. The dirt road forded the river about four hundred feet above the house, and they thought maybe Verlin Walker was crossing the river in his old truck. They waited but nothing came down the road. After a few minutes, Al Cline told them to go up the road and see what was causing the sound. When they reached the crossing, nothing was there. But when they got back to the house, the noise started again. It went on for another ten or fifteen minutes, then slowly faded away. Recalling the experience, Michael Perry said, "Man, my skin crawled!"

The bridge over the Guyandotte River near where Old Thump has been heard.

The people of Codger Town continued to hear Old Thump, especially at night, into the 1960s. At that time, the community became part of the R. D. Bailey Lake Wildlife Management Area, which was established along the Guyandotte between Justice and Baileysville. The creation of this wildlife area included construction of the R. D. Bailey Dam in the vicinity of Codger Town. During work on the dam, workers drilled into an underground river beneath the Guyandotte riverbed. People began to speculate that Old Thump was caused by the movement of rocks and sand echoing from the subterranean river. We don't know if Old Thump has put in an appearance recently, but there are fewer people in the vicinity to hear anything nowadays.

We should add that Old Thump was never confined to the Codger Town area. Local resident Zionel Walker told Michael Perry that people said they had heard Old Thump as far up river as Big Cub Run, by Coal Mountain, ten miles away as the crow flies. Although peculiar conditions in an underground river might give rise to a localized noise, could they really extend as far as ten miles? Or does something else lurk in the Guyandotte?

How to Get There: US-52 crosses the Guyandotte River at Justice. There is good parking and easy access to the river here.

SOURCES ~ BIBIOGRAPHY

NORTHERN PANHANDLE

EASTERN PANHANDLE

MOUNTAINEER COUNTRY

MID-OHIO VALLEY

POTOMAC HIGHLANDS

METRO VALLEY

MOUNTAIN LAKES

NEW RIVER GREENBRIER VALLEY

FIELD INTERVIEWS ~ INDEX

SOURCES

These sources are given in short form.
Full bibliographic data appears in the Bibliography.

CHAPTER ONE ✨EASTERN PANHANDLE

Harpers Ferry Haunts

Barry, Joseph. *The Strange Story of Harper's Ferry*.

Brown, Stephen D. *Haunted Houses of Harpers Ferry*, 41-44.

Dougherty, Shirley. "A Ghostly Tour of Harpers Ferry."

Furnas, J. C. *The Road to Harpers Ferry*.

Hearn, Chester G. *Six Years of Hell*, 39.

Jones, James Gay. *Haunted Valley*, 69-71.

Thomas, Dana. "On a Tour of Harpers Ferry's Favorite Haunts."

John Brown Marches On

Crane, Katie. Jefferson County Historical Museum. Field interview.

Furioso, Nan. Courthouse tour guide. Field interview.

Furnas, J. C. *The Road to Harpers Ferry*.

Perkins, Gene. Owner of the Gibson house. Field interview.

Sanders, David. "A Brief History of the Jefferson County Court House."

Thomas, Dana. "On a Tour of Harpers Ferry's Favorite Haunts."

The Haunted Inns of Charles Town

Anonymous. Waitress and other staff at Charles Washington Inn. Field interview.

Anonymous. Staff at Iron Rail Inn. Field interview.

Furioso, Nan. Courthouse tour guide. Field interview.

Quinn, George. Owner of the Iron Rail Inn. Field interview.

The Truth About Wizard Clip

Barry, Joseph. *The Strange Story of Harper's Ferry*, 178-188.

Bayless, Raymond. *The Enigma of the Poltergeist*, 35-36.

Brown, Jeanette. "Ghostly Remembrances: A Visit to Scollay Hall & Middleway," 65-69.

Brown, Stephen D. *Haunted Houses of Harpers Ferry*, 49-56.

Sources

Bushong, Millard Kessler. *Historic Jefferson County*, 95-98.

Comstock, Jim, ed. *West Virginia Heritage Encyclopedia*, vol. 3, 160; vol. 8, 174-177.

Curran, Rev. John A. "Haunted House Known Throughout the World," 2-3.

Finotti, Joseph M. *The Mystery of the Wizard Clip*.

Marshall, A. L. *Adam Livingston, the Wizard Clip, the Voice*.

Norris, J. E., ed. *History of the Lower Shenandoah Valley*.

Taylor, L. B., Jr. *The Ghosts of Virginia*, vol. 2, 98-103.

Haunted Hedgesville

Crites, Susan. *Lively Ghosts Along the Potomac*, 1-4.

Long, E. B. and Barbara Long. *The Civil War Day by Day*, 387, 482.

Berkeley's Haunted Castle

Berkeley Castle. "Visit Berkeley Castle."

"The Castle in Berkeley Springs," 24.

Lord, Suzanne and Jon Metzger, *The West Virginia One Day Trip Book*, 23-25.

Soltis, Stephen and Stacy Soltis. *West Virginia: Off the Beaten Path*, 24.

Chapter Two ~ Potomac Highlands

The Laughing Boys of the Cacapon River

Crites, Susan, *Lively Ghosts Along the Potomac*, 31-33.

The Old Stone House at Keyser

Cohen, Stan. *The Civil War in West Virginia: A Pictorial History*, 26, 103, 107, 111.

Giffin, Vernon O. *The Witch of Hooker Hollow*, 16-17.

Musick, Ruth Ann. "Folktales Depicting the American Revolution and the Civil War," 22.

Wolfe, William W. *History of Keyser*, 3-10.

The Devil's Warning

Anonymous. Patron of the Hideaway Tavern, Burlington. Field interview.

"Ghosts and Strange Happenings," 2-3.

Swetnam, George. *Devils, Ghosts, and Witches,* 60-61.

West Virginia Folklore, vol. 13 (1), 14.

The Cole Mountain Lights

Anonymous. Librarian, Hardy Co. Library, Moorefield. Field interview.

Hauck, Dennis William. *The National Directory of Haunted Places,* 382.

Musick, Ruth Ann. *Coffin Hollow,* 65-67.

Charles Sager (Never) Sleeps Here

Anderson, Ellen. "The Story of Lost River State Park."

Johnson, Robert Ray II. "Sir Walter Raleigh's Lost River State Park," 11-12

"Lost River State Park."

Taylor, Dee, Superintendent, Lost River State Park. Field interview.

The Maysville Market Haunt

Gainer, Patrick W. *Witches, Ghosts and Signs,* 78-79.

Hoverville, Mary. Maysville Market. Field interview.

Kiplinger, Sharon. Maysville Market. Field interview.

Hidden in Halliehurst

Scheidhaur, Lynn. "Ghost in Halliehurst: Fact or Fiction?" 5-8.

Schoonover, Susie. Davis & Elkins College employee. Field interview.

National Register of Historic Places Inventory—Nomination Form.

The Werewolf Hitchhiker

Baughman, Louisa Belle. Quoted, 8.

Cunningham, Vicki. Manager of Days Inn, Elkins. Field interview.

Gainer, Patrick W. *Witches, Ghosts and Signs,* 66.

Goss, Michael. *The Evidence for Phantom Hitch-Hikers.*

The Ghosts of Rich Mountain

Cox, Jacob D. "McClellan in West Virginia," 126-149.

Lamers, William M. *The Edge of Glory,* 28-30.

Musick, Ruth Ann. *Coffin Hollow,* 52-53.

Rich Mountain Battlefield Foundation. *Rich Mountain Battlefield Civil War Site.*

Sources

The Ghosts of Droop Mountain

Heuey, Johnson, Jr. "Who Goes There."

Johnson, Skip. "Droop Mountain Battlefield Ghosts."

Jones, James Gay. *A Wayfaring Sin-Eater*, 36-39.

Keen, Johnnie. "The Ghosts of Droop Mountain."

Lowry, Terry. *Last Sleep: The Battle of Droop Mountain*, 249-252.

Poliafico, Chuck. "Local Man Baffled by Ghostly Vision."

Schlefstein, Carol. *Memoirs of Droop Mountain Battlefield State Park*.

Smith, Mike. Superintendent, Droop Mountain Battlefield State Park. Field interview.

West Virginia State Parks and Recreation. "Droop Mountain Battlefield Map and Trail Guide."

Chapter Three ~ Mountaineer Country

The Rivesville Headless Horseman

Cohen, Stan. *The Civil War in West Virginia*, 94.

Long, E. B. and Barbara Long. *The Civil War Day by Day*, 387, 482.

Lough, Glen D. *Now and Long Ago*, 640-655.

Tichenor, Bertha. Quoted, 6-7.

Morgan's Premonition

Core, Earl L. *The Monongalia Story*, 13-14.

De Hass, Willis. *History of the Early Settlement and Indian Wars of Western Virginia*, 247-251.

Barrackville Boogies

"Ghosts," 14-15.

Lough, Glen D. *Now and Long Ago*, 291, 388.

Musick, Ruth Ann. *The Telltale Lilac Bush*, 132-134.

Pratt, William. Quoted, 71-72.

Fairmont's Headless Ghost

George, Diana. Owner of the Fairmont Motor Lodge. Field interview.

Musick, Ruth Ann. *The Telltale Lilac Bush*, 124.

The Atheist's Revenge

Anderson, Mr. & Mrs. William. Carolina residents. Field interview.

Lemley, Trudy. Carolina resident. Field interview.

Swetnam, George. *Devils, Ghosts and Witches*, 85-86.

West Virginia Folklore. Vol. 16, #1-2 (1965), 37-38.

Some More Coal Mine Ghosts

Musick, Ruth Ann. *Coffin Hollow*, 110-111.

———. *The Telltale Lilac Bush*, 78-80.

Nash, Robert J. *The Darkest Hours*, 710-720.

The Coffin Riders

Anonymous. Monongah residents. Field interviews.

Anonymous. Robin. Eldora resident. Field interview.

Lemley, Trudy. Carolina resident. Field interview.

Musick, Ruth Ann. *Coffin Hollow*, 9-11.

———. "Folk Tales Depicting the American Revolution and the Civil War," 71-72.

———. *The Telltale Lilac Bush*, 71-72.

The Ghosts of Prickett's Fort

Barrow, Thoma. Prickett's Fort story teller. Field interview and unpublished notes.

DeMay, John A. *The Settlers' Forts of Western Pennsylvania*, 103-105.

Prickett's Fort State Park and Pricketts Fort Memorial Foundation. Untitled pamphlet.

"Tall Tales," 2-3.

Withers, Alexander Scott. *Chronicles of Border Warfare*, 161.

The Hoult Water Monster

Lough, Glen D. *Now and Long Ago*, 13-16, 86-87, 168, 170, 176.

The Ghosts of Benton's Ferry and Vinegar Hill

Musick, Ruth Ann. *The Telltale Lilac Bush*, 81-82, 89, 91.

The Cunningham Massacre

Lough, Glen D. *Now and Long Ago,* 609-614.

Rinehart, Robert D. Quoted, 65-69.

Sturm, Glen, Jr. Cunningham relative. Field interview.

Withers, Alexander Scott. *Chronicles of Border Warfare*, 367-373.

Chapter Four ~ Mountain Lakes

The Old School Spirit

Jones, James Gay. *Appalachian Ghost Stories,* 74.

———. *A Wayfaring Sin Eater,* 73-75.

The Flatwoods Monster

Brandon, Jim. *Weird America,* 238-239.

Clark, Evert. "You Can't Get One Out at Night by Hisself."

Clark, Jerome. *The UFO Encyclopedia,* vol. 1, 409-412.

Davis, L. T. Flatwoods resident and owner of the monster site. Field interview.

Jones, James Gay. *Appalachian Ghost Stories,* 93-96.

Leavitt, Dale. "This Is Becoming More Monstrous by the Hour."

"The Monster of Braxton County."

Sanderson, Ivan T. "Report on the Passage of a Number of Unknown Aerial Objects."

———. *Uninvited Visitors,* 37-52.

Sutton, John Davison, *History of Braxton County,* 107-108.

The Phantom Wagon of US-19

Gainer, Patrick W. *Witches, Ghosts and Signs,* 67-68.

Roberts, Nancy. *Appalachian Ghosts,* 54-58.

The Ghosts in the Valley

Jones, James Gay. *The Haunted Valley,* 18-19.

Matheny, H. E. *Wood County West Virginia During Civil War Times,* 43, 51-53, 188, 239-241, 270.

Wonderful West Virginia, March 1979.

Chapter Five ➤ New River/Greenbrier Valley

Footsteps in the Air

Anonymous. Montgomery mayor's office personnel. Field interviews.

Gwin, Adrian. *Rovin' the Years with Our Man Gwin*, 70-74.

The Colonel at the Glen Ferris Inn

"The Glen Ferris Inn."

Phillips, Dave. Glen Ferris Inn, Glen Ferris. Field interview.

The *Genius Loci* of Hawk's Nest

Atkinson, George. *History of Kanawha County*, 23-25.

Carpenter, Charles. *West Virginia People and Places*, 42.

Cavalier, John. *Panorama of Fayette Co.*, 209-210.

Comstock, Jim, ed. *Commonplace Book*, 115.

Gwin, Adrian. *Never Grow Old with Our Man Gwin*, 39-43.

Miller, James H. *History of Summers County*, 15, 45.

Rowh, Mark. "The Hawk's Nest Tragedy: Fifty Years Later," 31-33.
West Virginia Folklore, fall 1952, 9.

The Ghostly Drummer of Big Sewell Mountain

Deitz, Dennis. *The Greenbrier Ghost*, 140-142.

McKinney, Tim. *Robert E. Lee at Sewell Mountain*.

Phillips, Dave. *A Soldier's Story*.

McKinley's Face

Andre, Richard, Stan Cohen and Bill Wentz. *Bullets & Steel*, 133, 136, 140.

Domby, Shirley. *Historical Notes of Fayette County*, 24-26.

Lord, Susan and Jon Metzger. *West Virginia One Day Trip Book*, 98.

Soltis, Stephen & Stacy. *West Virginia: Off the Beaten Path*, 60-61.

Williams, T. Harry and Stephen E. Ambrose. "The 23rd Ohio," 22-25.

The Haunted Highway

Anonymous. Larry, Highway worker, I-64/77, Kanawha Co. Field interview.

Allen, Vicky. Manager of Morton's Truck Stop. Field interview.

Deitz, Dennis. *The Flood and the Blood.*

———. *The Greenbrier Ghost,* 152-165.

Goss, Michael. *The Evidence for Phantom Hitch-Hikers.*

Shaffer, P. H. State Trooper. Field interview.

The Sandstone Light

Costa, Jimmy. "Ghost Light at Richmond's Ferry," 68.

Beckley's Haunted Theater

Anonymous. Scenery painter, Soldiers Memorial Theater. Field interview.

American Legion Post 32. "Program for Memorial Day Dedication."

Untitled account of the dedication of the Soldiers Memorial.

Zegeer, Jill. "Soldiers Memorial Theater Boasts Very Own Ghost."

The Spirit of a Steel-Driving Man

Chappell, Louis W. *John Henry: A Folklore Study,* 14-15, 34, 37, 47, 70.

Jones, James Gay. *The Haunted Valley,* 97.

Motley, Charles B. *The Gleanings of Monroe County,* 48, 51.

Roberts, Nancy. *Appalachian Ghosts,* 37-42.

Wheeler, Linda. "Probing the Musical Mystery of John Henry's White House," D7.

Zona Shue, the Ghost That Testified

Deitz, Dennis. *The Greenbrier Ghost,* 9-29.

Guiley, Rosemary Ellen. *The Encyclopedia of Ghosts and Spirits,* 146-148.

The Angelic Army of Lewisburg

Floyd, Randall. "Many Reported Apparition of Angels During Civil War."

Chapter Six ～ The Northern Panhandle

The Jennings Gang

Jones, James Gay. *Appalachian Ghost Stories,* 100-103.

McEldowney, John C. *History of Wetzel County,* 110-127.

The Ghost Who Failed to Appear

Gamble, Brent. "The Ghost of Gamble Run."

McEldowney, John C. *History of Wetzel County,* 128-130.

The Wells Inn Spook

Mountain Trace, 40.

"The Historic Wells Inn."

Smith, Nel. Wells Inn employee. Field interview.

Chapter Seven ~ Mid Ohio Valley

The Virgin Mary in the Ohio Valley

Pemberton, Robert L. *The History of Pleasants County,* 64-65.

Wonderful West Virginia, March 1979, 493.

Silver Run's Woman in White

Price, William B. *Tales and Lore of the Mountaineers,* 33-38.

Shepard, Susan. Haunted Parkersburg tour guide. Field interview.

Shepard, Susan and Richard Southall. "Haunted Parkersburg Tour Notes."

Southall, Richard. Haunted Parkersburg tour guide. Field interview.

Haunted Parkersburg

Matheny, H. E. *Wood County West Virginia in Civil War Times,* 161-181.

Shepard, Susan. Haunted Parkersburg tour guide. Field interview.

Shepard, Susan & Richard Southall. "Haunted Parkersburg Tour Notes."

Southall, Richard. Haunted Parkersburg tour guide. Field interview.

The Lady in White - Haunted Blennerhassett

Elliot, John Carroll and Ellen Gale Hammett. *Charged with Treason.*

Lord, Susan and John Metzger. *The West Virginia One Day Trip Book,* 157.

Lowther, Mimi Kendall. *Blennerhassett Island in Romance and Tragedy,* 27, 105, 113.

Schneider, Norris F. *Blennerhassett Island and the Burr Conspiracy.*

Shepard, Susan. Haunted Parkersburg tour guide. Field interview.

Shepard, Susan and Richard Southall. "Haunted Parkersburg Tour Notes."

Southall, Richard. Haunted Parkersburg tour guide. Field interview.

Swick, Ray. *An Island Called Eden.*

The Parkersburg Aerial Apparition

Fort, Charles H. *New Lands,* in *The Complete Books of Charles Fort,* 457.

New York Times, July 8, 1878, 2.

The Ghost in the Ravenswood Theater

Anonymous. Manager of Almeda's. Field interview.

Musick, Ruth Ann. *Coffin Hollow,* 30-33.

Soltis, Stephen and Stacy Soltis. *West Virginia: Off the Beaten Path,* 85.

Chapter Eight ⚊ Metro Valley

Chief Cornstalk's Curse

Atkinson, George. *The History of Kanawha County,* 65.

Comstock, Jim, ed. *West Virginia Heritage Encyclopedia, Supplemental Series,* 5:16.

De Hass, Willis. *History of the Early Settlement and Indian Wars of Western Virginia,* 162, 170, 173, 217, 218.

Howe, Henry. *Historical Collections of Virginia,* 364.

Jones, James Gay. *The Haunted Valley,* 30.

Lough, Glen D. *Now and Long Ago,* 295-296.

Newton, J. H., G. G. Nichols and A. G. Sprinkle. *History of the Pan-Handle,* 87-92.

Point Pleasant Battle Monument Commission. *The Battle of Point Pleasant,* 11-12.

Taylor, L. B., Jr. *The Ghosts of Virginia, Vol III,* 185-190.

Whithers, Alexander Scott. *Chronicles of Border Warfare,* 196, 232-235.

The Point Pleasant Ghost Blimp

Berliner, Don. "19th-Century Airship Mystery," 2-6.

Fort, Charles H. *New Lands,* in *The Complete Books of Charles Fort,* 470.

Horton, Edward. *The Age of the Airship,* 86-122.

Mangiacopra, Gary and Carl Pabst. "The Blimp that Wasn't There," 91-94.

Sinclaire, Louise. Middlebourne Museum. Field Interview.

Toland, John. *The Great Dirigibles,* 81-147.

Mothman: Space Alien or Old-Fashioned Haunt?

Bord, Janet and Colin. *Alien Animals,* 123.

Brown, Riki. "Highlanders Omen of Death," 56.

Jones, James Gay. *The Haunted Valley,* 27-35.

Keel, John. *The Complete Guide to Mysterious Beings*, 263-265.

———. *Strange Mutants,* 64-69.

Schorer, C. E. *The Indian Tales of C. C.   Trowbridge,* 10, 99.

Shuker, Karl P. *From Flying Toads to Snakes with Wings,* 115-117.

Spence, Lewis. *North American Indian Myths and Legends,* 110-111.

Yates, William Butler. *Irish Folk Stories and Fairy Tales,* 89-106.

The Other Lost Colony

Conley, Phil. *West Virginia Reader,* 146-154.

Washington, George. *The Diaries of George Washington,* vol. 1 (1748-1770), 400-449.

The Hatfield's Repentance

Jones, Virgil Carrington. *The Hatfields and McCoys.*

Spence, Robert Y. *The Land of Guyandot,* 157-160.

Swain, George T. *History of Logan County, West Virginia,* 194.

Thomas, Jean. *Blue Ridge Country,* 199-202.

Old Thump

Brumfield, Col. Darrell G. & Flossie Hatfield Smith, eds. *Stories About Gilbert,* 272-273.

BIBLIOGRAPHY

American Legion Post 32. "Program for Memorial Day Dedication of Raleigh County's Soldiers and Sailors Memorial." Beckley, WV, 1932.

Anderson, Ellen. "The Story of Lost River State Park." Photocopy ms., Lost River State Park, n.d.

Andre, Richard, Stan Cohen and Bill Wentz. *Bullets & Steel: The Fight for the Great Kanawha Valley, 1861-1865*. Charleston: Pictorial Histories, 1995.

Atkinson, George. *The History of Kanawha County*. Charleston, West Virginia: 1876.

Barrow, Thoma. Unpublished notes. Prickett's Fort State Park, n.d.

Barry, Joseph. *The Strange Story of Harpers Ferry*. 1903. Reprint, Shepardstown, WV: The Women's Club of Harpers Ferry District, 1974.

Baughman, Louisa Belle. Quoted in *West Virginia Folklore*, fall 1952.

Bayless, Raymond. *The Enigma of the Poltergeist*. New York: Ace, 1967.

Berkeley Castle Society. "Visit Berkeley Castle." Brochure. Berkeley Springs, WV, n.d.

Berliner, Don. "The 19th-Century Airship Mystery." *INFO Journal*, May-June 1978, 2-6.

Bord, Janet and Colin Bord. *Alien Animals*. Harrisburg PA: Stackpole, 1981.

Brandon, Jim. *Weird America*. New York: Dutton, 1978.

Briggs, Katherine. *The Vanishing People: Fairy Lore and Legends*. New York: Pantheon, 1978.

Brown, Jeanette. "Ghostly Remembrances: A Visit to Scollay & Middleway." *Goldenseal*, Fall 1982, 65-69.

Brown, Rikki. "The Highlanders Omen of Death." *Fortean Times*, October-November 1994, 56.

Brown, Stephen D. *The Haunted Houses of Harpers Ferry*. Harpers Ferry, WV: Little Brown House, 1976.

Brumfield, Col. Darrell G. and Flossie Hatfield Smith, eds. *Stories About Gilbert, West Virginia and Surrounding Communities.* Baltimore: Gateway, 1993.

Bushong, Millard Kessler. *Historic Jefferson County.* Boyce, VA: Carr, 1972.

"The Castle in Berkeley Springs." *Wonderful West Virginia,* September 1979.

Carpenter, Charles. *West Virginia People and Places.* West Virginia Heritage Encyclopedia, ed. Jim Comstock, vol. 22, suppl. series. Richwood, WV: Comstock, 1974.

Cavalier, John. *Panorama of Fayette County.* Parsons, WV: McClain, 1985.

Chappell, Louis W. *John Henry: A Folklore Study.* Jena, Germany: Frommansche Verly, 1933.

Clark, Evert. "You Can't Get One Out at Night by Hisself." *Washington Daily News,* September 19, 1952.

Clark, Jerome. *The UFO Encyclopedia: The Phenomenon from the Beginning.* 2nd ed. Detroit, MI: Omnigraphics, 1998.

Cohen, Stan B. *A Pictorial Guide to West Virginia's Civil War Sites and Related Information.* Charleston: Pictorial Histories, 1990.

―――. *The Civil War in West Virginia: A Pictorial History.* Charleston: Pictorial Histories, 1996.

Coleman, Loren. *Curious Encounters.* Winchester, MA: Faber & Faber, 1985.

―――. *Mysterious America.* London and Boston: Faber & Faber, 1983.

Comstock, Jim, ed. *Commonplace Book.* West Virginia Heritage Encyclopedia, ed. Jim Comstock, vol. 14, suppl. series. Richwood, WV: Comstock, 1974.

―――. *West Virginia Heritage Encyclopedia.* Vol. 3. Richwood, WV: Comstock, 1973.

―――. *West Virginia Heritage Encyclopedia , Supplemental Series.* Richwood, WV: Comstock, 1973.

Conley, Phil. *West Virginia Reader: Stories of the Early Days.* Charleston: Education Foundation, 1970.

Bibliography

Core, Earl L. *The Monongalia Story: A Bicentennial History, II. The Pioneers.* Parsons, WV: McClain, 1976.

Corliss, William R. *Handbook of Unusual Natural Phenomena.* Glen Arm, MD: The Sourcebook Project, 1977.

————. *Lightning, Auroras, Nocturnal Lights and Related Luminous Phenomena.* Glen Arm, MD: The Sourcebook Project, 1982.

Costa, Jimmy. "Ghost Light at Redmond's Ferry." *Goldenseal,* Fall 1992, 68.

Cox, Jacob D. "McClellan in West Virginia." In *Battles and Leaders of the Civil War,* vol. 1, ed. Robert Underwood Johnson and Clarence Clough Buel. 1887. Reprint, Edison, NJ: Castle Books, n.d.

Crites, Susan. *Lively Ghosts Along the Potomac.* Martinsburg, WV: Butternut, 1997.

————. *Lively Ghosts of the Eastern Panhandle of West Virginia.* Martinsburg, WV: Butternut, 1991.

Curran, Rev. John A. "Haunted Houses Known Throughout the World." *Wonderful West Virginia,* October 1971, 2-3.

De Hass, Wills. *History of the Early Settlements and Indian Wars of Western Virginia.* Wheeling, VA: H. Hobtelgell, 1851.

Deitz, Dennis. *The Flood and the Blood.* South Charleston, WV: Mountain Memories Books, n. d.

————. *The Greenbrier Ghost and Other Strange Stories.* South Charleston, WV: Mountain Memories Books, 1990.

DeMay, John A. *The Settlers' Forts of Western Pennsylvania.* Apollo, PA: Closson Press, 1997.

Domby, Shirly. *Historical Notes of Fayette County, West Virginia.* Privately printed, 1958.

Dougherty, Shirley. *A Ghostly Tour of Harpers Ferry.* EGMID Publishing Company, 1982.

Drapper, M. S. S. "Border Forays, Sketches of Cornstalk." *Ohio Archaeological and Historical Quarterly.* April-July 1912.

Elliot, John Carroll and Ellen Gale Hammett. *Charged with Treason, Jury Verdict: Not Guilty.* Parsons, WV: McClain, 1986.

Finotti, Joseph M. *The Mystery of Wizard Clip.* Baltimore: Kelly Piet, 1879.

Floyd, Randall. "Many Reported Apparition of Angels During Civil War." Unidentified Augusta, Georgia newspaper, June 20, 1993.

Fort, Charles Hoy. *The Complete Books of Charles Fort.* 1919-1932. Reprint, New York: Dover, 1974.

Furnas, J. C. *The Road to Harpers Ferry.* New York: William Sloan, 1959.

Gainer, Patrick W. *Witches, Ghosts and Signs.* Grantsville, WV: Seneca, 1975.

Gamble, Brent. "The Ghost of Gamble Run." In *History of Wetzel County, West Virginia.* Wetzel County Genealogical Society, 1983.

Gardner, Mabel Henshaw and Anne Henshaw. *Chronicles of Berkeley.* Durham, NC: Services Press, 1938.

"Ghosts." *West Virginia Folklore,* fall-winter 1965, 14-15.

"Ghosts and Strange Happenings. *"West Virginia Folklore,* fall 1958, 2-3.

Giffin, Vernon O. *The Witch of Hooker Hollow and More Folklore.* Easton, MD: Economy, 1981.

"The Glen Ferris Inn." Brochure. Glen Ferris, WV, n.d.

Goss, Michael. *The Evidence for Phantom Hitch-Hikers.* Wellingborough, England: Aquarian Press, 1984.

Guiley, Rosemary Ellen. *The Encyclopedia of Ghosts and Spirits* (New York and Oxford: Facts on File, 1992.

Gwin, Adrian. *Never Grow Old with Our Man Gwin.* Charleston: Jalamap, 1981.

———. *Rovin' the Years with Our Man Gwin.* Charleston: Jalamap, 1982.

Hauck, Dennis William. *The National Directory of Haunted Places.* Sacramento, CA: Anthanor Press, 1994.

Haymond, Henry. *History of Harrison County, West Virginia.* Morgantown, WV: Acme, 1910.

Hearn, Chester G. *Six Years of Hell.* Baton Rouge, LA: Paperback Editions, 1999.

Heuey, Johnson, Jr. "Who Goes There?" *Wonderful West Virginia,* November, 1982.

"The Historic Wells Inn." Brochure. Sistersville, WV, n.d.

Horton, Edward. *The Age of the Airship.* Chicago: Henry Regnery, 1973.

Bibliography

Howe, Henry. *Historical Collections of Virginia.* Charleston: Babcock, 1846.

Irving, Washington. *Hearthside Tales.* Schenectady, New York: Union College Press, 1983.

Johnson, David E. *A History of Middle New River Settlement and Contiguous Territory.* Huntington, WV: Standard, 1906.

Johnson, Robert Ray II. "Sir Walter Raleigh's Lost River State Park." *Wonderful West Virginia,* November 1971, 11-12.

Johnson, Skip. "Droop Mountain Battlefield Ghosts." *Charleston Gazette Mail*, September 18, 1977.

Jones, James Gay. *Appalachian Ghost Stories and Other Tales.* Parsons, WV: McClain, 1975.

———. *Haunted Valley and More Folk Tales of Appalachia.* Parsons, WV: McClain, 1979.

———. *More Appalachian Folk Stories.* Parsons, WV: McClain, 1993.

———. *A Wayfaring Sin Eater and Other Tales of Appalachia.* Parsons, WV: McClain, 1983.

Jones, Virgil Carrington. *The Hatfields and the McCoys.* 1948. Reprint, Marietta, GA: R. Bemis, 1974.

Keel, John A. *Our Haunted Planet.* Greenwich, CT: Fawcett, 1971.

———. *Strange Creatures from Time and Space.* Greenwich, CT: Fawcett, 1970.

———. *Strange Mutants.* Global Communications, 1989.

———. *The Complete Guide to Mysterious Beings.* New York: Doubleday, 1994.

———. *The Eighth Tower.* New York: Signet, 1975.

———. *The Mothman Prophecies.* 1975. Reprint, Avondale Estates, GA: IlluminNet Press, 1991.

Keen, Johnie. "The Ghosts of Droop Mountain." Typescript of phone interview, c. 1990.

Keightley, Thomas, *The Fairy Mythology.* 1880. Reprint, London: Wildwood House, 1981.

Lamers, William M. *The Edge of Glory.* Baton Rouge, LA: Louisiana State University Press, 1999.

Leavitt, Dale. "This Is Becoming More Monstrous by the Hour," *Washington Daily News,* September 22, 1952.

Lee, Marguerite DuPont. *Virginia Ghosts.* Berryville, VA: Virginia Book Co., 1966.

Long, E. B. and Barbara Long. *The Civil War Day by Day.* Garden City, NY: Doubleday, 1971.

Lord, Suzanne and John Metzger. *The West Virginia One-Day Trip Book.* McLean, VA: EPM, 1993.

"Lost River State Park." Tour handout. Lost River State Park, WV, n.d.

Lough, Glen D. *Now and Long Ago: A History of the Marion County Area.* n.p., 1969.

Lowry, Terry. *Last Sleep: The Battle of Droop Mountain.* Charleston: Pictorial Histories, 1996.

Lowther, Minnie Kendall. *Blennerhassett Island in Romance and Tragedy.* Rutland, VT: Tuttle, 1936.

Mangiacopra, Gary and Carl Pabst. "The Blimp That Wasn't There," *Fate,* August 1979, 91-94.

Marshall, A. L. *Adam Livingston, the Wizard Clip, the Voice.* Kearneysville, WV: Livingston, 1978.

Mathney, H. E. *Wood County West Virginia in Civil War Times.* Parkersburg, WV: Trans-Allegheny, 1987.

Maxwell, Hu. *The History of Barbour County, West Virginia.* Morgantown, WV: Acme, 1899.

McEldowney, John C., Jr. *History of Wetzel County, West Virginia.* n.p., 1901.

McKinney, Tim. *Robert E. Lee at Sewell Mountain: The West Virginia Campaign.* Charleston: Pictorial Histories, 1990.

———. *The Civil War in Fayette County, West Virginia.* Charleston: Pictorial Histories, 1988.

Miller, James H. *History of Summers County from Earliest Settlement to the Present Time.* Hinton, WV, 1908.

Morton, Orin F. *The History of Pendleton County, West Virginia.* Franklin, VA, 1910.

———. *A History of Monroe County, West Virginia.* Staunton, VA, 1916.

Bibliography

Motley, Charles B. *Gleanings of Monroe County West Virginia History.* Danville, VA, 1913.

Mountain Trace, winter 1976, 40.

Musick, Ruth Ann. *Coffin Hollow and Other Ghost Tales.* Lexington, KY: University of Kentucky Press, 1977.

————. "Folktales Depicting the American Revolution and the Civil War." *West Virginia Folklore Journal*, July 1977.

————. *The Telltale Lilac Bush and Other West Virginia Ghost Tales.* Lexington, KY: University of Kentucky Press, 1965.

Nash, Jay Robert. *Darkest Hours.* New York: Pocket Books, 1976.

National Park Service. "National Register of Historic Places Inventory—Nomination Form." Photocopy of National Park Service document. Davis and Elkins College, Elkins, WV, n.d.

Newton, J. H., G. G. Nichols and A. G. Sprinkle. *History of the Pan-Handle: Being Historical Collections of the Counties of Ohio, Brooke, Marshall and Hancock, West Virginia.* Wheeling, WV: J. A. Caldwell, 1879.

Norman, Michael and Beth Scott. *Historic Haunted America.* New York: TOR, 1995.

Norris, J. E., ed. *History of the Lower Shenandoah Valley.* Chicago: Warner, 1890.

North, E. Lee. *Red Coats, Red Skins and Red-Eyed Monsters.* Cranberry, NJ: A. S. Barus, 1979.

Pemberton, Robert L. *The History of Pleasants County.* n.p., 1929.

Phillips, David. *Daring Raiders: Little Known Tales of Courage.* New York: Metro, 1998.

————. *A Soldier's Story: The Double Life of a Confederate Spy.* New York: Metro, 1998.

Point Pleasant Battle Monument Commission. *The Battle of Point Pleasant, First Battle of the American Revolution, October 10, 1774.* Point Pleasant, WV: Mattox, 1995.

Poliafico, Chuck. "Local Man Baffled by Ghostly Vision." *The Parkersburg News*, December 23, 1990.

Pratt, William. Quoted in *West Virginia Folklore*, Summer 1955, 71-72.

Price, Charles Edwin. *Haunts, Witches and Boogers.* Winston-Salem, NC: John F. Blaire, n.d.

Price, William B. *Tales and Lore of the Mountaineers.* Salem, WV: Quest, 1963.

Prickett's Fort State Park and Pricketts Fort Memorial Foundation. Untitled pamphlet. Prickett's Fort State Park, WV, 1999.

Rich Mountain Battlefield Foundation. *Rich Mountain Battlefield Civil War Site.* Brochure. n.p., n.d.

Rinehart, Robert D. Quoted in *West Virginia Folklore,* Summer 1955, 65-69.

Roberts, Nancy. *Ghosts of the Southern Mountains and Appalachia.* Columbia, SC: University of South Carolina Press, 1988.

————. *Civil War Ghost Stories and Legends.* Columbia, SC: University of South Carolina Press, 1992.

————. *Appalachian Ghosts.* Garden City, NY: Doubleday, 1978.

Roth, David, ed. *A Guide to the Haunted Places of the Civil War.* Columbus, OH: Blue and Gray Magazine, 1997.

Rowh, Mark. "The Hawk's Nest Tragedy: Fifty Years Later." *Goldenseal,* January-March 1981, 31-33.

Sanders, David. *A Brief History of the Jefferson County Court House.* Brochure. Charles Town, WV, n.d.

Sanderson, Ivan T. "Report on the Passage of a Number of Unknown Aerial Objects Over West Virginia on the 12th of September, 1952." Photocopy of manuscript in the authors' possession.

————. *Uninvited Visitors.* New York: Cowles Education Corp., 1967.

Scheidhaur, Lynn. "Ghost in Halliehurst: Fact or Fiction." *Forward,* winter 1978, 5-8.

Schlefstein, Carole M. *Memoirs of Droop Mountain State Park.* Unpublished manuscript. Droop Mountain State Park, WV, n.d.

Schneider, Norris F. *Blennerhassett Island and the Burr Conspiracy.* Zanesville, OH: Courier, 1938.

Schorer, C. E. *The Indian Tales of C. C. Trowbridge.* n.p., n.d.

Shuker, Karl P. N. *From Flying Toads to Snakes with Wings.* St. Paul, MN: Llewellyn, 1997.

Shepard, Susan and Richard Southhall. "Haunted Parkersburg Tour Notes." Photocopy of tour guide notes in the authors' possession.

Spence, Lewis. *North American Indian's Myths and Legends*. 1914. Reprint, New York: Avenel, 1986.

Spence, Robert Y. *The Land of Guyandot: A History of Logan County*. Detroit, MI: Harlo, 1976.

Soltis, Stephen and Stacy Soltis. *West Virginia: Off the Beaten Path*. Old Saybrook, CT: Globe Pequot Press, 1995.

Sutton, John Davison. *A History of Braxton County and Central West Virginia*. Sutton, WV, 1919.

Swain, George T. *History of Logan County, West Virginia*. Logan, WV: G. T. Swain, 1927.

Swetnam, George. *Devils, Ghosts and Witches, Occult Folklore of the Upper Ohio Valley*. Greensburg, PA: McDonald/Swärd, 1988.

Swick, Ray. *An Island Called Eden*. Parkersburg, WV: Parkersburg Printing, 1996.

"Tall Tales." *West Virginia Folklore,* Fall-Winter 1965, 2-3.

Taylor, L. B. *Civil War Ghosts of Virginia.* N.p.: Progress Printing, 1995.

———. *The Ghosts of Virginia.* N.p.: Progress Printing, 1993.

———. *The Ghosts of Virginia, Vol. II*. N.p.: Progress Printing, 1994.

———. *The Ghosts of Virginia, Vol. III*. N.p.: Progress Printing, 1996.

Tennant, Diane Casto. "Blennerhassett Island" *Goldenseal*, April-June 1980, 53-58.

Thomas, Dana. "On a Tour of Harpers Ferry's Favorite Haunts." *Washington Post*. October 31, 1989, C1.

Thomas, Jeane. *Blue Ridge Country*. New York: Duell, Stone and Pearce, 1942.

Tichenor, Bertha. Quoted in *West Virginia Folklore,* Fall, 1952, 6-7.

Toland, John. *The Great Dirigibles: Their Triumphs and Disasters*. New York: Dover, 1972.

Tucker, George Holbert. *Virginia Supernatural Tales*. Norfolk, VA: Donning, 1977.

United Press Dispatch. "The Monster of Braxton County: Around the Bend They Saw a Pair of Bulging Eyes," *Washington Daily News*, September 15, 1952.

Untitled account of the dedication of the Soldiers Memorial in Beckley, West Virginia. Hand-written ms., n.d. Raleigh County Library, Beckley, WV.

Waddell, Joseph A. *Annals of Augusta County, Virginia.* Bridgewater, VA: C. J. Carrier, 1902.

Warren, Harlow. *Beckley USA.* Beckley, WV: Harlow Warren, 1955.

Washington, George. *The Diaries of George Washington, 1748-1799* , ed. John C. Fitzpatrick. Vol. 1. Boston: Houghton Mifflin, 1925.

West Virginia Folklore, Fall 1952, 9.

———. Vol. 16 (1-2), 1965, 37-38.

———. Vol 13 (1), 1962, 14.

West Virginia State Parks and Recreation. "Droop Mountain Battlefield Map and Trail Guide." Brochure. Droop Mountain State Park, WV, n.d.

"What a West Virginia Farmer Saw." *New York Times,* July 8, 1878, 2.

Wheeler, Linda. "Probing the Musical Mystery of John Henry's White House." *Washington Post,* December 8, 1998.

Withers, Alexander Scott. *Chronicles of Boarder Warfare.* Parsons, WV: McClain, 1994.

Williams, T. Harry and Stephen E. Ambrose. "The 23rd Ohio," *Civil War Times Illustrated*, May 1964.

Wolfe, William W. *A History of Keyser, W. Va., 1737-1913.* Keyser, WV: Keyprint, 1974.

Wonderful West Virginia, March 1979.

Wood, Warren, *The Tragedy of the Deserted Isle.* Boston: C. M. Clark, 1909.

Yates, William Butler. *Irish Folk Stories and Fairy Tales.* New York: Grosset & Dunlap, n.d. Reprint of *Fairy and Folk Tales of the Irish Peasantry* 1888.

Zegeer, Jill. "Soldiers Memorial Theater Boasts Very Own Ghost." *Beckley Register Herald,* undated photocopy.

Field Interviews

Allen, Vicky. Manager of Morton's Truck Stop, I-64/77, Kanawha Co.

Anderson, Mr. and Mrs. William. Carolina residents.

Anonymous. Highway worker named Larry, I-64/77, Kanawha Co.

————. Librarian, Hardy Co. Library, Moorefield.

————. Manager of Almeda's Clothing Store, Ravenswood.

————. Monongah residents.

————. Montgomery mayor's office personnel.

————. Patron of the Hideaway Tavern, Burlington.

————. Robin. Eldora resident.

————. Scenery painter. Soldiers Memorial Theater, Beckley.

————. Staff at Iron Rail Inn, Charles Town.

————. Waitress and other staff, Charles Washington Inn, Charles Town.

Barrow, Thoma. Prickett's Fort story teller.

Crane, Katie. Jefferson County Historical Museum, Charles Town.

Cunningham, Vicki. Manager of the Elkins Days Inn.

Davis, L. T. Flatwoods resident and owner of Flatwoods Monster site.

Furioso, Nan. Jefferson County Courthouse tour guide.

George, Diana. Owner of the Fairmont Motor Lodge.

Hoverville, Mary. Maysville Market.

Kiplinger, Sharon. Maysville Market.

Lemley, Trudy. Carolina resident.

Perkins, Gene. Owner of the Gibson house, Charles Town.

Phillips, Dave. Glen Ferris Inn, Glen Ferris.

Quinn, George. Owner of Iron Rail Inn, Charles Town.

Schaeffer, P. H. West Virginia State Trooper.

Schoonover, Susie. Davis and Elkins College employee.

Shepard, Susan. Haunted Parkersburg tour guide.

Sinclaire, Louise. Middlebourne Museum.

Smith, Mike. Superintendent, Droop Mountain Battlefield State Park.

Smith, Nel. Wells Inn employee, Sistersville.

Southall, Richard. Haunted Parkersburg tour guide.

Sturm, Glen Jr. Cunnningham relative, Harrison Co.

Taylor, Dee. Superintendent, Lost River State Park.

INDEX

C

L

M

N

S

Z

Point Pleasant Battlefield Monument
~Metro Valley~